CHOOSE WISELY

CHOOSE WISELY

Rationality, Ethics, and the
Art of Decision-Making

Barry Schwartz
Richard Schuldenfrei

Yale
UNIVERSITY PRESS
NEW HAVEN & LONDON

Published with assistance from the foundation established in memory of
Amasa Stone Mather of the Class of 1907, Yale College.

Copyright © 2025 by Barry Schwartz and Richard Schuldenfrei.
All rights reserved.
This book may not be reproduced, in whole or in part,
including illustrations, in any form (beyond that copying permitted
by Sections 107 and 108 of the U.S. Copyright Law and except by
reviewers for the public press), without written permission
from the publishers.

Yale University Press books may be purchased in quantity
for educational, business, or promotional use. For information, please email
sales.press@yale.edu (U.S. office) or sales@yaleup.co.uk (U.K. office).

Set in Yale and Alternate Gothic No2 type by Integrated Publishing Solutions.
Printed in the United States of America.

Library of Congress Control Number: 2025932977
ISBN 978-0-300-28399-0 (hardcover)

A catalogue record for this book is available from the British Library.

Authorized Representative in the EU: Easy Access System Europe,
Mustamäe tee 50, 10621 Tallinn, Estonia, gpsr.requests@easproject.com
10 9 8 7 6 5 4 3 2 1

From Barry: To Levi, Nico, Louis, Eliza, and Ruby, my beloved grandchildren. Not one of them is a devotee of rational choice theory, but each of them is wonderfully rational. In addition, to the memory of Daniel Kahneman, whose lifetime of brilliant work changed how we think about thinking.

From Richard: To my wife, my parents (of blessed memory), and my daughters, with infinite gratitude.

CONTENTS

Preface ix

Introduction: A Day in the Life 1

Chapter 1: How We *Should* Decide: Rational Choice Theory 10

Chapter 2: Rational Choice Theory: Specification of Options and Attributes 39

Chapter 3: Quantifying Probability 63

Chapter 4: Quantifying Value 80

Chapter 5: Rational Choice Theory and the Framing of Decisions 104

Chapter 6: Framing, Leakage, and Substantive Rationality 120

Chapter 7: Interim Summary of the Argument 139

Chapter 8: Why Rational Choice Theory Is Dangerous 144

CONTENTS

Chapter 9: An Alternative to Rational Choice Theory   171

Chapter 10: Rational Choice Theory and History   209

Chapter 11: Rational Choice Theory and Ideology   234

Conclusion   254

Coda   258

Bibliography   265
Index   271

PREFACE

A philosopher and a psychologist walk into a bar. No, just kidding; this book did not begin in a bar. Instead, it began with an innocent email from Rich to Barry on July 28, 2023. "I'm in the middle of *Thinking, Fast and Slow* [Nobel laureate Daniel Kahneman's comprehensive best-seller on the psychology of decision-making] and finding it very interesting. I have a question that I hope you can answer for me."

Barry answered the question as best he could (Rich asks hard questions), and another question followed . . . and another . . . and another. Sometimes Barry's answers were adequate. Sometimes they were flimsy. And sometimes all Barry could say was "I never thought about that." The back-and-forth continued via email until either Barry or Rich (we don't remember who) suggested that maybe we should talk instead. There ensued a string of phone conversations, from one coast to the other, with emails scattered in between. The topic, ostensibly, was always Kahneman's book, but the issues ranged all over the place. We would agree on some matter at the end of one conversation only to discover in the next that we hadn't quite agreed

PREFACE

after all. But we seemed to be making progress. We reached a point when Barry suggested to Rich, "We may have a paper here."

Thus began the writing, as the emails and conversations continued. When the dust cleared, we had a manuscript of more than two hundred pages—no longer a paper but a short book, the first draft of what you have before you. In the course of this development, there were over one thousand emails, scores of conversations, and many versions of our arguments. And it all began with an innocent question via email.

Well, no, not really. This book "began" more than fifty years ago, when Barry joined Rich on the faculty at Swarthmore College. Rich had been hired a few years before to teach moral and political philosophy and the philosophy of social science. Barry came to the psychology department to teach the brand of psychology most famously and radically offered by behaviorist B. F. Skinner, then perhaps the most influential living psychologist. Barry was mostly critical of Skinner's ideas about human nature, but Barry's view was that the proper sort of criticism would come from a rather narrow dissection of what the research in the field actually showed, as opposed to what it claimed to show. Rich was also very critical of Skinner's view of human nature and the world, but his criticism was much broader, emphasizing the historical, cultural, and economic context in which Skinner developed his theories. So we two started talking. Rich's email question to Barry about Kahneman was merely the latest chapter in a conversation that has been going on continually for more than half a century. The seeds of the arguments in this book were truly planted back then, in conversations about Skinner.

Soon after we started talking back in the Swarthmore days, we enlisted Rich's philosopher colleague Hugh Lacey, a philosopher of science, to join in. These three-way conversations eventually led to

PREFACE

a course, several papers, and a book co-authored by Hugh and Barry. We rehearse some of the arguments the three of us developed back then in chapter 10 of this book.

So, our collaboration for this book started many years ago. This was true not just of the substance of our conversations, but also of how we conducted them. Rich's approach to whatever issues were on the table was more expansive than Barry's. He taught Barry to think a bit more expansively too. Barry's approach tended to stick closer to the data. He taught Rich that even if data weren't everything, they were nonetheless relevant. We disagreed often, but usually came to a shared understanding of whatever we were discussing. What made our shared understanding possible, when it was achieved, was our deep mutual respect for what each of us contributed to the conversation. Among the results of these conversations were two books by Barry (*The Battle for Human Nature* and *The Costs of Living*) that offered broad criticisms of the Skinnerian view of the world (a view shared in important respects by economists) — books that would never have been possible without Rich.

Choose Wisely is merely the latest manifestation of this fifty-year conversation and collaboration. Both Rich and Barry retired from Swarthmore, and Barry moved west, so contact between the two became less frequent and less intense. But when Rich sent that innocent email, things quickly returned to how they had been a half century earlier. Yet it's certain that without the experience of those early days, there would be no book.

What you have before you is, we hope, not the end of our conversation but a new beginning that will extend beyond the two of us. Rich's training in philosophy has led him to expect that before you publish anything in philosophy, you need to develop an argument that gets decisively to the heart of the problem. Barry is a bit

PREFACE

easier on himself, having come to believe that progress in science is the result of just "one damn mistake after another." Yes, it is true that science corrects its mistakes, but those corrections have mistakes in them too. This book does not reach the standard that Rich sets for himself. We may not have gotten quite to the heart of the problem. Very likely if we had kept trying to attain that goal there would never have been a book. But our hope is that what we have produced will serve to invite others to join the conversation and make the arguments better.

Barry wishes to thank Adam Grant, Dan Keys, Hugh Lacey, Ken Sharpe, and Amy Wrzesniewski—colleagues and/or former students whose past collaborations with Barry are reflected and discussed throughout this book. He is especially grateful to his life partner Myrna Schwartz, whose close reading of this book (and all his others) has improved the arguments and the exposition immeasurably. Rich also wishes to thank Hugh Lacey as well as Ben Plotkin-Swing. Together, we thank Don Moore for offering a critical reading of an early draft of the book, editor Seth Ditchik for helping sharpen the argument, and copyeditor Robin DuBlanc for correcting our stylistic errors and sweetening our prose. We also thank our spouses, Helen Plotkin and Myrna Schwartz, for keeping us at it after the occasional frustrating email or phone call that left both of us discouraged.

This book is a critical examination of what is called "rational choice theory," an extremely influential model for how to choose rationally that comes out of economics. We will argue that rational choice theory fails as a description of how people choose and that it fails as a description of how people *should* choose. We will also argue that rational choice theory is not simply wrong but also dangerous, as its influence on our thinking continues to grow. And we will sketch an alternative model of what it means to be rational, one that differs

PREFACE

radically in both form and content from rational choice theory. We believe deeply that many of the issues we raise in the book are critical to our understanding of our society and ourselves, and that these issues have thus far been given far too little attention. We believe, as Willy Loman's wife Linda says at the end of Arthur Miller's play *Death of a Salesman*, "Attention must be paid."

CHOOSE WISELY

INTRODUCTION

A Day in the Life

This is a book about deciding, so let's begin with a decision. Imagine waking up on a Saturday morning, gazing out the window to see the sun shining, and asking yourself, "What should I do today?" You quickly review your various obligations and responsibilities and discover that there's nothing you have to do; the day is yours. Complete freedom awaits. So you do some stock taking. Will you be facing any challenges at work next week that maybe you should get a jump on? Are there chores around the house that you've been putting off? Is there any shopping that has to be done? No, no, and no. No constraints. Nothing obvious that a responsible person "should" be doing. You're free as a bird.

Now what? It looks like a beautiful day, so perhaps you should do something outside. There's a hike you've been meaning to take. It would be a challenging adventure in a gorgeous setting. You feel up for it—but are you up *to* it? You've neglected your cardio for the last few weeks and the inclines may exhaust you. Besides, the day looks so promising that the trail may be very crowded—and full of unleashed dogs. How about spending the day getting your garden

INTRODUCTION

started? On the other hand, you've had a tiring week. Perhaps you should just relax and enjoy yourself. Any good sports on TV? A movie to stream? But if you do something like that, you'll hate yourself after spending a day sitting passively in front of the tube. If you're going to relax, then at least do something worthwhile. Catch up on the news by spending the day watching cable? These are tumultuous times and you've been neglecting the larger world. But cable news is so damn polarized. It raises your blood pressure. And you never know who or what to believe. Okay, then: relax by reading a book? Not a mindless potboiler, but one that actually teaches you something. If you do that, you can both relax and better yourself, and end up feeling like you had a productive day. But you suspect that a day spent reading will end up as a day spent mostly napping. Then you'll really hate yourself.

Whew! Who knew that all this freedom of choice would be this hard? You could occupy the whole day just deciding what to do. And you've only gotten started. Actually, one of us (spoiler alert: it's Barry) already knew it could be this hard. He wrote a whole book about it — *The Paradox of Choice* — more than twenty years ago, when life was simpler compared to now because there were fewer options. Maybe it's time to clear your head with a cup of coffee.

Now that the coffee's brewing, you resume your reflections about how to pass the day. "Everything I've been thinking so far is just about me. Is that how it should be? Should this be a 'me day' or a 'we day'? I haven't talked to my daughter in a week, and right now she's probably packing boxes to get ready to move to her new apartment, with a new roommate, next week. I bet she's a little overwhelmed, and maybe also a little nervous about how the new roommate situation will work out. Maybe I should call her and invite myself over to help her pack, calm her down, and keep her company."

INTRODUCTION

This thought makes you feel a lot better. You can fill your day doing something productive that also helps someone you love. That makes a lot of sense. But now you've opened a can of worms. Your mother has been down in the dumps lately. Her health has not been great, and she spends a lot of time alone. She's never really recovered from the depression that set in when she moved to an assisted living facility. Perhaps you should take her out to lunch, go for a little stroll. That will probably cheer her up. Which of these loved ones will benefit more from your visit? Who needs you more? And which option will give *you* more pleasure?

This is getting hard. Perhaps the caffeine will help. But as you sip your coffee, something else occurs to you. Why just choose between a "me day" and a "we day"? How about a "they day"? You've been active in a few organizations concerned with social justice. These activities are important to you, and the organizations operate on a shoestring. Perhaps you can do some useful office work for one of them. But which one? Or perhaps you can do some reading to get up to speed on one or more of the issues that concern these organizations. This would be a productive way to spend the day. But do you really want to be productive on this particular day? Yes, this seems like a good idea.

But just when you think you've resolved your dilemma, another thought occurs to you. You've been thinking very short term. Shouldn't thinking about how to spend the day be embedded in a larger project — like how to conduct your life, or what kind of person to be in the world? Lord knows that the busyness of everyday life affords little opportunity to take the longer view. Today you seem to have the chance. Maybe this is the day to take stock. "How am I doing? Am I the kind of person I thought I would be? The kind of person I hoped to be? If not, what's missing? And how can I cultivate

INTRODUCTION

aspects of the self I want to have but have been neglecting? If not now, when? I'm not getting any younger. Maybe it's time to do some major reflecting on the big things. Change of career trajectory? Change in my intimate life? Why not put everything on the table?"

There is something very important to notice about the "me day" versus "we day" and the "short-term" versus "long-term" perspectives we just introduced. They are very different from the "Should I take a hike or work in the garden?" options we identified. Thinking "me day" versus "we day" establishes a context within which your final decision will be made. It puts a frame around the possibilities, with some possibilities very much inside the frame and others very much outside it. If you decide to frame this Saturday as a "we day," suddenly all kinds of options move off the table. You're not asking, "What should I do today?" but rather "What 'we' thing should I do today?"

We will see that the effects of decision framing have been much examined in the science of decision-making. We will also see that for the most part, framing has been viewed as an obstacle to good decision-making. What we will be arguing, in contrast, is that framing is an important ingredient — perhaps the most important ingredient — in good decision-making. Many details of our argument will come later. For now, it is important to note that some of the possibilities you are thinking about are, in effect, possibilities that try to answer the question "How should I frame my day?" while others try to answer "Within the frame I have chosen, what should I actually do?"

We could go on and on enumerating possible ways to spend a free Saturday, but we don't want to make you impatient, silently screaming, "Just do something!" What we *do* want to do is illustrate just how potentially complex an apparently simple, everyday decision

INTRODUCTION

about what you should do today can be. This book is about how we actually make such everyday decisions. What do we think about? What moves do we make to turn seemingly intractable decisions into manageable ones . . . or the reverse? It is also about how we *should* make such decisions. What does science tell us about how decisions *should* be made, and about how they actually *are* made? The scenario we've just described suggests that at least sometimes making a decision can involve all of our cognitive and emotional resources – all that we know, and all that we aspire to. But we will see that the dominant approaches to decision-making aim to reduce this potential complexity to an almost algorithmic, mechanical process. Our aim in this book is to argue that such simplification is a serious mistake – that to understand decision-making is to understand almost everything about human thought.

There are many ways we might go about answering the question "What should I do today?" depending on our character and our inclinations at the moment. We might simply do what strikes us – whimsically and almost impulsively. We might act in accordance with our habits and community customs – traditionally. We might simply use common sense, taking account of the obvious facts of the situation and taking our initial inclinations at face value. We might try to decide systematically and scientifically, creating some sort of spreadsheet that considers the various possibilities along with our assessment of the aspects of each possibility that seem to matter to us. We might think about it seriously, using our reflective intelligence to consider who we are and who we want to be. We might decide socially, thinking about who we can be helpful to and what our community expects of us. We might decide hedonically, thinking about what will give us the most pleasure. We might decide instrumentally, thinking about what will serve us best in the long run. Or we

INTRODUCTION

might decide more or less directly on the basis of some overarching value — philosophically.

The discussion to follow will focus on two distinct approaches to making everyday decisions — intelligent reflection on the one hand, and some type of formal, mechanical decision process on the other. Much of the rest of this book will focus on the latter; but for now, let us discuss briefly what we mean by intelligent reflection.

To begin thinking seriously about what to do, you ask yourself, "What would I like to get out of this day? Fun? Rest? Exercise? Fresh air? Errands done? Responsibilities fulfilled? Social interaction? A clean house?" This is effectively another instance of choosing a frame within which to make a decision. As you go through the list, some options may strike you as nonstarters. Housework is boring, and exercise is too much physical effort. In addition, good examples of other options present themselves — visiting your mother or helping your daughter (socialize, fulfill responsibilities), finding a nice spot in the park to read (fresh air, relaxation, edification), watching sports on TV (fun and relaxation). Then, imagining these options, you might think of considerations that rule out some of them (too many noisy children to read in the park). You have now come up with a set of two options to consider seriously: watching sports and visiting your mother or daughter.

Watching sports is very tempting. It is virtually effortless, no physical exertion involved and no obstacles to overcome. And it is fun and doesn't cause any harm to anyone. But you have a sense that there is something wrong with it. It appears that some of its "virtues" are actually undesirable. Yes, it requires no effort, physical or intellectual, but doesn't that encourage a kind of laziness and passivity that you do not particularly approve of? Yes, it hurts no one, but that is partly because it is a solitary endeavor. And it may strengthen

INTRODUCTION

antisocial tendencies that you have noticed in yourself recently. The pleasure it yields is basically insipid and kind of meaningless. It leads nowhere and contributes nothing but a few moments of pleasure to your life. There's nothing wrong with experiencing pleasure, but there's more to life, or at least there should be. It is also habit forming, and when you think of yourself being glued to the tube, it feels degrading. In that sense, it actually does cause harm, even if only to you. It is a bit like taking opioids. The analogy with opioids, although exaggerated, helps you to understand what is going on when you watch sports; and but for your lack of self-control, you would rule it out.

Visiting your mother is not, initially, a very appealing option. She is a pretty negative person these days, both about her own life and about yours. She believes you to be directionless and for that reason nags you about your career and your social life. On the other hand, she is lonely, and you have not fulfilled your responsibilities to her. You visit her occasionally, but not often enough. Here your judgment tells you that you should visit your mother, and but for your lack of self-control, you would. Visiting your daughter might be a perfect compromise: true, she needs you less, but it will be much more pleasant to spend the day with her than with your mother.

Intelligent reflection allows you to see multiple aspects of a decision. It allows you to compare options that seem to have little or nothing in common. It allows you to consider the ways in which a simple decision of how to spend a Saturday says something about who you are and what you value. It allows you to ponder what kind of shadow your decision about today may cast on your future. Intelligent reflection speaks not only to *what* you decide, but also to *how* you decide. We do not always have the luxury (or the burden) of intelligent reflection. Much of the time, the demands of daily life press on us, taking much of our freedom of choice away. But even when that happens, it is intelligent reflection that may enable us to decide that these demands on us come up too often, and that they lead us away from doing the things we most want to do, or the things we should want to do. It not only enables us to be who we are; it enables us to change who we are.

The distinguished twentieth-century philosopher Ludwig Wittgenstein once said that "to know a language is to know a form of life." What he was trying to suggest, we think, is that the meanings conveyed by language are so deeply embedded in our everyday practices that when you wrench the language out of those practices — say, by translation into another language — much is distorted or left behind. In a certain sense, to know anything about a language you need to know everything about the culture that uses it. Analogously, we think that to understand a decision is to understand a way of thinking about the issue you face. Isolating decision-making from the context of the decision being made distorts the options and leaves much behind. And yet, that is what most of the thinking, theorizing, and research on decision-making has done. In what follows, we hope to point out how impoverished thinking about decision-making is, and also to illustrate how it can be enriched.

Let's zoom out from how to spend a Saturday to how to spend a life. Should you try to acquire as much money as you can? Then work on Wall Street. Should you strive to have the best relationships you can with the people (family, friends, and community) in your life? Then cultivate those relationships and also develop the aspects of your character that you will need to establish and sustain those close relationships. Should you strive to experience as much pleasure as you can in life? Then choose an undemanding job, and minimize social entanglements (no spouse or kids) to pursue what you want,

INTRODUCTION

when you want. Should you attempt to attain the admiration of your community? Then consider politics or charity work. These life paths are not *necessarily* in conflict, but can easily become incompatible, so let's assume you have to choose between them. We believe that many young people today have *exactly* this kind of decision to make, and many of them are tortured by it. So, how *should* we decide what to do with our lives? We'll examine a theory of decision-making that underpins much of the thinking (by social scientists, at least) about how we make decisions, and how we *should* make decisions, and show why it falls very short as a way to think about decision-making in our own lives. That theory of decision-making, known as rational choice theory, offers us a formal, quantitative alternative to intelligent reflection. In the discussion to come, we will describe what rational choice theory is and how influential it has become. We will discuss the ways in which everyday decisions must be transformed in character, losing much of their complexity, in order for rational choice theory to be applied to them. We will illustrate some of the ways in which rational choice theory fails as a description of how people make decisions, and how it also fails as a *prescription* for how people *should* make decisions. We will also show how, despite its inadequacies, rational choice theory has grown ever more influential in modern society, with the result that it has become dangerous. And we will offer an alternative model for decision-making — both descriptive and prescriptive — that replaces the formal, quantitative aspirations of rational choice theory with considered, thoughtful judgment.

Chapter 1

HOW WE *SHOULD* DECIDE

Rational Choice Theory

Our introduction illustrated various ways that we might go about answering the question "What should I do today?" We hope that you found most of our musings familiar. In this chapter, we will focus on one particular method for deciding what to do today, and many other things, that has become the normative standard for making "rational" decisions: rational choice theory (RCT). In the rest of this book, we will be arguing that RCT is not, in fact, all that rational. Let us examine what RCT actually tells us to do when we are faced with decisions.

From the perspective of RCT, the presumed goal of a decision is to maximize utility or preference. What "utility" means has been debated for centuries without clear resolution. Unlike something like money, "utility" is clearly subjective — it is in the eye of the beholder. Though extremely vague, its virtue is that it captures more than just pleasure. Utility could be pleasure in some decision settings, but it could be usefulness in others. Two hours in the weight room may not give the professional athlete much pleasure, but it can be useful in making the athlete better at her sport. The term "utility" functions as a way of acknowledging the diversity of things that are valued. Though pleasure and money capture much of what most people value, and almost all of what *some* people value, most people value things that are neither of those, such as health or achievement or meaningful social relationships. "Preference" often substitutes for utility, in response to dissatisfaction with the vagueness of the latter term. It too is subjective, and virtually content free. The way we know what someone "prefers" is by observing what someone chooses. Almost by definition, what people choose is what they prefer.

RCT assumes that people bring well-articulated preferences with them to the decision process — in other words, that preferences are exogenous (they exist prior to the occasion on which a decision must be made). People then array the options before them, or construct a set of options, analyze them into relevant attributes, and assess the importance each attribute should have in influencing their decision. For example, someone might decide that a car's reliability is much more important than the color of its upholstery and give reliability extra weight in deciding what car to buy. Then, people assess how good each attribute of each alternative is; they assign each attribute a value. Next, they try to determine how likely it is that if they choose a given alternative, their goals with respect to the target attributes will actually be realized.

For example, they might think, "The value of going to the beach is great if it is sunny, but there is some significant probability it will rain, and in that case the value will be greatly decreased." The value of the options and the probability of attaining those values are given numerical specifications. You multiply those specifications, and the product of the values and the probabilities is the *expected utility* of that option. "The value of the beach in good weather is 100, the value of the beach if it rains is 10. The chance of good weather is 80%, of rain, 20%." Rational choosers then just do the math: 80% of 100 is 80, and 20% of 10 is 2, so by adding them together we get the expected utility of the trip to the beach. One could imagine using this framework, as we will describe later, to decide where to go to college, what to study, what job to take, where to go on vacation, what investments to make, what house to buy, what city to move to, and perhaps whether (and when) to marry, and whether (and when) to have children. RCT is meant to be essentially an all-purpose tool for making complex and often difficult decisions. It is a tool for asking and answering two very important questions: what are you trying to attain with this decision, and how likely is each of the options on the table to enable you to attain it?

RCT has a better known and more influential "cousin" in what is called "cost-benefit analysis." With cost-benefit analysis you assess the plusses and minuses of each available alternative to get a net value, and then choose the alternative with the highest net value. Not only is cost-benefit analysis meant to guide individual decisions, it is also meant to guide government decisions (for example, which program to reduce greenhouse gases should be implemented; which prescription drug plan should be adopted) and business decisions (for example, which new product should be developed; which marketing campaign should be pursued).

Why assess probability in addition to value? Because little in life is certain, and every decision is a prediction. You may choose a college because you sat in on a couple of biology classes and loved them. But are all the biology teachers as engaging as the ones you heard? You may choose to vacation at a national park because of its beauty and serenity. But what if it's extremely crowded? You may choose a job because it seems that your colleagues will be great people to work with. But how much can you tell on the basis of one day spent at the company? Thus, probability assessment is essential.

This description of RCT is admittedly highly schematic, but it enables us to highlight a few key points. First, the structure of RCT is entirely formal; one could substitute variables for actual alternatives and attributes and have a recipe that applies to all decisions. Second, deviations from this normative model will also be formal. That is, decision inconsistency, intransitivity (for example, preferring A to B, and B to C, but C to A), preference reversals (preferring A to B at one moment, but B to A later), and lack of descriptive invariance (making decisions that are affected by the way in which the options are described, even if the different descriptions are of the same underlying reality) are all identified as "errors" because of their failure to match the formal normative model. Finally, rationality is typically judged (with the exception of work on "current and future selves" and how people do and should weigh future or long-term consequences of a current decision) in respect to the circumscribed decision itself and not by assessing how the particular decision fits into the decider's life as a whole.

Let's look at how RCT deals with some examples. First, what we will call the *gambling paradigm*.

Consider the choice between the following two gambles:

A. A 50% chance of winning $10 and a 50% chance of losing $6.
B. A 25% chance of winning $20 and a 75% chance of losing $2.

RCT proposes to solve this choice problem with relatively simple mathematical calculation.

HOW WE *SHOULD* DECIDE

A. 50% of $10 = $5. 50% of $-6 = $-3. $5-$3 = expected value of $2.
B. 25% of $20 = $5. 75% of $-2 = $-1.50. $5-$1.50 = expected value of $3.50.

Since the expected value of B is greater than the expected value of A, B is the rational choice. Notice that the question of which gamble it is rational to choose is turned into a purely mathematical problem. Every element of the problem is mathematical. As a math problem, the reasoning is formal. There are, as a result, no empirical questions relevant to its solution. There is no basis for questioning the process of solving the problem and therefore the determination of the rational choice. In addition, all the variables are clear and precise. There is no relevant vagueness or ambiguity. There is also no need to deal with the contents of your (or anyone else's) mind, in the sense of beliefs, desires, understanding, purpose, or the formulation of fundamental opinions or goals, no consideration of how to determine options or important attributes.

You should note that we described what we calculated above as expected *value*. This is not the same as expected *utility*. To focus on expected utility, we have to take into account the fact that the more money you have, the smaller the utility of a given additional amount. Technically, this phenomenon is called "the diminishing marginal utility of money," and it captures the obvious point that $100 means a lot more to someone with nothing than it does to someone with thousands of dollars. And what is true of money is true of most things people value. When you have no oranges, the value of an orange is larger than it will be if you already have a half dozen. There are tools for calculating the diminishing marginal utility of money and thus inferring expected utility from expected value. But these tools are based as much on theory as on empirical evidence. So, the realistic version of this gambling problem is not as purely mathematical as the use of the formula above implies. But it is very nearly purely mathematical.

The practical significance of the inclusion of the diminishing marginal utility of money in the determination of the rational choice may be small, but in certain ways it is the camel's nose under the tent. It turns a purely precise mathematical problem into a problem that is empirical (how much does the value of money diminish?) and concerned with "mental" things (values rather than money). The thinking involved in solving this new problem is also not all formal, as purely mathematical problems are. Throughout the book, we will be examining the use of RCT with normal real-world decisions and watch carefully as the rest of the camel follows its nose into the tent.

People who work within the framework of RCT do not explicitly endorse the idea that all decisions, if made rationally, are mathematical. They neither make nor defend such a claim. What they do suggest, or at least imply, is that the closer we can come to transforming decisions into close analogs of the gambling paradigm, the closer we come to being rational decision makers. The influence that RCT gains from this notion that decision problems can be solved mathematically, or nearly so, can hardly be overestimated, and we believe that it remains even when examples show clearly, as we hope to, that the claim is unfounded. Moreover, treating decision problems this way under normal circumstances interferes with good decision-making rather than facilitating it. We hope to demonstrate that the gap between the mathematical aspirations of RCT and the unmathematical nature of human decision-making is "bridged," so to speak, by oversimplification, sometimes arbitrary.

Decision scientist Keith Stanovich wrote a lovely short introduction to the science of decision-making several years ago. The book, *Decision Making and Rationality in the Modern World*, begins with a problem closely related to our gambling problem.

Consider the following two gambles:

> Gamble A. Win $10 if a red card is drawn from a standard deck of cards; lose $6 if a black card is drawn.
> Gamble B. Win $20 if a heart is drawn from a standard deck of cards; lose $2 if a heart is not drawn.

To get from Stanovich's problem to our gambling problem, "Win $10 if a red card is drawn from a standard deck of cards..." needs to be changed to "A 50% chance of winning $10...," and similarly with the other factors formulated in terms of the deck of cards. This is a virtually trivial change for anyone who knows what a standard deck of cards is.

Advocates of RCT suggest that the decision problem we have just discussed, the gambling problem, is typical, not an exception; it is a model for all normal decisions, though of course normal decisions will be rather more complicated. The reason they regard the gambling problem as typical is that it contains the two essential components of any decision: an estimate of value (money) and an estimate of likelihood (probability). This is a bold claim, in part because, aside from the trivial quantification of probability with reference to a standard deck of cards — a process that anyone familiar with a standard deck would go through almost automatically — and accounting for the diminishing marginal utility of money, the problem is a purely mathematical one. So, the implicit claim is that not only can decision problems generally be solved rigorously, but they can be solved basically by formula. To our knowledge, the presumption that all decision problems can be solved mathematically, though never stated explicitly, is the clear implication of the claim that the gambling case is a typical one, and we believe it is the impression left by such examples. We believe that the prestige that RCT gains from this implication/impression remains even when other examples show clearly that the claim is unfounded. How, for example, do we reduce the "What should I do today?" question to a simple matter of mathematical calculation?

People who work within the framework of RCT suggest, or at least imply, that the more we can transform everyday decisions into close analogs of gambles, the closer we can come to being rational decision makers. What does such a transformation require? RCT proper can be applied when and only when a manageably sized set of options has been specified. The construction of this set we will call *specification*. This is the first process of RCT that we want to identify. "Specification" is one form of the framing process we introduced in the introduction. "What should I do today?" fails to meet that standard, though with some deliberation that prunes the almost infinite set of possibilities into a much smaller number, RCT may then be deployed. And not just the options, but the relevant "attributes" of the options need to be specified: how much fun will I have, will it improve my health, how much effort is required, will I get a sunburn, what will it cost . . . ?

We are anticipating quantifying all the relevant considerations so that we can calculate the answer to our question of what to do, and quantification requires eliminating vagueness and ambiguity in both the options and the attributes. We call this process *clarification*. Getting exercise and going for a walk in the park "overlap" (a walk in the park *is* exercise) so we might reformulate the options as "getting exercise in the gym or by walking in the park." If exerting effort is often fun for the decider, various options that seem like fun will have to be made distinct: fun without effort and fun with effort. We call this third aspect *disentanglement*.

Probability and utility have to be quantified ("the probability of rain is 20%" replaces "there is a possibility of rain." "If it doesn't rain, the beach will be worth 100 units of utility, and going to the movies will be worth 60.") *Quantification* is the fourth aspect of transformation. These four processes — specification, clarification, disentanglement, and quantification — taken together we will call the process of preparation or *closure*. When we have brought closure to the problem "What shall I do today?" we are ready to calculate the rational choice.

What do we mean by "closure"? What does it mean for a decision problem to be "closed"? First, specific options have to be articulated. RCT cannot work directly on a problem formulated like "What shall I do today?" The problem needs to be reframed in something like the following way: "Shall I go to the beach or the movies?" Initial framing often results in these aspects of closure. Next, for a formal system like RCT to be used effectively, the various alternatives facing the decider must be specified with clarity and precision. The aim of RCT is to enable quantitative, formal conclusions to be the result of the analysis. This is difficult to achieve when components of the alternatives are vaguely or incompletely specified or if they overlap. It is not good enough to say that a job you are considering offers a fair amount of autonomy or decent chances for advancement. It is no doubt often useful to be clear and precise in formulating alternatives, but the actual world does not always cooperate. Often, the vagueness of the open system in which we live will not permit the clarity and precision that closure offers without introducing serious distortion.

In addition, for the system to be closed, the decision has to be framed in a context-independent way. That means that the relevant factors have to be specified precisely. Decisions are often made in a context that has an almost unlimited number of relevant factors. The choice between having red meat or fish for dinner, in addition to considerations of how much pleasure each will provide, might also include matters of health and the environmental consequences of supporting the raising of beef or the farming of fish. Very often all but a relatively few factors will be insignificant, but what factors are significant has to be judged. The factors that will be relevant to the decision must be chosen from among a potentially unlimited set of possible considerations. Since the context contains an unlimited number of such factors, the RCT method requires taking the decision out of context. We note that formal RCT cannot do this work, which is essentially a framing job. In other words, RCT can operate only *after* a decision has been suitably framed. In the gambling examples discussed above, that framing is done by the setting of the problem. In normal life, setting the problem is frequently one of the most challenging aspects of making a decision.

Furthermore, RCT requires that decisions meet a set of formal properties to be considered rational. We enumerated some of them above. The mathematician L. J. Savage formulated these properties about seventy years ago. We will not discuss the so-called Savage postulates here, but they include such features as transitivity of preference, independence of preference from the presence of "irrelevant" alternatives (if A is preferred to B, then adding C, which is inferior to both A and B and thus irrelevant to the decision, should not alter one's preference between A and B), and independence of preference from the way in which options are described, as long as the various descriptions are formally equivalent. Many decision "errors" studied by decision researchers are cases that violate one or more of these postulates.

This is a rough characterization of the sort of reframing needed to transform an everyday problem that does not present itself in a form that makes formal RCT productive. We can get a small taste of what that process is like by discussing another example taken from Stanovich, of a family deciding whether to go to the beach or to the art museum. His presentation of the beach/museum example leaves the impression that this more familiar type of decision can be solved by RCT with just minor adjustments for complexity. We believe that impression is misleading in important respects.

In Stanovich's example, the Weather Channel says it might rain, which would totally ruin the trip to the beach. The museum trip would not be as good as the beach trip on a beautiful day, but it would be much better than the beach on a rainy day. Are the essentials of this real-life decision well captured by the examples of monetary gambles?

Let us compare the two sets of choices — the choice of monetary gamble and the choice of weekend activity. The impression that Stanovich (and most researchers like him) gives is that with respect to the use of RCT, the choices are similar; and from the point of view of RCT there is a lot of truth in that assumption. But is there enough truth to justify the claim that RCT is generally applicable?

The beach/museum problem is presented as specified and partially formalized (that is, clarified). Formalization is a prerequisite for the next step, quantification:

> Gamble A (Go to the beach): 80% chance of 100 units of utility and 20% chance of 10 units of utility. (The chances depend on whether it rains.)

Gamble B (Go to the museum): 80% chance of 60 units of utility and 20% chance of 50 units of utility. (If it rains, you won't be able to have a picnic lunch in the museum's lovely sculpture garden.)

Here we can see important differences between the gambling paradigm and "normal" decision problems. Unlike the gambling case, the beach case, even though it is presented as largely closed, requires additional closure. First, the probability of bad weather has to be quantified. "The Weather Channel says it might rain" becomes "There is a 20% chance of rain." Here, we are taking a non-numerical acknowledgment of uncertainty and giving it a numerical value. There is a considerable element of arbitrariness in this quantification. Given that "it might rain," can we infer that the chance of rain is 20% and not 45%? On what basis? Forecasting the weather is not nearly as precise as forecasting the chances of drawing a heart from an ordinary deck of cards. How imprecise is the weather forecast? Does this imprecision matter? Is assigning a probability to rain a strictly logical inference? Clearly not. It is, in a sense, an interpretation of "it might rain" as "there is a 20% chance of rain." So, we can already see a substantial difference between the gambling example and the beach example: the latter requires something substantial other than mathematical calculation — interpretation. And given that it requires interpretation, is it as rigorously precise as RCT implies?

A second kind of imprecision, or vagueness, that needs to be made precise is illustrated by the question of what length or kind of rain will count as ruining the trip to the beach. Without an answer to this, we can't reasonably determine a probability of rain. Will it be a shower that lasts for five minutes, a steady rain lasting most of the day, or something in between? In other words, we have to clarify what is to count as rain. We discuss the pervasive implications of this problem in chapter 3. Thus, the likelihood of hidden arbitrariness or vagueness in "there is a 20% chance of rain" is substantial. The rigor of this process is called into doubt.

The quantification of utility has somewhat related problems. "The museum trip would not be as good as the beach trip on a beautiful day, but it would be much better than the beach on a rainy day." This stipulation, framed the way that a normal set of valuations of such things is likely to be, requires precision and quantification. The vague formulation gets interpreted as "On a sunny day the ratio of the utility of a beach trip to a museum trip is 100 to 60, and on a rainy day it would be 10 to 50." We can ask the same questions here that we ask in connection with the quantification of the probability of bad weather. Is this quantification a rigorous inference? If so, what is its empirical basis? If not, what justifies making the inference? These questions of how one transforms commonsense comparisons into quantified ones and how one resolves the ambiguity of "might" and "rain" were not part of our gambling problem, and thus they introduce new questions.

The decisions we face typically in our everyday lives do not come to us closed and quantified. And they do not always come to us well specified. "What should I do today?" is neither specified nor closed, let alone quantified. To understand the difference between using RCT on a gambling problem and on a common everyday issue like the beach problem, we have to investigate the processes of specification and closure in addition to the process of quantification. This is often very difficult to do, and when it can't be done, the apparent rigor of RCT is called into question.

We have seen that the gambling example is atypical in that it does not require specification, formalization, or nontrivial quantification; or, perhaps more accurately, it has specification, formalization, and quantification built in. We shall see that normal decisions differ from the gambling paradigm not just in using additional processes that produce closure. There are also very important differences involved in the way the processes are used, depending on the content of the decision. We can see this in the beach/museum example.

The necessary calculations in the beach/museum example are virtually identical to those in the gambling example, but it takes some work to get there. How does Stanovich get the beach case into a form that matches the deck of cards case? He tells us that the first preference of everyone is for the beach, but (1) the Weather Channel says it might rain; (2) rain would totally ruin the trip to the beach; and (3) the family would not have time to backtrack from the coast and go to the museum in the city. Moreover, (4) the museum trip will not be as good as the beach trip on a good day; but (5) it will be much better than the beach on a rainy day; and (6) the museum on a rainy day is almost as good as the museum on a day that is not rainy, but not quite. The reason is that (7) there is a neat sculpture garden at the museum that would have to be missed if it were raining. This reasoning allows Stanovich to put the choice in semi-closed form, though the assignments of value of the two options and probability of achieving that value are somewhat arbitrary. They capture the conditions under which one option will be preferred to the other, but the magnitude of the preference is essentially invented.

Evidence for proposition 1 might have been readily available. Propositions 2, 4, and 5 are perfectly obvious, and comparable to the common sense we used in the deck of cards gamble, perhaps even simpler and easier. Even so, they have to be kept in mind as the comparisons of utility are made. Proposition 3 might also be obvious, or it might require calculation; how often do you drive from the

HOW WE *SHOULD* DECIDE

beach to the museum? How much time at the museum is required to enjoy the visit (minus time in the sculpture garden)? How tired will you be after driving first to the beach and then to the museum? How bored will the child be after all that driving? Propositions 6 and 7 might also require some thought.

Now, we have to consider that while simply knowing that one option is preferred to another might be sufficient to use RCT on some problems, it is not enough in this and many other cases. We need to know how much better a given option is. The devil here is in the details. Stanovich reformulates the possibility of rain affirmed by the Weather Channel as a 20% chance. Perhaps the Weather Channel actually said that the chance of rain was 20%, and if so, no additional work is required. That the beach is preferable to the museum on a sunny day seems easy enough to determine as a subjective fact, but a finer-grained analysis tells us that the beach is 40% better. Is it really? If it were only 10% better, the choice of activity would probably flip to the museum. Does anyone have easily accessible and reasonably accurate knowledge that something is subjectively 40% preferable to something else? Perhaps $100 is 40% preferable to $60, and 10 potatoes are 40% preferable to 6 potatoes, but in those cases the comparison is between similar things, easily quantified. That you prefer the beach to the museum is perfectly reasonable. But do you prefer it 40% more than the museum, not 39% and not 41%, but 40%? It is hard not to think this is arbitrary. And if we admit that such quantification is needed and makes sense, to be other than arbitrary such a claim would require a lot of work to be "evidence based," even on a very loose notion of evidence.

We discuss this simple example that Stanovich uses to move from monetary gambles to real-life decisions to illustrate that even when the real-life decisions are pretty simple, it takes a lot of work to turn them into decisions that parallel monetary gambles. For RCT to be persuasive as a normative model for making actual decisions, such work is necessary, but it is not obvious that one can make the parallel without assigning quantitative values rather arbitrarily, and without leaving important things out, thus oversimplifying the decision. Moreover, transforming a real-life decision into one that parallels a monetary gamble is itself not the rational part of RCT; just the calculations are. So, it is fair to say here that RCT has contributed less than it appears to the making of this choice. RCT relies on other kinds of thinking to be in a position to do its work.

Now, let us modify slightly the beach example. One of Stanovich's stipulations dramatically simplifies the example and unrealistically seems to confirm the generality of the usefulness of RCT. Stanovich tells us that the family agrees about the greater utility of the beach on a nice day. But suppose there had been disagreement—say, the father preferred the museum. The resolution of the disagreement would have added enormous complexity to the decision. The utility of going to the beach would be a complicated function of the utilities of the family members and their interactions (how happy will Mom be if Dad is forced to go to the beach, and how happy will the child be if Mom and Dad are not happy?). We could calculate the utility of each option separately for each family member and then just add the utilities up. A problem with that approach, however, is that the utilities for each family member may interact. The utility of going to the beach may drop for the child if Dad is unenthusiastic about it, or if continuing to discuss it creates uncomfortable tension between Mom and Dad. The interaction among utilities requires more than just adding them up. It requires the use of very different thought processes than are reflected by RCT, or at least raises issues that may not be precisely soluble. We believe that it reflects an important fact about RCT that examples involving interaction between people based on their beliefs and values are seldom if ever examined carefully. So, in addition to the fact that different processes are central in normal decisions than are used in the gambling paradigm, as the substance of the decision and the relevant considerations change, qualitative differences emerge between the gambling paradigm and other decision problems. We will examine this issue in greater depth in later chapters.

Let's add a little more complexity by pursuing further the possible disagreement between the parties. Disagreement could arise about almost any of the relevant factors — how rewarding the beach is relative to the museum, whether you could get to the museum in time if the beach didn't work out, whether the zoo should be considered. Let's suppose that the issue came down to a choice between the beach, the museum, and video games. The child wants to play video games. The parents know that that would be much preferable to the other two options in the child's opinion, but the kind of enjoyment that the child gets from the video games is, they think, unhealthy. It is physically passive, isolating, and it orients the child to fantasy worlds rather than the real world. If they believe it is unhealthy enough, the parents may decide to discount substantially the enjoyment the child gets from video games. How is such a decision possible on the basis of RCT, and how much work is involved that is not RCT? If the parents discount the enjoyment of playing video games, what will be the child's reaction? Will the child think of this as a kind of punishment? Will the child think it is a trivial matter? If the child regards it as punishment, how much "disutility" should the parents expect from having to deal with the child's response? All this has been simplified out of the picture by ignoring both the process of coming up with an appropriate range of options and the possibility of disagreement between the people involved. And these sorts of considerations further reduce the significance of RCT in coming to a final decision. One can only imagine how much truer this would be if, as proposed by Stanovich, the whole family, including other children, are involved, without the assumption that they all agree.

We have elaborated this simple beach/museum example for a reason. When the core of a decision is understood to involve essentially two considerations — how likely am I to get the outcome I'm hoping for, and how good will that outcome be for me — how closely our decisions conform to the norms of RCT can be stripped away from the complexities of real-life decisions and studied in much simpler situations. This sort of strategy is standard operating procedure in science. If you want to understand genetics, study peas or fruit flies, not people. Fruit-fly genetics are simpler than human genetics and the reproductive cycle of fruit flies is much faster. Having figured out fruit-fly genetics, you can move on to the much more complex human case. One could imagine thinking of the gamble as the fruit fly of research on decision-making. True, normal decisions usually do not come packaged as closed and context free. But starting simple and then adding complexity is a standard scientific strategy.

And there is even something to be said for treating the beach/museum decision as a close analog of the gamble. By ignoring the complexity of interpersonal interactions and pretending that both the probability and the value of the options can be specified with the same precision as with a gamble, one may help people clarify decisions for themselves. Start out neat, precise, and simple. Figure out what you prefer in this unrealistic setting. Then, and only then, add some or all of the complexities in deciding between the beach and the museum. Starting simple may provide clarity, and as long as you don't stay simple, it may do no harm. None of this is unreasonable. We will suggest, however, that starting simple like this can and does do harm. And we will argue that the difference between the gambling paradigm and everyday problems is not a quantitative difference between simple and complex, but a qualitative one requiring a whole different kind of thinking.

We have presented a sketch of RCT that was intended to show two things. First, in certain kinds of cases, those that are "naturally" framed as closed and quantified, RCT seems to work well. But second, there are important differences between these cases and those that, to allow for calculation, must first be specified, closed, and quantified. In later chapters we will show more fully that the processes of specification, closure, and quantification, when examined carefully, raise important questions with regard to whether the gambling paradigm is typical, and whether RCT is as useful as it claims to be in the general case.

Rational Choice Theory Meets Heuristics and Biases

Before addressing this problem in detail, we will first address a different one: whether RCT accurately describes the way we actually do our thinking. However good RCT is as a normative theory — a theory of what people *should* do — how does it fare as a descriptive theory — a theory of what people *do* do? In the last half century or so, a part of psychology known as behavioral decision-making, or judgment and decision-making (JDM), has grown into a major enterprise, the central purpose of which is to describe and explain how decisions actually get made and look for discrepancies between what

HOW WE *SHOULD* DECIDE

RCT tells us to do and what we actually do. And, as a result of this research, a more refined idea of RCT has emerged. The field of JDM has developed an ever-growing catalogue of the mistakes human beings are susceptible to when they use a variety of heuristics, or shortcuts, rather than RCT, or in preparation for the use of RCT, to evaluate information, make decisions, and then calculate the expected results of those decisions. Much of the time, these heuristics work fine, but sometimes they introduce bias. Taken together, these mistakes or biases are subsumed under "System 1" (S1) in Daniel Kahneman's synoptic *Thinking, Fast and Slow*. S1 works outside of consciousness, rapidly delivering results to consciousness that are produced by these heuristics. In other words, S1 provides answers to the questions we may have. Afterward, a second, slower process, which is conscious, effortful, and rule-governed, may go to work using logic, probability theory, and other formal systems. This second system, S2, of which we are aware, may take the results of S1 and analyze them, sometimes leading to a different decision than S1 has produced on its own. Perhaps because S2 is slow, effortful, and conscious, it is usually what we have in mind when we say we are thinking a decision over. But in fact, the fast-acting S1 may already have made the decision before S2 even gets started.

In his book, Kahneman analogizes S1 to many perceptual processes. Think about driving in city streets. You want to turn left, but a car is approaching from the other direction. Do you have enough time to make the turn? How far away is the car, and how fast is it going? Your visual system answers these questions for you very fast, and typically very accurately. But when the passenger sitting next to you — a teenage beginning driver — asks you how you knew that you had the time to make the turn, you have nothing to say. So it is with S1-type decision-making processes. They deliver answers, but the conscious you typically has no idea how they arrived at those answers. And because S1 is so fast, it may answer a question for you before you have even fully formulated it.

Kahneman spent a quarter of a century doing research on S1 processes, most of it in collaboration with Amos Tversky. Their focus was on elucidating the ways in which S1 goes wrong. But studying the errors of S1 required that there be some standard—some normative theory—of how judgments and decisions *should* be made. To provide that standard, Kahneman and Tversky, like most other researchers in their field, relied on the RCT model we just described to provide a contrast with S1 processes. RCT is at the heart of how economics captures decision-making, and provides the background against which heuristics, biases, and other S1 processes are evaluated.

RCT is the province of S2 and is slow, effortful, and logical. A decision maker need not accept the results of the automatic S1 processes as competent or definitive, but these processes deliver answers upon which consciousness acts. One of Kahneman's main arguments is that people think they are using S2 when faced with problems of judgment and choice when in fact S1 is doing much of the work—automatically, effortlessly, rapidly, but not always accurately.

We cannot overestimate the significance of Kahneman's body of work (with Tversky as well as other collaborators) mapping out various S1 processes and relating them to S2. Among the characteristics of S1 processes are these: they turn inarticulate impressions, feelings, and inclinations into beliefs, attitudes, and intentions; they create a coherent pattern of ideas in memory; they distinguish surprising events from normal events; they take the ease of information processing to be evidence of the truth of what has been processed; they infer causes and intentions; they neglect ambiguity and suppress doubt; they exaggerate the consistency of the information being processed; they focus on what is present in a situation and largely ignore what is absent, even when absent information is relevant to the task at hand; they respond more to changes in the environment than to steady states; they overweigh the significance of rare events; they are more affected by potential losses than potential gains from a baseline state; they tend to frame the decisions being faced narrowly. And they are always working. This list of attributes is impressive, but hardly exhaustive. The research that Kahneman and Tversky did launched an explosion of interest in heuristics and biases and their effects on decision-making (see the work of JDM researcher Gerd Gigerenzer for many examples studied from a somewhat different perspective). By some counts, at this point more than one hundred different heuristics and biases have been identified and studied. The exploration and explication of S1 processes has been quite a growth industry.

For beginning this line of research that countless others have followed, Kahneman deservedly won the Nobel Prize in Economics in 2005 (Tversky would surely have shared it had he not died prematurely). A few years later, economist Richard Thaler also won a Nobel, for work very much inspired by Kahneman and Tversky. But our aim in what follows is not to describe various S1 processes and explain how they lead us astray. For that, *Thinking, Fast and Slow* is pretty definitive.

Kahneman and others have offered serious criticisms of the notion that RCT in its pure form can adequately capture judgment and decision-making. But they are proposing, in our view, modifications of RCT rather than basically different ways of understanding what thinking is about. Their critique of RCT is essentially that it fails as a *description* of decision-making, not that it fails as a *norm* for decision-making. We think this approach is inadequate to capture the scope of the problem. We will argue that what is needed is a different, nonformal conception of judgment and decision-making, and we sketch such an alternative in chapter 9. Kahneman's articulations of the limits of RCT lead only to a variant that defines itself by differences from RCT, and in that sense keeps RCT as the central model. And RCT remains the basic prescriptive model, the proffered guide to good judgment and decision-making. Another way of stating our objective going forward is this: economists and many other social scientists had assumed that human beings are "rational" decision makers. Research has shown that people are not nearly as rational as these researchers assumed. And RCT is a deeply inadequate account of what it means to be rational. We will develop our critique largely with Kahneman's book *Thinking, Fast and Slow* as our touchstone.

We will suggest that the view of S2, largely governed by RCT, as overseeing and correcting the errors of S1 mischaracterizes both the relation between the two systems and thinking in general. We believe that rather than being a corrective to the errors of S1, S2 (and RCT in particular) is *parasitic* on S1. Without S1 doing crucial work, the RCT-driven processes of S2 could not get off the ground. Furthermore, RCT mischaracterizes what we mean, or should mean, by "thinking." Thinking, and thus rationality, is much more than what RCT provides the norms for. And with a more comprehensive understanding of thinking in mind, S1 processes loom even larger.

The focus in what follows is not on whether people adhere to the normative standard set by RCT; they do not. Rather, we question whether the normative standard *should* be normative. We think it should not. Our basic reason is that RCT requires that we frame our decisions in a "closed" and formal way. "Framing" will have a prominent role in much of the discussion that follows. For JDM researchers, framing is a paradigm case of S1 bias. Indeed, one of Kahneman and Tversky's most celebrated papers is titled "The Framing of Decisions and the Psychology of Choice." So, framing phenomena are typically considered to be obstacles to rational decision-making. In taking this stance, decision researchers have typically had a specific handful of examples of framing in mind, examples in which people frame the decisions they face more narrowly than they should. We might call these examples of "narrow framing" (or, more accurately, "too narrow framing," since any instance of framing narrows the range of possibilities). In contrast, we think framing, understood more broadly as imposing limits and context on a decision, is essential to RCT in particular and rationality in general. For RCT to work, the options need to be limited. They need to be clearly defined, unlike the terms that frame much of ordinary life. The decisions people face need to be separated from the larger context in which they are, in reality, often embedded. And data and preferences must be homogenized—squeezed into a common framework that facilitates comparison, even among very different things. The data must be homogenized so as to be amenable to evaluation with quantitative methods. Preferences must be homogenized so that quantitative methods can be used to assess them. What the focus on RCT and S1 deviations from it have in common is that they take a system (thinking) that is highly varied in form and substance, and extremely sensitive to context, and they *close the system* to make it manageable and formalizable.

As we said, Kahneman and most other researchers in JDM describe framing as a significant source of bias or deviation from RCT in decisions. We believe, in contrast, that while framing sometimes leads us astray, it is central to almost all thinking and decision-making. In many cases, good framing is itself the goal. And there is no inquiry or deciding without it. This point is often overlooked or underappreciated, in part because it is thought that rigorously presented examples, like monetary gambles, that call for the use of RCT are themselves unframed. It is central to our view that the standard RCT cases, though thought to be unframed, are in fact framed: they are framed to the extent that they can be treated as closed.

Expressed slightly differently, our view is that framing is a *prerequisite* for the operation of RCT; without framing, RCT procedures can't even get started. In addition, RCT requires quantification of both probability and value, which we believe cannot be done within the bounds of RCT, at least not without framing. In many situations in real life, attaching probabilities to outcomes is at best wishful thinking and at worst sheer fantasy. In addition, assignment of value to the options we face often depends on framing, and since RCT can't tell us much about how decisions should be framed, it can't tell us much about how alternatives should be valued. These points will be elaborated in later chapters. Finally, in a paper with Daniel Keys, then an undergraduate at Swarthmore College, Barry argued that frequently the frames that operate at the time of decision continue to operate after the decision is made, affecting the subjective quality of the chosen experience, a process they call "leakage." And when decision frames leak into experience, it becomes very difficult for RCT to claim that a mistake has been made as a result of framing.

By now, almost everyone who studies decision-making knows that RCT is an idealization that does not match how many decisions are actually made. The work of Kahneman and Tversky has had profound effects. Indeed, perhaps, speaking practically, RCT is not even a good model for how decisions always *should* be made. Going through the process of RCT decision analysis may be more costly in time and cognitive resources than the decision is worth. And an outcome that is utility maximizing in an individual decision may be destructive when cumulated, so that individual decisions must be considered in terms of the long-term consequences they may have. This acknowledgment has led some researchers, in the spirit of Herbert Simon (another Nobel Prize winner), to modify the rational choice norm and speak of "bounded rationality," which highlights the cognitive (and emotional) limitations of human beings. The notion of bounded rationality leaves the normative status of the model of rational choice intact, simply describing the ways in which finite organisms actually make decisions with processes that fall short of the normative standard. Thus, the normative standard exerts a powerful influence on the research that is actually done, on what investigators find interesting and noteworthy, and on the prescriptions that are offered to improve decision-making. Perhaps most significant, the normative standard makes certain important questions about rationality essentially invisible to researchers and policy makers alike. In what follows, we will try to make them visible.

Two Inadequate Defenses of RCT

We suspect that there are many RCT enthusiasts who will disagree with the sketch we have just presented. First, with regard to RCT's failures as a descriptive theory, it might be said that economics, the disciplinary home of RCT, has always been concerned with predicting and explaining aggregate behavior, not individual behavior. In other words, economists are interested in the behavior of markets and economies as a whole, not in the behavior of individual participants in those markets. Deviations from RCT in practice are just "noise" in the system, noise that washes out when the behavior of millions of individuals is aggregated. This defense is inadequate for two reasons. First, Kahneman (accompanied by Tversky and many others) and Thaler did not win Nobel Prizes for identifying noise. The driving force of research in JDM has been to show that deviations from RCT are systematic, not random. These deviations are displayed by the vast majority of people, and in aggregate, they change how economies work. Moreover, as a normative rather than descriptive theory, RCT is very much concerned with individuals. RCT, it is argued, is how decisions *should* be made, by each and every one of us, in most if not all situations. So this defense, we believe, fails.

Second, as we indicated above, defenders of RCT might argue that it is standard and good scientific practice to articulate theories or models that oversimplify the domain they are trying to explain. Oversimplification gets the process of explanation started, and then complexities are added as the theory develops. Start with the genetics of fruit flies and move, fitfully, to the genetics of human beings. This is a fair defense, as long as the introduction of complexity does not fundamentally undo the principles with which the simplified theory started. Our belief is that, unlike the fruit fly, the gambling paradigm with which RCT began is a fundamental distortion of decisions as we face them every day, and of rationality as understood more comprehensively. The gambling paradigm does not merely simplify reality; it distorts reality. Because of this, developing RCT into more complex forms is like eating fruit from a poisoned tree. Moreover, the gambling paradigm is not an incidental starting point for RCT, it is essential. This point is well illustrated by Annie Duke's recent book *Thinking in Bets*. Duke is a psychologist, decision scientist, and world champion professional poker player, and the book is an extended argument that our decision-making would be vastly improved if we thought of our decisions in the way we think about placing bets (that is, gambling).

We do not mean to suggest that starting simple and then adding complexity as progress is made is not a good way to develop a theory. But it is not *always* a good way. If the simple theory you start with has fundamental flaws, it is unlikely that adding complexity will correct or eliminate those flaws. And our belief is that an RCT built on the gambling paradigm has just such fundamental flaws. It may even obstruct recognition of those flaws, as pre-Copernican astronomy preserved the notion that the Earth is the center of the planetary system by adding epicycles to its theory of planetary motion.

An individual decision can be evaluated with the help of a model of an ideal decision, and we take RCT to be such a model. And a whole life can be evaluated with the help of a model of an ideal whole life. Often the evaluation of a decision, and always the evaluation of a life is not a yes-or-no, good-or-bad matter based on whether it is ideal or not. No life will fully measure up to an ideal model. Rather, the model facilitates our assessment of a life in something like the way that geometry helps us understand the physical world. There are no objects in the world that are perfect geometrical shapes. Nonetheless, it is still useful, for example, to understand the movement of a baseball, basketball, or golf ball on the assumption that it approximates a sphere. To understand the behavior of the actual object, however, we must make accommodations necessitated by the fact that the object is not exactly a sphere, but an approximation of a particular kind: it may have (approximately) concave indents almost covering its surface in an irregular pattern, or stitching that disrupts the smoothness of the surface; it has a certain degree of elasticity; it moves through the air with a certain degree of resistance; and so on.

To understand the movement of the approximately spherical object, we need to take into account all these things, yet the model of a sphere is still very helpful in understanding the movement of the object. What the models from geometry do is put us in the right ballpark. It's a great start, but it must be reconciled with the empirical facts on the ground. Thus, the process of rational thinking and deciding is one that shuttles back and forth between the ideal and the real — between the simplified formalisms of a discipline like geometry and the bumps and ridges of lived reality. As we will see, among the things that RCT is missing is this back-and-forth. It impoverishes decisions by analogizing them to gambles (conceptually equivalent to geometric spheres) and stops there, rather than fitting them back into reality (baseballs and golf balls).

Chapter 2

RATIONAL CHOICE THEORY

Specification of Options and Attributes

In the last chapter, we tried to accomplish three things. First, we presented rational choice theory as a normative approach to making decisions and showed that the canonical form it works with is the gambling decision, in which the value of a win or loss and the probability of a win or loss are the two key parameters. Second, we discussed briefly some of the ways in which RCT fails as a descriptive theory, focusing on empirical research on heuristics and biases spearheaded by Kahneman and Tversky. And third, we explored the mismatch between the form of the sorts of decisions we face every day and the canonical gambling paradigm that RCT depends upon. This chapter will expand on this third point. What does it take for an everyday decision to become the kind of decision that RCT is comfortable with?

Specification

Calculation of expected utility (value times probability) is the culmination of RCT, and quantification is a prerequisite for that calculation.

Quantification itself has prerequisites in the form of specification — specification of options and of relevant considerations.

Stanovich's beach/museum example illustrates these two prerequisites. First, he specifies the options — beach or museum. Then, he formalizes considerations by enumerating them (utility, weather, and so on) and refining them (disambiguating them, removing or ignoring overlap, and omitting lots of possible complications). Let's dig deeper into how one might get to that stage with a somewhat more complex example.

Mia is a high school junior, living in Delaware, who is thinking about what to do after high school. Between pressure from her parents and the attitudes of all her friends and acquaintances, going to college is largely a foregone conclusion rather than a decision. However, she is confronted with the decision of where to go. This is a typical unspecified decision — more consequential than most. To apply RCT to her decision, the decision needs to be formulated as a choice between specific options. Our concern here is with how she gets from the unspecified "Where should I apply to college?" to a specified decision problem.

We will compare two versions of her process of specification. The first will meet the standards of RCT, but not more. If we follow the RCT method as described in chapter 1, specification will come in two stages — first, the specification of the relevant options and then the specification of the relevant attributes of the options. RCT as a formal method typically says nothing about the best way to specify the options. So Mia takes the options that come to mind, perhaps the obvious ones, perhaps the ones her friends are thinking about, as the relevant list to start with.

Her next step will be to identify the relevant attributes, those by which she will evaluate the options. Here again RCT as a formal method can say little or nothing about specifying the attributes well, so again, Mia starts by taking the considerations that come readily to mind. In other words, Mia does not give much thought to determining the right way to specify options and attributes. After clarifying the things on her lists rather informally, she proceeds to what she considers to be the real work, quantification and calculation.

Now imagine a second version of the decision process. Suppose that Mia, even though she intends to quantify and calculate according to RCT, does not neglect the importance of specification by undervaluing it relative to quantification and calculation.

Rather than going directly to listing the options from which she will choose the schools to apply to, Mia examines some college guides — lists of "best" colleges — and consults people whom she thinks are likely to know about colleges. And rather than just listing what factors seem important to her, she thinks about what she really wants. She dismisses fraternity life as unimportant and includes distance from home. At this stage the number of options and considerations are so large as to make it impossible for her to apply RCT to them rigorously, so she sets about paring down both lists.

The *Wall Street Journal* lists Babson College as the second-best college in the country. But when Mia considers that, she sees that the *Wall Street Journal* is ranking on the basis of how well colleges prepare you for financial success. This leads Mia to ask herself why she is going to college. Her first thought is the conventional one — because she wants an education — but she realizes that she hasn't thought much about what that means. Perhaps she is actually going because all her peers are going. So Mia reflects, and on reflection, she decides that getting an education is actually a good reason to go to college, so now it is her real reason. But what kind of education? She realizes that while financial success is tempting, it is not the primary thing she wants out of life. What she really wants is to contribute to her community, and that suggests being a social worker, a lawyer, a teacher, a doctor, or a political activist, among other similar things. Mia thinks a liberal arts education rather than a vocational education will prepare her well for these possible future paths.

Swarthmore College has come up high in many rankings for liberal arts colleges, but upon thinking about it, she concludes that it is too intellectual – too high pressure – and that she is not smart enough or committed enough to academics to thrive at Swarthmore. Michigan has also come up high in several rankings, but those rankings are based on things like graduation rates and faculty publications, which, on reflection, she does not think are particularly indicative of a college that will appeal to her and prepare her for the life she wants to lead. Moreover, thinking about how far away Michigan is, she considers how disappointed her parents will be. She will, of course, have to break with her parents at some time, but a break at this time would be sharper and sooner than she wants. Penn State is a possibility that is closer to home, but reading college guides and talking with her friends suggests to Mia that sports and partying play too big a role in campus life there. "Is that what I want from college, a good time? Why am I going to college? To get an education, find out about the world and where I fit in it." She tries to picture what her life would be like at Penn State, and the picture suggests to her that she will be marginalized there because she does not have that much interest in sports or partying. She wants to be with students who, like her, are there for an education. Boston University and NYU have been highly ranked so she compares them, debating with herself by first trying to make the case for one as opposed to the other, and then vice versa. She also asks other informed people, perhaps graduates or current students of one or the other, for their opinions about how the schools compare, and discusses that with them.

Let's look at what Mia has done in this second case. She has learned from sources — books and people that have more knowledge than she has. She has thought about what she really wants and believes, rather than taking outside assessments at face value. She has thought about the limits of her abilities. She has thought about the beliefs and desires of others (her parents), and the effects of her decision on them. She has constructed conceptual pictures of life at given colleges — thought experiments, as it were — and rejected some on the basis of what she learned, like a scientist constructing a hypothesis and rejecting it when it fails experimental testing. She has compared and debated the options with herself (perhaps with others as well). We propose to call this process "deliberation." Mia was motivated to deliberate and capable of doing so because she had certain qualities, among them patience, thoughtfulness, intelligence, reflectiveness about herself, honesty about herself, capacity for self-knowledge, and concern for others. Without these qualities, she might have been unmotivated to deliberate, or incapable of worthwhile deliberation.

Little of what Mia did in the course of her deliberations is congenial to the process of RCT. Deliberation is, essentially, a nonformal process, while RCT, as we saw, aspires to formality. Some of what she did is probably inconsistent with RCT, and much is marginal at best. Mia has changed her preferences in the course of her deliberation, and that is logically excluded by formal RCT, since RCT assumes that preferences are exogenous, meaning that we have and know our preferences before the RCT exercise begins. She has changed her options in the course of deliberation, which is almost never considered in research on or exposition of RCT. Change of options in the course of deliberation is surely likely. Is there a reader who has not agonized over a choice between two movies, only to have the problem solved by the discovery of a third option?

The quality of Mia's choice of where to apply depends greatly on how well she specifies her options and their relevant attributes. If, objectively speaking, Ursinus College is best for Mia, but does not make it onto the list of options, there is a limit to how good her decision will be, whatever happens in later stages of deciding. The same is true if she ignores a significant attribute, such as an intrusively political atmosphere on campus or access to city life. The first version of Mia's choosing where to apply, without deliberation, is very likely to contain mistakes of this sort that raise the question of whether it was actually rational, even if the formal calculation was done correctly. It was certainly not a good decision process, and was unlikely to contribute to a good decision. If we insist on calling it rational because it conformed to the standards of RCT, we are faced with the question of why we should aspire to be rational in that sense. The point here is that the quality of "specification" contributes a great deal to the rationality and quality of the decision process — perhaps equal to or even greater than quantification and calculation. If we compared the Mia who calculated but did not deliberate with the Mia who deliberated but did not calculate, who would we say was more rational? In our opinion, it would be the latter.

Our description of the college-selection process seems arduous, and perhaps a little tedious, which suggests that decision makers will be reluctant to go through this process no matter how much it improves the decision, and will be inclined to carelessness and oversimplification. As confirmation, every year, in the first meeting of his undergraduate course on decision-making, Barry displayed a complex college-choice spreadsheet and asked the students how many of them had gone through such a process in choosing where to go to college. Over at least a dozen years, which encompassed about six hundred students, only one student ever owned up to having generated a spreadsheet (both of her parents were economists)! This tediousness may also explain why examples of the use of RCT rarely if ever consider such a process in detail.

Arduous though it may be, the second process is better and more rational than the first. Mia actively explores and considers her lists. She researches and evaluates her sources. She takes into account important considerations, like the feelings of others. She carefully imagines life at the various options, recognizing new and important factors as a result. She substitutes better for worse options. And she asks the right questions, deep questions, about her real motives and goals.

How much better and more rational her process is actually depends in large part on how she answers the questions she raises. Her answers might be arbitrary, and that would undermine the idea that her process has been rational. She might have, for example, simply accepted her first response to the question "Why am I going to college?" — that is, that she is going for an education — and left it at that. However, she did not do that.

The reason she didn't lies in qualities we have attributed to her: rather than impatience to reach an answer, thoughtfulness, intelligence, reflectiveness, and self-knowledge. How would they manifest themselves? Thoughtfulness manifests itself as the disposition to ask and think about questions; intelligence, as the ability to think well; reflectiveness, as the inclination to examine one's own life rather than just external circumstances. And self-knowledge — a certain amount of understanding of oneself, one's strengths, one's biases and limitations — is a product of the previous three qualities.

Of course, it is by now clear that Mia is an extraordinarily serious and intellectual young woman, and no one expects all or even most high school graduates interested in college to go to these lengths. Even super-serious Mia might also have cared about the quality of social life, extracurricular activities, and how good the food was in making her decision. But several things are quite clear. First, the closer one comes to this sort of process, the better the decision will be. Second, RCT has little in general to contribute to this kind of decision-making; it is almost irrelevant. Third, the rigorous and rational use of RCT, without oversimplification, other than in a small number of specific cases, is qualitatively more complex and difficult than the gambling paradigm makes it appear because so much thinking is required before a proper RCT decision matrix can even be set up.

Perhaps the takeaway from this discussion of Mia's thoughts about where to go to college is to do the hard thinking first, and then use RCT. But some of the ways of thinking that Mia has used (for example, nonquantitative research and evaluation of sources) are too informal to live up to RCT standards of rationality, some (for example, reflection on oneself and one's real wants) are simply outside the spirit of "scientific" RCT, and some may even be sources of bias in the final decision. To incorporate deliberation into RCT in any capacity would be to change the nature of RCT at its core, making it dependent on another kind of thinking altogether. To fail to do so raises questions about whether RCT as such (without deliberation) is the best way — or even a good way or a truly rational way — to make a decision in all cases.

We want to emphasize that this process of deliberation has resulted in a decision—the decision of which schools to investigate "rigorously." So, we have identified a decision process that is not RCT, but on which RCT depends whenever the decision problem does not already come in specified form, which is quite common, perhaps normal. In addition, the quality of deliberation is crucial to the success of the decision process as a whole. If rationality requires including for explicit consideration the best options, then to be rational, the deliberation on which RCT depends, which leads to specification, must be done well. Yet RCT plays little or no role in it.

Vagueness and Clarification

Proper specification in order to use RCT requires eliminating vagueness in its key parameters. We have already mentioned the problem of vagueness and the need for clarification in connection with the attributes in the beach/museum decision. The stipulated attribute was rainy weather, but that is a placeholder for *suitable* weather, which is thoroughly vague as a quantifiable concept. Windy or chilly weather could also ruin the trip to the beach. But what temperature is to count as chilly for these purposes? How much rain would ruin the trip? How much wind? It seems obvious that there is no formal way to draw the lines that need to be drawn here. To turn the concept of suitable beach weather into a quantifiable concept is complicated. Nor will two rational people necessarily agree with each other about how to quantify it. And our purposes will have to be taken into account. Suitable beach weather for swimming is different from suitable beach weather for sunbathing, or for taking a long walk and experiencing the sights and sounds of the ocean. The resemblance of even so simple a case as the beach/museum decision to the gambling paradigm is disappearing. Informal reasoning, vagueness, purposes, and desires: the camel's nose is well under the tent.

There are two kinds of vagueness we will discuss — qualitative and quantitative. Qualitative vagueness is ambiguity. Quantitative vagueness is imprecision. "Big" is an example of both kinds of vagueness. If we say someone is very big, do we mean that they are tall or heavy? Once we have answered that question and resolved that ambiguity, we are still left with the question of just how tall or heavy a person has to be to be big: the problem of imprecision. Both kinds of vagueness are relevant to assessing the appropriateness of RCT, as we'll see.

Let us return to Mia and her college decision. Having specified the elements of her decision, Mia must now try to clarify them. There are different aspects of clarification. Mia, as we said, wants to go to a good school, but "a good school" is an ambiguous notion. There are different kinds of good schools. There are schools that are good because they are likely to lead to a good job — good vocationally — and there are schools that are good because they will broaden and deepen your understanding of your world and its history, and the world of others — typically, schools with strong liberal arts programs. Mia, we stipulated, wants a liberal arts education, so when she considers the various lists of top schools, she will know which lists to take seriously because she has disambiguated the notion "good school" to disregard the *Wall Street Journal*'s list of good schools, which is explicitly vocationally oriented. She will also view the *U.S. News* rankings of good schools with suspicion because she thinks *U.S. News* puts too much emphasis on graduation rates and financial considerations rather than broadening and deepening students' understanding of the world.

Even within the set of good liberal arts schools, the notion of a good liberal arts education needs further clarification. It is still vague. Is the liberal education Mia will get at one good school better than the liberal education she will get at another? Different, yes, but better? "Good liberal education" is ambiguous. To determine "better," she needs to know what "a good liberal education" is. How does she determine that?

Does a good liberal arts school need to teach Greek and Latin? These subjects were once at the heart of a liberal education. Without them you could not read the Bible in the original and were at the mercy of biased translators and/or interpreters. You also did not have direct access to classical Greek and Roman cultures. But the Bible does not play the role in the contemporary world that it did for much of the last two thousand years. And classical culture does not play the role that it played for several hundred years after the Renaissance. While the classics are still important to understanding Western history, perhaps they are not as important today as understanding the cultures of India, China, and the Islamic world. So, we may want to define a good liberal arts school as one that teaches the latter rather than the former. Or we may want to define it, given the technological age in which we live, as an education with a strong emphasis on the natural sciences.

This kind of clarification requires judgments that are not only difficult, but that may be impossible to make using only the form of thinking most congenial to RCT—formal, quantitative thinking. Can formal thinking tell you that there are two kinds of "good" colleges? Can it tell you whether a scientific/technical education defines a third kind of good college, or is that one of the two we already identified? Formal thinking will not answer such questions. Nor will it tell us whether the classics are essential for a liberal education. This also is a matter for sophisticated judgment rather than formal thinking.

Indeed, you may need the kind of education Mia is deciding about to develop the judgment you would need to decide what kind of education you want. Not a few college graduates lament, a few years after graduating, that they wish they could do college all over again.

When we realize the ambiguity of "big" we stop asking whether a tall person or a heavy person is bigger. We consider why we are asking the question. If we are creating a basketball team, height will be the relevant meaning. If we are creating a football team, it will be weight. Analogously, clarification will substitute deciding what Mia wants out of an education for deciding which school is likely to give her a good education. Does she want to come out of college prepared to increase our knowledge of the physical world, equipped with a broader and deeper understanding of contemporary culture and her place in it, or prepared to get a well-paying job?

This is, indirectly, the decision of what kind of life she wants to lead (though, of course, she may change her mind about this, more than once). When she chooses between the different kinds of life, it will almost certainly exert a significant influence on her decision about which schools to apply to. Will the formal techniques of RCT be of help in categorizing and understanding the important qualities (and shortcomings) of different kinds of education? We think it will be of little help, if any. Deliberation, as we described it earlier, will be necessary for Mia to make a good decision. It may be useful to point out that the *U.S. News* ranking, oriented as it is to formal methods, ignores this kind of question.

Vagueness: Fuzzy Categories

Vagueness is one of the most important obstacles to dealing with decision-making using the formal, quantitative techniques of RCT.

It is not a side issue, a nuisance detail. But despite our best efforts to eliminate vagueness, it is pervasive.

In *Practical Wisdom*, Barry and co-author Kenneth Sharpe discuss vagueness as one reason why judgment, rather than well-specified rules, is needed to make decisions. "Treat all people fairly" is a tough rule to follow if the concept of "fairness" itself is more than a little vague or fuzzy.

Not all of our concepts are as vague and fuzzy as "fairness." For example, there is a rule for computing the area of a rectangle: length times height. No problem. The question is, when should that rule be applied? Again, no problem. It should be applied to all rectangles, and we can specify exactly what makes a geometric form a rectangle: four sides, joined by right angles. When we encounter a geometric shape, it either is or is not a rectangle. If it is, we apply the rule. If it isn't, another approach is required. We can say, more technically, that the definition of a rectangle includes necessary and sufficient features so that we can always know whether a geometric shape belongs to the class or not. Not only that, but every rectangle is as much a rectangle as any other. We hasten to add that, as in the case of the "spheres" we discussed in chapter 1, the real world contains no actual rectangles. Nonetheless, many objects are close enough to being rectangles to be treated as such in definition, classification, and quantification.

Now consider the medical ethical principle of telling the truth to patients. The central concepts or categories in this principle — "truth" and "lie" — are not like rectangles. Whatever these words mean, they do not mean the same thing in every situation. They should not always be applied in the same way. And this is true for virtually all moral rules and principles — injunctions involving respect, harm, contracts, kindness, fair wages or living wages, patience, loyalty, and so on depend on categories that are fuzzy because the issues they involve are fuzzy. Instead of a clear, unambiguous, yes-or-no relationship between the core categories in a rule and the circumstances in which we consider using it, we find a "more-or-less" relationship, a *graded* relationship. Not telling a very elderly patient about a cancer diagnosis unless the patient asks directly is a lie of one kind but not of another kind.

It might seem at first that this fuzziness is a problem characteristic only of abstract or moral categories. If only the categories were more concrete or tangible, like "fruit" or "birds," we could be clear about what is in the category and what isn't. But fuzziness is a feature of most of the categories we use. "Fruit," for example, is less like "rectangle" than we might think. Though biologists might be able to provide a rectangle-like definition of fruit (for example, the seed-carrying part of a plant), that's not the one that most of us carry around in our heads. Instead, we think of fruits as edible parts of plants, usually juicy and often sweet. Not only that, but some fruits are "fruitier" — more typical — than others. If we asked you what comes to mind as an example of fruit, you'd probably say an apple or a pear or an orange. These are typical fruits. You certainly wouldn't say cumquat or persimmon or pomegranate. The category of "fruit" has a set of core examples, or core features. No one of these features "defines" fruit, but the more critical features an example has, the better an example of fruit it is. Some fruits are great examples; other fruits (pomegranate) are less good examples. And there are some foods we think of as non-fruits (avocados, for example) that are "almost fruits." We often call these core examples "prototypes," and they turn out to be very important in how we categorize.

About seventy years ago, the philosopher Ludwig Wittgenstein made the important argument that most of our everyday categories are like "fruit" and "truth" and decidedly not like "rectangle." These everyday categories have come to be called "natural" categories ("natural" just because of their everydayness) to distinguish them from more formal, precisely defined categories like "rectangle." More than fifty years ago, psychologist Eleanor Rosch started subjecting such natural categories to psychological research. Over the years, much has been learned about the structure of natural categories. And we know now that the mind has a tremendous capacity to deal with categories like these.

Natural categories are very different than formal categories like rectangle. They have "graded" membership—that is, there are degrees of "fruitiness." They also have fuzzy boundaries. At the boundaries, people might disagree about whether something is a fruit. This was the problem exemplified in the last chapter in our discussion of "suitable" beach weather.

Wittgenstein's most celebrated example of a natural category is "game." If asked to define game, you might start with an example—say, tag. Tag is usually played by children, has rules, is engaged in for fun, has multiple players, is competitive, and takes place during periods of leisure. This is a good start on a definition. But what about the Olympic Games? They are dead serious and most of the players are adults. What about solitaire or video games, usually played alone? What about professional sports? The problem here isn't that you started with the wrong example. No matter what example you started with, there would be lots of games that did not share all the relevant features of your start-off example.

The Dynamic Nature of Categories

In addition to being fuzzy, categories change as our experience changes. Kiwis were once a very bad example of a fruit; as they have become more common in American groceries and restaurants, they have become a pretty good one. If we encounter lots of modern chairs, we may change our prototype, or add these chairs to our set of examples, or extract from them important features that many modern chairs share (like being uncomfortable), adding them to our feature list and thus revising our category of chair. We saw an example of the dynamic nature of categories in discussing Mia's decision about where to apply to college. The category Mia is trying to create might be something like "colleges worth applying to." As she deliberates, refining her understanding about what matters to her in a college, some new schools go on her list and old ones go off it.

Categories and Purposes

Often, the way we shape a category will depend on our purposes in establishing the category, as in the case of Mia and the category of "colleges worth applying to." Members of a category need to be similar to one another in ways that matter. Most of the time, in real life, it will be pretty obvious what the "ways that matter" are. So, most of the time we will classify objects into categories effortlessly. But this depends on the context and the purpose of our categorization at least as much as it depends on the properties of the objects themselves.

Take the distinction between "truth" and "lie." Consider these statements:

> "I have a million papers to grade."
> "The average life expectancy with your condition is two years, but statistics don't tell us anything about individual cases."
> "You look great in that dress!"
> "You did a fine job on that assignment."

"Two objects dropped from the same height will hit the ground at the same time."

"I did *not* have sex with that woman."

Which of these are lies?

The first statement is an exaggeration. The speaker's intent is to communicate that she has a lot of work to do. Is an exaggeration a lie?

The second statement is a distortion. Statistics *can* tell us something about individual cases. If the average life expectancy of someone with your condition were fifteen years, you'd have good reason to walk out of the office feeling a lot better than if it were fifteen months. What the doctor was trying to do with his comment was communicate two things: first, averages do not *determine* your fate because there is variability; second, don't give up. Was this distortion a lie?

The third statement, made even when you think your friend doesn't look so good in her dress, is a lie in that it is contrary to what you actually believe, and it is intended to deceive. But it isn't intended to harm; it's intended to aid and comfort. Is a "white lie" like this still a lie? Does a commitment to always telling the truth extend to white lies?

The fourth statement is incomplete: what the teacher really thinks is "you did a fine job on that assignment (for you, a pretty mediocre student who has been struggling all semester)." Does withholding part of the truth count as a lie?

And what about gravity? Is oversimplification a lie? Are we supposed to tell fourth graders the whole complicated story of what, other than gravity, determines how fast objects fall to the ground? If oversimplification is a lie, then every teacher, at every level, spends most of every day lying to the students.

Finally, in the sixth statement, we come to a bona fide, prototypical lie (though even here, it depends on how you define "sex"). Someone who has transgressed is trying to deceive – not for the sake of others, but to protect his status and reputation. But what should be clear is that not all lies are created equal, and if we tried to come up with a rigorous definition of "lie" (as rigorous as the definition of a rectangle, specifying necessary and sufficient conditions), its lack of nuance and context sensitivity would make it close to useless when we're trying to judge the moral status of what others do, or when we're trying to figure out what to do ourselves. What we need is not a rigorous definition of lie, but a natural category, with some clear examples at the heart of our understanding, with less clear examples at the periphery, and with fuzzy boundaries between lies, incomplete truths, exaggerations, oversimplifications, kind distortions, jokes, and plain old mistakes. Lie as a natural category serves us well. Lie as a precise category does not.

So we are predisposed to categorize ordinary objects and activities (fruit and games) into categories that lack sharp boundaries, that reflect an appreciation of nuance, and that can change as a result of our experience and a function of our purposes.

The crucial point, in connection with the requirements of RCT, is that although clarification of our concepts is always possible, a certain amount of vagueness is ineliminable. And if that is true, it is not clear how the kinds of decisions we face in everyday life can ever be captured by the gambling paradigm. The coin lands either as heads or tails. The dice sum to six or to seven. We win or lose our gambles. There are no good or poor examples of coin flips or dice rolls in the way that there are good and poor examples of fruit, furniture, games, or good colleges. And beyond the fuzziness of category boundaries, there is another problem. Sometimes the categories overlap. An apple is a good example of fruit, but it is also a good example of food. And this overlap – this entanglement – poses its own problems for the precision that RCT aspires to.

Entanglement and Disentanglement

Mia's focus on liberal arts study raises the problem of entanglement. The quality of the social sciences and the quality of the academic program generally are not independent, and unless that can be clarified, the calculations of the quality of the school will be imprecise. For practical purposes, this may not be a problem, but to treat it cavalierly belies the assumption that RCT is precise in the way that the gambling paradigm suggests. With a gamble, the possibilities are discrete and mutually exclusive. This is not true of a school's overall academic program and its social science programs. Ignoring this problem is a significant indicator of potential oversimplification and arbitrariness in the actual application of RCT to real-life decisions. How exactly do we disentangle the relevant factors in a decision from one another? Disentanglement as a problem is by no means rare, as we saw in the need to disentangle going for a walk from getting exercise in the gym in deciding how to spend your day.

Quantification

The ultimate purpose of the processes of specification, clarification, and disentanglement we have discussed is to enable quantification of RCT's key parameters – probability and value. To calculate expected utility, you must be able to multiply a specific value by a specific probability for each option. Thus, having clarified and disentangled options, Mia must then quantify them, if RCT is to be used in making the college choice decision. How do we quantify overall academic quality? We could conduct a survey of how people evaluate quantitatively the academic programs of given colleges, average these ratings, and take the average as the quantification we are looking for. This sort of approach is pretty common in attempts to approach rigorously material that does not straightforwardly lend itself to rigor. It presents itself as a way of getting objectivity (the average rating) out of subjectivity (the individual evaluations). But the claim of objectivity needs to be examined.

It is, of course, an objective fact that the average evaluation is the result of the mathematical calculation, but this is objectivity about the subjective opinions of the sample, not about the actual quality of the academic program. If the sample consisted of people whose opinions were objectively well grounded, then the overall average might reflect something significant about the quality of the academic program, but objectively grounding such opinions is the problem we were trying to avoid with this method. If we knew that individual opinions were well grounded, calculating the average would be less important. The whole point of calculating the "objective" average is that we don't know how well grounded individual opinions are.

To see how far from objectivity the results of this method can be, imagine doing a survey of how good different brands of ice cream are, and averaging the results into a judgment of which is the best. Would the selection of the best brand by this method tell us anything at all objective about the ice cream itself, as opposed to the opinions of the sampled? What exactly would one know about the ice cream? The results of the survey about the quality of the academic program of a college is of the same character, giving no objective knowledge of the thing in question, only people's opinions about it. This problem reminds us of economist John Maynard Keynes's famous observation that the best way to predict the winner of a beauty contest is not by evaluating the physical features of the contestants, but by evaluating the evaluations of those physical features by the judges. It would be a happy accident if people's assessments of beauty aligned well with some objective specification of beauty. Whether the same is true of the quality of an academic program is an empirical question.

We are faced with a number of problems in attempting to find a way of making the quality of the academic program a quantifiable factor. One of them is coming up with a nonarbitrary way to rate the importance of different fields, such as physics, classics, sociology, and so on. Many difficult questions are raised if this problem is taken seriously. Is there a formal, rigorous method for answering the indefinitely large number of questions that will arise? It is fair to say that the answer is no. Intrinsically fallible judgment will be necessary. And that is true as well in the processes of constructing the limited set of factors to be considered. Ultimately, the process of refinement of the set of options and their relevant attributes will be based on many sorts of inferences outside RCT proper – and finally, on judgment. And if the judgment is not good, no amount of RCT methodology at later stages can make the decision a good one, except by luck. We discuss the difficulties inherent in quantifying value in greater detail in chapter 4.

In addition to quantifying value, we also must quantify probability. This too is a major challenge – one we have illustrated in our discussion of the vagueness and fuzziness of natural categories. Without knowing unambiguously what counts as a game, it is impossible to quantify how many different sorts of games there are. Without being able to quantify unambiguously whether a dice roll was a six or a seven, we can't quantify the probability of obtaining a seven with a roll of the dice. We will turn to a discussion of the problems inherent in attaching probabilities to outcomes in our everyday decisions in the next chapter.

Substitution

Ultimately, the combined processes of specification and clarification exemplify what Kahneman called *substitution*, the replacement of a difficult question with an easier one. In fact, each stage of this process is a substitution. And the appropriateness of the substitution needs to be established. Is there an RCT-approved way of judging a substitution as appropriate? We doubt it. Substitution is a form of interpretation, and a good substitution has to preserve the crucial aspects of the meaning of the thing substituted for. Whether a substitution has done that is, as we said before, not a question that can be answered formally. It may in fact often be impossible to answer uncontroversially. Substituting an easier question for a harder one has its virtues. It may offer insights into the decision at hand that would otherwise be obscured by its complexity. It may enable one to overcome decision paralysis caused by the uncertainty surrounding a complex, important decision. But substitution, even when helpful, must be understood as a step in the process, not the goal of the process. And it should be clear that the kinds of substitutions we described when it comes to choosing a college are by no means unique to that decision. The same processes operate when we are deciding what job to take, who to hire, or whether to give a faculty member tenure. How does one measure the objective quality of an academic colleague's (or a potential colleague's) teaching and research? RCT may give you *an* answer, but it won't give you the *right* answer unless you have done a lot of non-RCT thinking first.

Gambling and Normal Life

In the last chapter, we pointed to RCT's implicit claim that the paradigmatic gambling decision problem is a model for all decisions, always assuming there would be additional complications. In this chapter, we have been examining the complications, and we have seen that they deserve a lot more respect than to be treated as afterthoughts. In coming chapters, we will examine much more carefully the complications of quantifying probability and quantifying utility or value. We will discuss the very significant role that framing plays in specifying a list of options, in determining relevant factors and in refining those factors to eliminate vagueness and overlap. We are now in a position to affirm that the difference between the gambling paradigm, in which the problem can be solved by using fairly elementary math, and choosing colleges to apply to, which cannot, is not a small quantitative matter but a substantial qualitative one. Many stages of substitution are required, and the appropriate substitutions require several different kinds of thought and inference. To imply that the gambling paradigm, with only minor qualifications, is an appropriate model for solving our decision problems in general is very misleading.

Two Cheers for RCT

A good deal of hard work is needed to put an everyday decision problem into a format amenable to RCT analysis. If your plan to use RCT to make the ultimate decision motivates this hard work, then this is to RCT's credit. We often avoid asking ourselves hard questions, especially when we know that we will not find certain answers, and anything that induces us to do something difficult but critically important is good. We suspect that very few high school students go through anything like the process we have described for Mia, and that decisions about where to apply and to go to college are often made on the basis of very capricious considerations. If RCT disciplines anyone to think more seriously about a serious decision, then good for it.

In addition, to be fair to RCT, not every decision we face requires *all* the preliminary work that choosing a college does. Deciding where to go on vacation, what neighborhood to look for housing in, what restaurant to go to, what team to support in the NFL playoffs, what kind of health insurance to buy, and many other decisions may be more amenable to an RCT approach than choosing where to go to college, because many of the relevant considerations in these other decisions are already specified, disentangled, and quantified. But even in these cases, some work must be done to fit the decision you face into the gambling paradigm, as we saw in discussing whether a family should go to the beach or the museum. Even the college decision may be amenable to RCT analysis if a variety of factors (for example, family assets) serve to narrow the possibilities and the relevant considerations dramatically. And an RCT approach may sometimes lead to better decisions — decisions that include assessments of relevant factors that you might have overlooked if you simply went with your gut (whatever that means). So, we want to be clear that RCT has its place. But we also want to be clear that what it takes to turn a complex decision into one that is RCT-appropriate can often distort the character of the decision almost beyond recognition.

Chapter 3

QUANTIFYING PROBABILITY

We have seen that in order to use RCT to produce a good answer to a decision problem, it is necessary to frame the problem as a choice between a manageable number of reasonable alternatives, which themselves need to be specified clearly and precisely. Needless to say, that is not the only prerequisite for the use of RCT. Another is the assignment of probabilities to those alternatives, both the probabilities that they will occur and the probabilities that they will yield the expected results. In this chapter, we are going to highlight two obstacles to assigning such probabilities: vagueness and radical uncertainty.

Our discussion of natural categories in the last chapter was intended to show that for categories to be useful in our everyday lives, they often need a certain vagueness and fluidity. There is, of course, a price to be paid for this vagueness. Two people engaged in a conversation may use the same words but mean different things. Or they may differ on the centrality and significance of certain features of whatever they are discussing. Many serious disagreements in life derive from people thinking they are talking about the same thing when they aren't. The imposition of a frame, or a specific context, can reduce ambiguity and misunderstanding. When you are contemplating what to have for dessert, a tomato is unlikely to come to mind as a fruit. When you hit your opponent hard in the back of the head with the ball in a racquetball rally, and your opponent angrily says, "This is a game, right?," you know what feature of "games" your opponent has in mind. Thus, framing reduces (though it does not eliminate) fuzziness. In this respect, when it comes to rational discourse, framing is a feature, not a bug. And it is, of course, unavoidable.

In addition, framing helps us make probability estimates more precise. The fuzzy boundaries of natural categories means that there is inherent ambiguity about what is or is not a member of the category. It is very difficult to estimate the probability of an X without knowing what counts as an X. The probabilities of heads or tails in a coin flip assume that the coin flip won't count if the coin should happen to land on its edge. The probability of 00 on a spin of a roulette wheel can be specified precisely because spins of the wheel in which the ball jumps the table won't count. The less precise the category boundaries are, the less meaningful probability statements are, and the more likely misunderstandings are. Nonetheless, natural categories have the enormous virtue that they capture the world as it is.

Having established the pervasiveness of vagueness in ordinary thought, we need to emphasize its special relevance to RCT. Proper use of RCT requires eliminating vagueness. We have already mentioned the problem of vagueness and the need for clarification in connection with the attributes in the beach/museum decision. The stipulated attribute was rainy weather, but that is a placeholder for suitable weather, which is thoroughly vague relative to a quantifiable concept. What is suitable beach weather, defined in quantifiable terms? And our purposes will have to be taken into account. Suitable beach weather varies depending on the planned activity: swimming, sunbathing, or taking a long walk. And without providing an answer to questions like these, we really can't estimate the probability that we will have suitable weather.

The same issue arises when Mia tries to estimate the probability that a given college will provide a good education. This can't be done without a clear criterion for calling a college good. But "good" is quite a vague notion. Mia buys a college guide, which has a list of the best colleges. But when she investigates what the authors of the book mean by "good college," it turns out that they judge primarily by various measures: graduation rates, financial resources, the publications of the faculty. "Is that what defines a 'good' college?" she asks herself. "Is that what it means to be a good college?" Two things are necessary here to answer these crucial questions: understanding what a good college is and knowing whether a definition in quantifiable terms captures what is important about being a good college.

Having decided that a "good college," for her, means a "good liberal arts college," Mia needs to be able to specify a "good liberal arts college" more precisely. What determines just how good a liberal arts college is, and how good an education one gets at it? Is it a matter of the quantity and diversity of courses? Is a school that has an excellent history department but a poor art department better or worse than one that has an excellent art department and a poor history department? And what makes a good department? Is it the number and content of the courses or the quality of the teaching? What content makes the department a good one? And how do you measure the quality of the teaching? Is it by the publication record of the faculty of the department (as some rankings seem to assume)?

Is it the average teacher evaluations provided by students? Is it the average size of classes? To answer the question "How likely is college X to be good?" Mia needs answers to these questions.

At the very least, it is clear that these determinations, if they are performed in a sufficiently rigorous way to be called rational even in a broad sense, would be prohibitively time consuming. We say "at the very least" because it is also clear to us that it is simply impossible to use primarily formal or quantitative methods to rigorously make these sorts of determinations. But if this is true, what are the people who do in fact use RCT to address these decisions actually doing? We believe they are making largely arbitrary determinations, often with no articulate justification, to get on to the methods on the basis of which they will claim rationality. They are arbitrarily substituting a gambling problem for a complicated and difficult problem that requires deliberation and judgment to deal with well (if imperfectly), like a teacher who throws the exam papers up the stairs, grades on the basis of how far up each paper landed, and claims objectivity for her grading. They have no choice. To make these kinds of determinations is not the trivial exercise that it is often thought to be. It is very complicated and difficult. And when rationality is restricted to the rigorous use of primarily formal methods, the problem is made much more difficult.

"How do I even determine what a good college is?" Mia wonders. "Do I read and think about college education? What is it that I should read?" If "what is a good college?" is understood to mean "what do people *think* is a good college?," it may be an empirical question about which Mia could try to find data. But taken literally, it is not merely an empirical question. It requires an understanding of what knowledge is, what kind of knowledge is important and why, and other such essentially nonempirical, or not wholly empirical, considerations. These kinds of questions are not going to be answered by formal reasoning or statistical reasoning, or fully by empirical evidence. Determining the meaning of a concept is a very different kind of process. It is a process of defining, but not dictionary defining — not defining wholly determined by use. Unless Mia can decide what counts as a good college, so as to divide colleges into the categories "good" and "not good," she can't estimate the probability that she will get into a good college. If she uses very stringent criteria for identifying colleges as good, she may end up with such a rarified list of schools that the probability she will be admitted to any of them will be low.

And the evaluative aspect of "good college" is not crucial to our argument. If Mia wants to go to a college that is not too far from home, what does "far" mean? Is it just a matter of distance? If so, how much distance? But is it also relevant how difficult and costly travel home will be? Penn State is closer to Delaware than the University of Pittsburgh is; however, you can fly or take the train from the latter, but not the former. What exactly is convenience of travel, and which is "farther" in the relevant sense? So eliminating vagueness requires yet another kind of thinking — determining and comparing meanings. This exploration of meaning suggests something more like interpreting a text than doing mathematics. Here too, without answering these questions for herself, Mia can't estimate the probability that she will get into one of the colleges on her list, because she can't construct the list.

Suppose Mia's concerns about society's collective welfare and the common good have led her to think that she may best achieve her life goals by becoming a lawyer. She has seen two of her grandparents suffer significant financial manipulation and exploitation as a consequence of cognitive deterioration as they aged, and this experience has engendered in her a special concern about protecting vulnerable people. This leads her to think about not only how good various colleges are, but also how likely she is to get into law school coming out of one or another college.

So how should Mia proceed? To estimate her chances of getting into law school, she looks up the statistics on law school admissions from the various colleges she is considering. This seems straightforward enough. Divide the number of people who get into law school by the number of people who apply and you get the probability that Mia will get into law school from this or that college. But there is some ambiguity. Maybe Mia should include as "failed" law school applicants people who did not even apply because they knew they would not get in. That would increase the denominator and lower Mia's estimate of her probability of success. And should Mia include *all* successful applicants, including those whose parents both graduated from prestigious law schools themselves? How about applicants who were stars on their college football or basketball teams? Mia is in neither of these categories and does not have these advantages. If she excludes such people, the numerator in her calculation will get smaller. It might seem clear and obvious who counts as a successful or failed applicant. Either you applied or you didn't; either you got in or you didn't. But from Mia's point of view, the categories "successful applicants" and "failed applicants" are fuzzy in the sense that really, only some of the people in each category are probably relevant to Mia's probability estimates, and some people in neither category are also relevant.

There is an additional complication: using probability calculations from the past to predict probability in the future can also be problematic. One college has an extremely high rate recently of acceptance of its graduates to law schools, but before that it had a very spotty record, and just last year it had a very low rate of acceptance. How is she to extrapolate from those data? Is last year an exception to a rising trend, or the beginning of a return to its old erratic record? Also there have recently been a few highly publicized scandals involving the school's faculty, one concerning plagiarism and one the psychological abuse of certain students, and she needs to determine how likely this is to affect the acceptance rate. Many of the college's successful law school applicants have been political science majors, but she does not intend to major in political science. Further, the school is expensive, and Mia will have to contribute to meeting its costs by working during the school year and then earning as much as she can in the summer. Working during school may lower her GPA and thus hurt her chances of law school admission. And needing to earn money in the summer will prevent her from doing an unpaid internship in a legal clinic or even for a law firm. Maybe Mia would be better off going to a less expensive and prestigious school, which would enable her to get better grades and do those internships. Or maybe she could take basic courses at a junior college for the first few years, saving even more money while outperforming many of the other students. Mia comes from a family of modest means. Neither of her parents have college degrees. How, if at all, will that affect her chances?

To add another complication, politics has started to have a negative influence on the reputations of schools, even such prestigious ones as Harvard. Which, if any, of the schools she proposes to apply to will be the victim of such a decline, and will it affect the success of their students in getting into law schools? These sorts of questions, we suggest, are indicators of far greater uncertainty than we face when throwing a pair of dice or picking a playing card out of a deck, because the probability of events of these kinds affecting Mia's future is almost impossible to quantify. Without being able to impose boundaries (frames) that identify unequivocally whether something is or is not a member of a category, probability assessment is at best an approximation of reality.

Radical Uncertainty

What Mia's complex decision and countless others we could describe have in common is that one is faced with a decision that has multiple dimensions, with outcomes that are uncertain and influenced by factors that are difficult to evaluate or sometimes even identify. And they are not merely uncertain in a probabilistic sense. In many cases, you cannot even attach probabilities to outcomes in a meaningful way. Economist Frank Knight distinguished between probabilistic risk and non-probabilistic "true uncertainty," as he called it. Daniel Ellsberg famously pointed out this distinction when he contrasted a container with fifty red and fifty black balls with a container that has one hundred balls, some of which are red and some black. If people can win $10 by picking a red ball while blindfolded, and nothing for picking a black ball, they typically prefer the first container to the second, favoring (probabilistic) uncertainty to what Ellsberg termed "ambiguity." The probability of winning with the first container is 0.5. But what is the probability of winning with the second? There is no way to know. We prefer to call Knight's "true uncertainty" and Ellsberg's "ambiguity" *radical uncertainty*. And when a situation is radically uncertain, RCT simply does not apply, since one of its two key parameters — probability — can't be specified.

We believe that most of the decisions people face in life involve radical uncertainty at least as much as probabilistic uncertainty. In conditions of radical uncertainty, the goal of utility or preference maximization is unreliable. Indeed, it may even be self-deceptive, in that it involves assigning probabilities to outcomes in a context in which probabilities cannot be determined.

What kinds of conditions are radically uncertain? Answering this question requires a brief excursion into the foundations of probability theory. Jonathan Baron, in his book *Thinking and Deciding*, nicely summarizes three different approaches to understanding what probability statements mean. The first we might call "logical." When the events that comprise a sample space are fully known, and their distributions can be specified, a probability statement is simply a matter of logic: in the sample space of outcomes of rolls of two fair dice, there are thirty-six equiprobable outcomes, of which six sum to "7." Thus, one-sixth of possible rolls (.17) will yield the outcome of 7. This is not an empirical matter. It is part of what it means to be throwing "fair" dice.

The second we might call "empirical." If you follow a sample of ten thousand men between the ages of, say, forty and seventy-five, and three hundred of them develop prostate cancer, you might infer that the chances of any particular man developing prostate cancer are 300/10,000, or .03. You use the frequency of the event of interest in the past to infer the probability of the event with respect to any particular case in the future. Thus, as we suggested, Mia might simply compare the various schools she is considering with respect to the percentage of pre-law students who gain law school acceptance, and use that frequency in the past as a gauge of her probability of success in the future.

The final approach to probability we might call "personal." You are asked in April, "Will Spain win the soccer World Cup this year?" You might answer, "I think they will." "How sure are you?" "I give them a 25% chance," you say. Because each World Cup competition is a unique event in ways that matter to prediction, you can't really rely on frequencies in the past to infer probabilities in the future, though they may be informative. The number you supply is merely an expression of your confidence. As Baron points out, some have argued that it makes no sense to attach probabilities to unique events. But of course, each throw of the dice is a "unique event," and each middle-aged man with prostate cancer is a "unique event," so distinctions among these three approaches to understanding probability statements are not so easy to make sharply. This is especially true when it comes to distinguishing frequency and personal approaches to probability.

So what, then, does it mean to call an event "radically uncertain" in a way that distinguishes throwing dice from choosing a college? What makes attaching probabilities to gaining admission to law school different from throwing dice, or even predicting the weather? It might be that if you pushed a high school senior, she would attach a number to how likely she was to get into law school with a degree from Yale. But would the number mean anything? And if not, is there information available so that if she collected it assiduously, the number she attached *would* mean something? Even if the answer to this latter question is yes, if the meaning of the number is not substantially resolved by the added information, then there is radical uncertainty. Sure, you might think it's obvious that you are more likely to get into law school with a degree from Yale than with a degree from your state university, but unless you can specify how much more likely, you can't multiply value by probability to come up with an estimate of expected utility, which RCT requires.

It seems unlikely that there will ever be models of success in college, however defined, that approximate the predictive power available in casino gambling or, say, in meteorology, but that is an empirical question. There is no doubt that people can know more or less about a domain in question, so that estimates of probability from frequency can be more or less well justified. In other words, in real-life decisions, we may never be confronted with the kind of uncertainty we face with Ellsberg's container, where any number of red balls, from zero to one hundred, is possible. But before we attach probabilities to outcomes, we need to assess which of Ellsberg's two containers the decision we face more closely resembles.

In a recent book, *Radical Uncertainty*, two distinguished British economists, John Kay and Mervyn King, made the argument that many, perhaps most, decisions we face in life involve uncertainty to which we can't assign probability. This, they suggest, is true even in fairly circumscribed financial situations, in which probability assessment and utility assessment, the two key parameters of RCT, are the coin of the realm. One of their chapter titles is "Radical Uncertainty Is Everywhere," which conveys a sense of what they think is the magnitude of the problem. Nonetheless, people do assign probabilities to outcomes, even radically uncertain ones. Do they realize that such probability assignment is virtually fictional? If so, why do they do it? Perhaps they derive some comfort and assurance by pretending that the world is more predictable than it really is.

Kay and King point out that Jimmie Savage, the prominent statistician we mentioned in chapter 1 whose work did much to formalize RCT, acknowledged himself that his statistical formulations only applied in what he called "small worlds" — worlds that have been simplified with processes like those we discussed in the last chapter to turn complex, real-life decisions into analogs of the gambling paradigm. They further suggest that models or theories like RCT have the virtue of turning "mysteries into puzzles." Puzzles can be solved; mysteries, not so much.

QUANTIFYING PROBABILITY

Disentanglement

As we saw in the last chapter, rigorous quantification also requires using categories that do not overlap, or perhaps whose overlapping can be measured precisely. Suppose that in evaluating a college, Mia is concerned about both the overall academic quality and the quality of the pre-law program. These overlap, and if she adds the utility of the overall academic program to the utility of the pre-law program, the area of overlap will be counted twice. Similarly, there will be overlap if Mia tries to assess the probability of getting into law school from a good pre-law program versus from a college with high overall quality. Perhaps under many or even most circumstances this is not a practical problem. Perhaps few of the categories we use in making decisions overlap, or if they do overlap, it's only to an insignificant extent. In principle, however, removing the overlap or giving it a quantitative analysis is crucial to the rigor of quantification – of both probability and utility. It can be, like other aspects of preparation for calculation, a complicated and difficult business, and this complexity creates a temptation, also as in the case of other aspects of preparation for calculation, to ignore the problem or to treat it unrigorously. Such temptation comes up often in preparation, and it is significant. Systematic lack of rigor, systematic because it is due to the complexity (impossibility?) of certain steps in preparation, undercuts the claim of RCT to be rational.

Kay and King, in their book, make arguments very similar to ours. From the point of view of normative theories of rational decision-making, the key idea is that one cannot do a conventional utility analysis without attaching probabilities to various outcomes. Inventing probabilities in the face of serious information gaps, because you have learned that that is the normatively correct way to make decisions, can lead you astray. And even if it doesn't, it is hardly rational to base a decision on probabilities that are invented. And what they and Jimmie Savage call "small worlds," within which probability estimates may be meaningful, we prefer to call *closure*. Without imposing frames around a decision and thus "closing" it to make much of its complexity invisible, adequate quantification is impossible. The gambling paradigm has the needed framing built in; real life does not.

Decontextualization

Specification and clarification prepare the way for quantification. They do so by narrowing Mia's focus. Specification of options narrowed her focus to a few schools. Specification of the relevant factors has narrowed her focus to specific features of those schools. By making the specified factors precise and limited, Mia's focus will be narrowed. The larger social and economic context within which Mia's decision will have to be made will be off the table. Here, we want to discuss the way this focusing leads to marginalizing, if not totally ignoring, the broader circumstances that form the context of Mia's decision.

The general state of the economy may well have a major effect on Mia's college life and her future job prospects, at the very least by affecting costs and her ability to meet them. There are many ways that could happen. To attempt to list them in order to quantify their probability is futile. The same is true of climate change, the situation in the Middle East, the domestic political situation, Mia's health, the stability of her parents' marriage, and an indefinite number of other factors. Any of these could take an unpredictable turn and any such turn could have an effect on Mia's college experience that could not be quantified, and perhaps not even specifically foreseen. If they can't be foreseen specifically, RCT will be unable to account for them. What this tells us is that the success of Mia's various efforts to make the college decision a rigorous, precise, and quantifiable process are context dependent. Thinking about whether and how her assessments might change if the context changed makes Mia's decision even less amenable to precise specification than we have already indicated. And deciding what context changes might occur, how likely they are to occur, and how they might change Mia's college preferences and college experience are not things RCT is set up to accomplish. Clearly, Mia will have to pull the trigger at some point, before she ages out of going to college altogether, but it will take judgment, not calculation (except, perhaps, for her age), for Mia to know when to stop.

Closing an Open System

The gambling paradigm is a "closed system." Nothing is relevant aside from probability and value. But most of our everyday decisions are made in an "open system," in which many factors may be relevant. The various steps we have described in this chapter and the previous one are intended to close an open system. What does it mean to close an open system? Among other things, it takes decisions that may well be context dependent and turns them into decisions that are context independent. For example, in the case of choosing a job, it may encourage arraying salary, benefits, chances for advancement, degree of autonomy, and other features in a kind of spreadsheet to facilitate analysis, leaving out such factors as what the person has heard about the company, what kinds of jobs the person has had in the past, how much the job will encroach on responsibilities for caring for three kids entering adolescence, how the job might affect the person's ability to engage in various hobbies, what kinds of financial obligations are looming in the future, and so on. These types of features, and others, could certainly be added to the analysis — that is, the system could be opened up to some degree — but how open should the system ultimately be? RCT can't tell us what is and what ought to be relevant to the decision. And sometimes the vagueness of the open system in which we live will not permit clarity and precision without introducing serious distortion.

Psychologists Will M. Bennis, Douglas L. Medin, and Daniel M. Bartels, writing about the limits of cost-benefit analysis (a first cousin to RCT that we mentioned briefly earlier and that is a key aspect of the decisions made by government agencies and private enterprises), said that it might be adequate given a set of "closed-world assumptions":

> The [decision] scenario is accepted as stated as complete and accurate with no other considerations or interpretations introduced. To satisfy closed-world assumptions, it is off limits to consider any alternative actions, to doubt that [the stated action] will have the intended consequences, to suspect that it may have other unintended consequences, to wonder if the action sets a dangerous precedent for other circumstances where the information may be less reliable, or to assign utility or disutility to things [that extend beyond the outcomes stated in the problem].[1]

1. Bennis, Medin, and Bartels, "Costs and Benefits," 189. For all footnotes in the text, see the full citation in the bibliography.

QUANTIFYING PROBABILITY

Consider the closing of the framework for deciding in connection with the domain of gambling. What bet does one make in roulette, craps, or at a horse race? There are better and worse bets in each of these arenas, with better and worse determined by the odds of winning (which can be specified precisely at the gambling table, though not so precisely at the racetrack), together with the size of the payoff for one or another bet. So far, so good. Calculate the expected value of a win (payoff × probability) and choose the option with the highest expected value. But what if we open the system a little? Suppose you need to win a certain amount of money to cover next month's rent and less than that amount won't do. Suppose that one of the horses in the race is owned by a friend and you don't want to be rooting against a friend's success, or against yourself. These modest openings of the system make the tools of RCT much less useful.

The process of closing an open system is itself a process of making a significant number of decisions: "I will limit myself to only these options"; "I will limit myself to considering only these attributes of the options"; "I will turn the qualitative, commonsense notion of this concept into a measurable one in this particular way"; and more to be considered later. These decisions are not and cannot be made by the methods of RCT. They require judgment, not formal thinking. Indeed, the process of closure (and quantification) is a process of using nonformal judgment in the preparatory stages of a decision to eliminate the need for nonformal judgment in the ultimate stage of the decision. Moreover, for that process to be used well and rigorously enough to justify calling it rational by RCT standards, and to avoid arbitrariness and oversimplification, it requires an enormous amount of work. Whether the "success" of the use of RCT in any given case is due to the formal methods of RCT or the prelimi-

QUANTIFYING PROBABILITY

nary work that enables RCT to be deployed is not clear, but we believe there is a good case for the latter.

In summary, at least one of the key parameters of RCT – probability estimation – suffers from a false precision. This in turn creates a false sense of how well the parameters of a decision can actually be quantified. As we'll see, the same problem applies to the quantification of value.

Chapter 4

QUANTIFYING VALUE

As we saw in the last chapter, a central component of RCT is the presumption that each outcome under consideration has an associated probability of occurring. Mia must estimate how likely it is that she will be admitted to the colleges she is considering and then to law school if she goes to this or that college. As we described in the example, owing to radical uncertainty and vagueness, calculating probabilities is, at best, a challenge, and at worst, a fantasy. Not only are many relevant factors radically uncertain, but there are also potentially relevant factors (summer internship possibilities, grade competition with other students, and so on) that might well contribute to Mia's overall probability of success by combining in highly uncertain ways.

But there is more complexity. In addition to this probability assessment, RCT requires a second one. Even when an outcome is certain when we make a decision, how good will it be? Will Mia love college? Will she love a liberal arts education? And will she love law school? In other words, for RCT to work, value must be quantified as well as probability. Remember, to compute expected utility, a quantified probability must be multiplied by a quantified value. And beyond this challenge to quantify the quality of her education, it is probably not the only thing that matters to Mia about college. She enjoys studio arts. What are the studio arts programs like at various schools? She is really into being in nature—hiking, boating, swimming, and experiencing beauty and tranquility. What possibilities will be available near each campus she is considering? She is very close to her family and will miss them a lot if she can't see them regularly. How much will she miss them, and how should that be factored in? And what will the social life be like? None of these features is as important to Mia as her education and law school prospects, but they aren't irrelevant either. And they may loom large if Mia comes to the conclusion that the colleges she is considering are pretty close to each other with regard to overall academic quality. These other factors may end up as tiebreakers.

Suppose that, instead of Mia, you (or one of your kids) have been fortunate enough to be admitted to a half dozen colleges. Now you sit down to decide which one to attend. How should you go about this process? RCT might recommend that you list all the things that matter to you about college (for example, size, location, reputation, quality of its program in economics, social life, studio arts department, housing, cost). Then attach a weight to each attribute, one that reflects its importance to you. If you are devoted to economics, the quality of the economics program may get a weight of 10, while other attributes get fractions of that weight. Next you should evaluate each school on each dimension: give it a score, say, from 1 to 10. Finally, multiply scores by weights, and do some addition. Then choose the school with the highest score. This kind of weighting is necessary because though you value many things about your upcoming college education, you don't value them all equally.

QUANTIFYING VALUE

This process can obviously be taxing and time consuming, and as we said in chapter 2, virtually none of Barry's students admitted to doing it. But the situation is even more complex. When you assign the values that are the basis for the scores for each school on each dimension, you're making guesses or predictions. Your assessments may be wrong. You may also be wrong about how important the various aspects of college life are (or will be) to you. You're only seventeen, after all, and people change. And even if your estimates of importance and quality are correct, you don't know how it will actually feel to experience being a student at a school that has the qualities of the one you choose. You are making a prediction about a future subjective state, and as psychologists Daniel Gilbert, Timothy Wilson, and their various collaborators have amply documented, such predictions are notoriously inaccurate (see Gilbert's book *Stumbling on Happiness*).

Can we rationally quantify our preferences in this way? We readily acknowledge that some of many people's preferences *can* be quantified. Consider someone whose life is centered around increasing personal wealth; what this person values most highly is money. Perhaps there are massive student loans to be repaid. Perhaps this person wants to live in an area where costs are high. Perhaps this person grew up in a home where money was always tight, causing a good deal of family stress and unhappiness. Perhaps this person just keeps score by counting financial assets. Whatever the reason, this person cares about making money. In this case, decision options can be rated and ranked in accordance with how much money they are likely to yield (assuming of course that the probability of their yielding it can also be calculated). There are nuances, such as the diminishing marginal utility of money — the fact that for many people, the more money they have the less each unit increase of money makes them happy — but that, too, can be quantified. There is also the problem that money obtained in one way (for example, by clever investing) may be more valuable, subjectively, at least at the time it is obtained, than money obtained in another (a bequest from a distant relative). But let us, at least for the moment, dismiss these as relatively unimportant considerations. For the people focused on money, a dollar is a dollar. For these people, it seems clear that preferences can be quantified. And RCT may be an ideal tool for doing the quantification.

But how many of us are like "these people," and how many of our preferences are like these people's preferences? What do we learn from the fact that certain people, those whose preferences center on wealth, can quantify their preferences? Should we learn that most preferences, especially important preferences, for most people can be quantified? If we take the individual concerned with wealth as a typical person facing typical decisions, the answer might seem to be yes. And we have very tempting reasons to take it to be typical. If we can treat our decisions like the decisions about wealth, we will have substituted a much simpler question for what may otherwise be a very complicated one that requires extensive and subtle thought and is often impossible to answer with complete confidence. Can we reasonably see most of our decision problems, and particularly our important decision problems, as analogous to the problems of the person focused on wealth?

There are research tools central to the study of decision-making that presume that pursuing wealth is a good approximation of many or even most of the things we value. One of them is called "contingent valuation." To assess the value to you of the *Mona Lisa* (or, to be realistic, a high-quality print of the *Mona Lisa*), you would ask a question like "How much would I be willing to pay for a print?" And if you already had a print, you would ask, "How much would I have to be paid to sell the print?" These seem like perfectly reasonable questions since prints of masterpieces are in fact available on the market. But how about "How much would I be willing to pay to get into the section of Psych 101 taught by the department's most popular teacher?" As far as we know, slots in popular courses are not yet available on the market, but an answer to this question could tell you whether the respondent values the slot more or less than a print of the *Mona Lisa*.

Examples like this can be produced endlessly with respect to things people value that are similar to goods or services that are routinely available on the market. And from the perspective of RCT, this is a virtue. It helps us quantify value.

But consider a different example — the case of an industrial accident. The victim has lost a leg due to the negligence of the company. Over the years of what remained of his working life, he would have earned, say, $2 million. What should the victim be awarded in compensation? A jury might award him that $2 million in compensatory damages. It might add another $1 million for pain and suffering. But if every loss in addition to what he would have earned is included in "pain and suffering," then this category is very complicated indeed.

Suppose the victim was a dancer. Now he cannot dance. What is the monetary value of that loss? Suppose he was a champion amateur dancer. Is his loss greater because he was a champion? He was past his peak. How much does that diminish the monetary value of his loss? Can the estimate take into account the pain of the blow to his ego as he gives up an activity at which he excels, as distinct from the loss of the pleasure he gains from dancing per se? And what if

QUANTIFYING VALUE

he had lost both legs? Would his pain and suffering have been doubled? If not, then increased by how much? To take these questions seriously and hope to answer them with precision is to fall down a rabbit hole and end up in Wonderland. There are circumstances under which we must attach a monetary value to such things, and we do, but to take these determinations to be accurate assessments of value — even if only monetary value — is silly, to say the least. Judgments like this are useful fictions; they are nothing like rigorously rational determinations of quantitative value. And they are not the latter because it is inconceivable that such a determination could be made with the sort of rigor RCT requires.

The issue is further complicated by the matter of scope. What about the pain the injured man feels for causing his wife trauma as a consequence of the accident? Is that something he should be compensated for? And what about the effects of his disability on his marriage in other respects?

And if the issue of the monetary value of his loss of dancing is impossible to assess rationally with any accuracy, consider that this is only a single dimension of the damage done to him. Suppose the victim was a serious hiker as well and that was the one activity that he and his children could enjoy together. But no longer. It seems that it might be easier to compare the values of aspects of his loss from the accident qualitatively than to quantify them. But even that seems out of the question here. How do we compare the pain of adjusting the terms of his marriage to the effect of the accident on his relationship with his children? Or to the blow to his ego from the loss of his leg? Can we compare these losses in anything but the vaguest terms? We think a thoughtful person would feel foolish trying to answer these types of questions, even if they are useful for some very limited purposes, just as the reader of this work may feel it is a waste of time to be asked them. Yet RCT depends on answering questions that are even less answerable than these.

Of course, valuations of this kind are made all the time. There are situations where there is no alternative. The company cannot return the leg of the injured man, so if he is to be compensated, he has to be compensated with something else that cannot be rigorously commensurable with being fully able-bodied, and money is the obvious candidate. So he is awarded a certain amount of money, but the fiction that there is an equivalence between the loss of the leg and the amount of money he is given is something that no one takes seriously. We are doing the best we can under impossible circumstances, not finding the real value, either objective or subjective, of the leg. A friend of ours was recently on a jury that found a corporation liable for the death of a woman from mesothelioma. When it came to determining the damages, there was virtually no attempt to examine her life and calibrate the damage award according to the specifics of her loss of life. There was no estimate of her pain, of the loss to her husband and children, of how long she was debilitated, of how long she would probably have lived. The damages were determined almost wholly by jury dynamics: who had made compromises earlier in the deliberations, the need to come to agreement, the prestige of the various jurors, and personal relations among them were the basis for negotiating the virtually arbitrary estimates that were the initial basis for discussion. Not completely arbitrary, of course — no one suggested $1 and no one suggested $1 billion — but arbitrary by the standards of accuracy and precision. And how could it have been otherwise?

In a similar, well-known example, lawyer Kenneth Feinberg was charged with the task of getting the families of victims of the

9/11 terrorist attacks on the World Trade Center to agree on compensation for their lost loved ones. His efforts are vividly displayed in the 2021 movie *Worth*. On the one hand, you could calculate the expected career earnings of each person who died and compensate the victims' families on that basis. The families of victims who worked, say, in finance, would get much more (to compensate for their loved one's lost earnings) than the families of janitors, food service workers, or firefighters. On the other hand, you could operate on the view that each human life has equal value and offer compensation on that basis. Or you could consider how old victims were, calculate the expected number of years of life lost, and compensate on that basis. Each of these approaches is reasonable, but they lead to very different judgments about compensation. The task of quantification is essentially impossible. But failing to solve this problem in some way would leave victims' families with nothing. *Worth* vividly depicts Feinberg's efforts to do the impossible while being fully aware that it *is* impossible.

Can Everything Be Quantified?

Pretty much anything can be quantified. Take the comparative aesthetic (as opposed to market) value of the *Mona Lisa* and Raphael's painting *The School of Athens*. To quantify their comparative value, we can place a grid of one-inch squares on each, and then, covering all but one square, ask a random sample of people how much, on a scale of 1 to 10, they like it, eventually coming up with an average number for each square of each painting. If we add up or average the numbers for each painting, we will come up with a number for how aesthetically pleasing each painting is, and we can say that they are of equal value or that one is more valuable than the other by this precise amount. We have in fact quantified the aesthetic value of the paintings. The trouble is that any reasonable person will correctly judge that if the numbers are any indicator of the aesthetic value, it is almost purely coincidental. Of course, we might say that since it can't really be measured, aesthetic value is simply a fanciful thing that should not be taken seriously. Or we might say that aesthetic value, like all value in RCT, is subjective and thus very difficult to criticize (as economists like to say, there is no accounting for taste). Or we might say that if what you are looking for is an objective scale of value, then market value (the price it will fetch) is the best you can do. We could do the same with values like justice, kindness, decency, loyalty, morality, love, and many more concepts, though there seems not to be much of a market for these values, in contrast to fine art. What would life be like if we stopped thinking about those values unless we could find or create a scale on which to measure and compare them?

There is an old (we hope apocryphal) story, which we mentioned briefly in an earlier chapter, that makes this point. When a teacher handed out the exam grades, a student judged that they seemed almost random, so the student asked the teacher on what basis the exams had been graded. The teacher said that she had been so harshly criticized for subjectivity in her grading in the past that she had graded this batch of papers objectively; she had thrown the papers up a set of stairs, giving the best grade to the ones that landed on the highest step, the next best grade to the ones that reached the next highest step, and so on. No subjectivity involved. The problem here is obvious, and the solution is absurd. The price paid for "objective quantification" is that the standard being used has no relation to the underlying value that it is taken to be a standard for. But the moral of the story is that we need to be on the lookout for less obvious cases involving the same kinds of issues.

Second-Order Values and Quantification

Consider this situation. Melinda is a heavy smoker, and often uses marijuana. She gets enormous pleasure from both. But she knows that her use of them could interfere with other things she values in her present and future life (good health, energy, motivation, clear thinking, treating friends and family well, doing her job effectively). If she takes the pleasure she gets from smoking and marijuana at face value, the question arises as to how, and how much, she should factor in that pleasure and the prices she pays for indulging in it. She believes drug dependence (including tobacco) to be a degrading thing, and her sense of self-respect tells her not to give such pleasures the same weight as the pleasure she gets from accomplishments in her efforts to help secure people's retirement as a financial advisor. Should she discount such pleasures? How much? Should she perhaps give them no weight, regard them as peccadillos that she cannot correct, but that should not play a role in her important decisions in life? Can this distinction between her better and worse self be captured quantitatively? And why is the self that has contempt for the value of drugs the better self? Perhaps it is in part because the value of smoking is the value of each moment of pleasure, and the moments do not add up to more than that, whereas the effects she can have on other lives in her efforts to assist clients have worth that is more than the sum of the value of individual moments.

Suppose we say that she has a desire not to desire tobacco and marijuana, what philosopher Harry Frankfurt called a *second-order preference*. Does that mean that she should simply weight her desire for these drugs against her desire not to desire them? We don't think so. It is not a simple desire, this desire not to desire something. It is a question of what kind of life she is to lead, and what kind of person she is to be. What role should pure sensual and other immediate pleasures play in her life?

Many of us, perhaps all of us, prefer things we would prefer not to prefer. Say we have a strong preference for smoking, but also a strong preference not to have that preference. If this "second-order" preference not to prefer smoking were effectively to diminish our first-order preference to smoke, our problem with regard to smoking might simply vanish. But preferences often do not work this way. Often a person strongly prefers smoking *and* strongly prefers not to prefer it. Does the second-order preference diminish the quantitative value we assign to smoking or not? If so, by how much?

These sorts of questions may be dismissed by RCT enthusiasts as concerning rare cases, or delicate and subtle issues that can be easily dealt with later, or simply by hand waving. But they are the common stuff of everyday life, and important. Hand waving here waves away struggles that many people face frequently in life. And it seems evident that the differences between the objects of these second-order and first-order preferences, and perhaps the preferences themselves, are qualitative, not quantitative, like the differences between a Leonardo and a Raphael painting.

Incommensurability of Values

Value is often complex and multidimensional. To decide where to go to college, Mia must assign value to location, studio arts, extracurricular opportunities, social life, later acceptance to law school, and more. Moreover, she must be able to assess these seemingly quite different sorts of values on a common scale, or else she will not be able to assemble her judgments into an overall score for each candidate school. As with Leonardo and Raphael, Mia can certainly assign scores (say on a 10-point scale) to each relevant attribute of each school she is considering. Then adding up the scores becomes a simple matter. But what do the scores mean? Does an 8 for studio arts mean the same thing as an 8 for social life? This seems to us extremely unlikely, without doing violence to the ways in which the various attributes Mia is thinking about are distinct. When someone attaches value numbers to attributes of options in deciding where to go to college, the operative assumption is that an 8 on a 10-point scale means the same thing whether one is considering the quality of the sociology program, the quality of the school jazz band, or the quality of the school football team. They are treated as fungible. One distinguishes them only by assigning each feature a weight based on its importance to the decider — for example, a high weight to the sociology program and a low weight to the jazz band. Like money, these rating numbers are treated as comparable. But are they? The problem with assessing values in this example is not complexity per se, but the possibility that various dimensions of value may be incommensurable: incomparable using a common metric.

Imagine this situation. Sarah brings a friend home from college for Thanksgiving dinner. The food is delicious and the whole meal is a pleasure in every respect. After the meal, Sarah's friend takes out a $50 bill and leaves it on the table for Sarah's mother, who not only cooked the meal but served it and cleaned up afterward. Everyone, including Sarah, is appalled. Why? Because there are forms of social interaction that are intimately connected with social relationships. Friends do not normally pay each other for the things they do for each other. When a doorman opens the door for us, we may tip him. When a friend opens the door for us, we don't tip him. It is not just a "mistake" to do so, it is a violation of the nature of the relationship — a social taboo. Psychologist Alan Fiske has systematized these sorts of taboos in his book *Structures of Social Life*. Fiske argues that there are four fundamental modes of social organization and interaction that characterize most societies. There is *communal sharing* ("what's mine is yours"), *authority ranking* ("we will allocate resources based on people's position in the social hierarchy"), *equality matching* ("you took care of my dog last weekend, so I'll take care of yours this weekend"), and *market pricing* ("Thanksgiving dinner was delicious; here's a $50 tip"). Societies differ, says Fiske, in which of these modes is dominant, and in which domains of social life each of the modes should operate. But operating from within an inappropriate social mode (the $50 tip to your friend's mother) is taboo, and offensive. Political philosopher Michael Walzer has made a similar argument in connection with justice. In *Spheres of Justice*, he argues that different principles for allocation and distribution of society's goods should operate in different domains. Perhaps in the domain of daily survival needs, justice requires adequate support for everyone, a kind of communal sharing. Perhaps when it comes to admission to highly selective colleges or jobs, justice demands allocation on the basis of merit, however it is measured. Both Fiske and Walzer acknowledge that there is room for disagreement among citizens about which activity belongs in which domain. They also agree that the boundaries between domains are fuzzy and dynamic, much like the natural categories we discussed in chapter 2. And they also agree that lumping all value (or justice) considerations into a single domain does violence to how people live (and should live) their lives and how societies regulate (and should regulate) social interactions. Walzer

QUANTIFYING VALUE

argues that societies dominated by one measure of value (for example, money) become tyrannized by that measure. And Fiske argues that breaking boundaries between modes of social relations is deeply offensive. It is offensive to give your friend's mother a $50 tip, and it is offensive to give your restaurant server a hug. It would be offensive to resort to market pricing ("What will it cost me in a donation to the college to get an acceptance?") or authority ranking ("Don't you realize that I'm the mayor of this town?") to get your child into college. In a paper written with psychologist Philip Tetlock, Fiske argues that often "to compare is to destroy," at least when comparison involves values that cross the boundaries of social regulation that he articulates (he calls such comparisons "taboo trade-offs"). Indeed, this may be what "incommensurable" means. Some values are "sacred," in the sense that they cannot be traded off against other values — as, for example, in the case of "donating" organs for money. But the complexity of values that are often involved in making decisions virtually demands that we compare features of the alternatives that are incommensurable, perhaps almost incomparable, and probably unquantifiable. We had a colleague in the economics department who having returned from an expensive vacation with his family, justified the expenditure by saying "it was cheaper than psychotherapy." We laughed at his joke, only to come to the realization that he wasn't joking.

    Think about a situation in which a lucky, privileged college student is trying to decide where to go for spring break. Hiking in the Rockies, sitting on a beach in Florida, and sightseeing in Europe are three of several candidates. One can imagine setting up a spreadsheet and comparing these possibilities to one another on a number of dimensions (weather, food, nightlife, culture, cost, and the like) and then doing the math and choosing. But there is one possibility that is not like the others on the list. It is going home to stay with her family (who love her and miss her) and hanging out with old high school friends. How can she compare this option with all the others? The categories of value do not line up. What will the spreadsheet compute such that going home compares meaningfully with these various exciting trips? When she chooses between these qualitatively different options, she is to some extent deciding what kind of person to be (a hedonist or a family-oriented person) rather than how to maximize utility.

A defender of RCT might say that the student will eventually choose, and that the fact of her choice will "reveal" her preference. So, if she decides to spend the week with her folks, that must mean that that option won in her calculations. We find this sort of argument quite unconvincing. The fact that aspects of the values of different options can't be compared quantitatively does not mean that a chooser will be paralyzed by indecision. What it means is that the chooser's decision, when she makes it, will not be the product of RCT-type thinking. A different kind of thinking is required.

Thus, we believe that quantifying the value of everything that is a factor in our decisions is impossible to do objectively and reasonably. It can of course be done objectively, however, as in the case of the teacher who throws student papers up the stairs to determine grades. The moral of that story is that "objectivity" has to be of a sort that reflects the nature of the situation, the purposes of the decider in that situation, and social norms that tell us which kinds of situations should be handled in which kinds of ways.

There is one other significant point to be made about the formulations of Fiske and of Walzer. In both cases, we can understand their arguments as defenses of framing writ large. Framed as an instance of market pricing, tipping your friend's mother is appropriate.

QUANTIFYING VALUE

The only question is how big a tip to leave. Framed as communal sharing, the tip is deeply disrespectful and inappropriate. And so if RCT is useful, it is only because of frames imposed and justified by some other kind of rational deliberations or traditional set of practices. Absent these supposed frames, which are often regarded as adding an irrational element to the otherwise rational RCT process, RCT is useless, if not absurd, and potentially quite destructive ("to compare is to destroy").

There is a great deal of convenience attached to being able to compare different types of values on a common scale, and the most obvious common scale at hand is money. But to compare on a monetary scale the values, say, of pleasure, convenience, honesty, and justice will lead not just to largely arbitrary consequences, but to immoral ones. It is a step on a path on which our society has already gone too far – the commodification of everything. In some traditions this is considered a sin, and there is a name for it: *simony*. Simon the Magus, who lived in the early days of Christianity, saw that the Christians had discovered something very important, and so he offered them money for a "franchise," as it were. The rejection of Simon's offer did not end the problem. The Catholic Church centuries later took to selling "indulgences," shortcuts to heaven, and disgust with that contributed significantly to the coming of the Reformation. We have largely lost the notion of simony as a sin, but residues of our disgust with it exist in the ways that Fiske illuminates. We may be on the verge of accepting the sale of sex as unproblematic, but we have not yet accepted the sale of our organs, and we will, we hope, never accept the sale of our children. Economist Alvin Roth has written thoughtfully about how what he called "repugnance" complicates the way in which markets for various kinds of goods and services work. Attitudes toward such "repugnant markets" are very much in the spirit of what Fiske and Walzer are suggesting. One view of this sort of repugnance is that it is a drag on the efficiency of market exchange. Another view is that it saves us from the monstrosity of unbridled market exchange. As we assume is obvious, we support this second view.

Fiske's analysis has important implications for the way we formulate decision problems. In *Thinking, Fast and Slow,* Kahneman regards formulations that are not suitable for the application of RCT prescriptions as being "framed" in a potentially biased way. In contrast, we have suggested that formulating a problem in such a way that it is amenable to RCT methods and quantitative calculation is, in most cases, a way of *reframing* the problem. Moreover, we suggest that it is a way of reframing that reflects an important "bias," as Kahneman would have it. Reframing probabilities and values into mathematically manipulable categories that RCT can handle reflects the genuine bias that Kahneman frames as "neglects ambiguity and suppresses doubt." Nothing removes ambiguities and introduces unrealistic clarity more than the quantification of most everyday uncertainties and values.

Closed-World Assumptions, Incommensurability, and Cost-Benefit Analysis

In the examples in this chapter, our intention was to highlight not only that decisions are often complex, but that the complexity is of a particular type, involving aspects of the decision and its consequences that can be compared only with great difficulty, uncertainty, and offense to our shared notion of boundaries. This, we suggest, is not an uncommon aspect of decisions, but a routine one. As we discussed earlier, Bennis, Medin, and Bartels, in their research on cost-benefit judgments, introduce a distinction between "open-" and "closed-" world assumptions. They suggest that rigorous, case-by-case cost-benefit analyses can be done only under closed-world assumptions, which can significantly distort the issues at hand. But what is the alternative? An obvious alternative to cost-benefit analysis is rules. An economist or policy maker does cost-benefit analysis. A rigid person just puts blinders on and follows the rules, whatever they are—for example, compensating families of 9/11 victims by calculating lost earnings. A less rigid person starts with the rules but has eyes open to possible exceptions, as Kenneth Feinberg did when he acknowledged that all lives have equal value *and* that they do not have equal earnings potential, *and* that both of these perspectives matter. And a wise person makes exceptions at just the right times, in just the right ways, for just the right reasons. But even among those open to exceptions, rules may provide the defaults—the anchors. Or, if not rules, then perhaps habits or social conventions, a main point of Fiske's analysis.

Rules don't tell us how to compute the real cost of a lost arm or leg, except perhaps arbitrarily. But then, neither does cost-benefit analysis. What is needed is a conversation about how much the "closed world" should be opened up. Such conversations may bring clarity, but there is no guarantee that they will help people reach agreement. And that is because to know how much to open up the world, one needs to know a lot—about the state of the world, the state of the people in it, the goals and purposes of those people, and perhaps what the goals and purposes of those people should be. With issues like these settled, a useful cost-benefit analysis is possible. But not before.

An instructive example of what we are getting at comes from research on moral development in children. Psychologist Lawrence

Kohlberg had a major influence on the field with his theory that moral development involved the development of ever more sophisticated moral principles. The most famous illustration of his theory involves a man who needs a very expensive drug that he can't afford in order to save his life. The druggist won't bargain about the price of the drug. And the question is, should the sick man or his family steal the drug? In answering this question, young children focus on such things as "they might get caught," or "it's against the law to steal." As moral development proceeds, reasoning shifts to arguments like "people have the right to do what they want with their property," or "you can't put a price on life." A critic of Kohlberg's view, Carol Gilligan, suggested that rather than relying on abstract high principles, some people address this sort of problem in a different voice — a voice that sees the world as "open." Such people look for a way to reframe the problem to respect both property rights *and* life, seeking a way to reconcile competing views. What Kohlberg regarded as the "highest" form of moral reasoning takes the problem as given and then calculates the "right" answer. One of Gilligan's young respondents even described these dilemmas as being like math problems. Yes, we can make them like math problems, but all the really hard work comes beforehand. So cost-benefit analysis has its place, but that place is not every place.

As Bennis, Medin, and Bartels point out, the field of judgment and decision-making makes much of the distinction between normative and prescriptive approaches. Normative standards tell us how people should make decisions on the assumption that they have unlimited capacity for evaluating the options. Prescriptive standards tell us how people should go about making decisions given the limitations of human information processing and rationality. Within this framework, it may seem natural to regard cost-benefit analysis as the normative ideal, but then acknowledge that finite creatures with limited time and cognitive resources may need to resort to rules or social norms.

We think this is the wrong view. The problem is not (just) in us, but in the world. Even people of unlimited processing capacity will have problems knowing how much to open up the system and in what ways. To do this unerringly is to be able to predict which types of "opening up" will be relevant in the future. It would not have occurred to very many of us fifty years ago to consider global warming in deciding what to have for dinner. Moreover, it may be impossible to attach probabilities to many relevant futures, because we don't know enough, and probably will never know enough, as the notion of radical uncertainty suggests. Closing the system and turning our decisions into versions of the gambling paradigm can solve this problem, but only at the cost of significant misrepresentation of what the decisions actually are like. And since one can't do cost-benefit analysis without being able to assign probabilities to possible outcomes, the limit on such analysis is a normative one, not a prescriptive one.

And among the futures we can't predict are those that arise as a result of cost-benefit analyses that treat incommensurables as commensurable, treat sacred values as mere preferences, and treat "taboo trade-offs" as permissible. What kind of place does the world become when people are willing to break all the rules and use cost-benefit analysis in their place? Cost-benefit analyses, if they become routine because everyone learns that they are the normatively correct way to make decisions, may cast a long and destructive shadow. If each citizen takes it upon him- or herself to do cost-benefit analyses to determine whether or not to follow a rule, life will be chaos, and the expenses of rule enforcement will explode.

There is an African proverb: "If a man does away with his traditional way of living and throws away his good customs, he had better first make certain that he has something of value to replace them."[1] Cost-benefit analysis has real value, but not nearly enough.

Should the Aim of Decision-Making Be *Maximizing* Utility?

As we said in chapter 1, RCT assumes that the aim of a decision is to maximize utility, or preference. We suggested that while the concepts of "utility" and "preference" have some desirable attributes, both terms are rather less informative than might appear. We left alone, at that time, the goal of maximizing. Maximizing seems like an uncontroversial goal. Why wouldn't you want to get the most you can out of a situation? This is especially true in the case of the gambling paradigm. It seems silly — maybe even a little crazy — to opt for the second- or third-best bet available. But one of the things that makes the gambling situation so atypical is that there is only one thing of value up for grabs — money (though even here, the thrill and excitement of betting on a long shot may offer rewards that compensate for it being a worse bet than the favorite). In contrast, the kinds of decisions we have been discussing in this chapter often involve different sorts of values, and even trade-offs among them. When Mia cares about liberal arts courses, extracurriculars, studio arts, social life, and being close to nature and to home in choosing a

---

1. Ruark, *Something of Value*, 3.

college, what does maximizing even mean? Should she strive for some of each of the things she values, as much as possible of each thing she values, as much as possible of the thing she values most, or something else?

Nobel Prize-winning economist/psychologist Herbert Simon argued some seventy years ago, in considering complex decisions with multiple options, each having multiple relevant attributes, that whereas maximizing might be the appropriate logical goal, it was not the appropriate psychological goal. Human beings, along with all other animals, just do not have the cognitive horsepower to calculate what would maximize utility, except in quite simple situations, like typical gambles. Instead, Simon argued that people *satisfice*, seeking out options that are "good enough," and stopping their search when they find an option that meets their standards. To maximize, you need to know what every possibility out there has to offer. To satisfice, you only need to know how high your standards are, and then evaluate possibilities one by one until you find one that meets your standards. Satisficing, unlike maximizing, is within human cognitive capacity.

Years later, one of us (Barry) suggested in *The Paradox of Choice* that not only is maximizing as a goal too hard, it is also self-defeating. People who seek to maximize suffer from analysis paralysis, and when they finally do pull the trigger and choose, they are almost always disappointed in the results. So satisficing, rather than maximizing, is the more sensible objective in most of the decision situations we face. Thus, perhaps RCT should be modified to suggest that the goal in a decision is to satisfice utility.

We think such a view is an improvement, but it does not go far enough. It doesn't tell us how Mia should go about weighing her different values in choosing a college. Satisficing is quantitative in the same way that maximizing is. More is better than less of anything we value. Satisficing just tries to hit an easier target.

Perhaps the right way to think about the goal of our decisions is that we should be seeking not the most, and not more, but the "right amount." Mia should seek the right amount of intellectual rigor, the right amount of liberal arts excellence, the right amount of studio arts, and the right amount of social life, proximity to nature, and closeness to home. What the notion of the "right amount" implies is that more is not always better than less. There can be too much of even good things. We mention this perhaps odd-seeming possibility for two reasons. First, as Barry showed in collaboration with Adam Grant, it seems to be true, at least in many consequential areas of human life. And second, the notion of a "right amount" bears more than a family resemblance to what Aristotle called the "mean." The mean, for Aristotle, is not the arithmetic average, but the right amount. Courage, for example, is the mean between cowardice (too little) and recklessness (too much). Moreover, what the right amount is will depend on context, which is a main reason why the arithmetic average won't do. What counts as physical or intellectual courage in one situation may be cowardice in another and recklessness in a third. And so Aristotle's mean is not quite as quantitative as the term suggests. We mention Aristotle and the mean here because his approach to rationality and decision-making will play a prominent role when we discuss our alternative to RCT later in the book.

Finding the right amount isn't easy, especially when it is context dependent what the right amount is. But it substantially reduces the problems posed by values that are incommensurable. When you are seeking the right amount of X, Y, and Z, there is much less need to be trading off a unit of X for a unit of Z. We will also see when we

QUANTIFYING VALUE

discuss Aristotle in more detail later that incommensurability of values is what he pretty much takes for granted.

We have criticized cost-benefit analysis, as we criticized RCT, for doing much less than it promises, and for ignoring the kinds of nonquantitative work we must do to turn a decision we face into a form that cost-benefit analysis may be able to handle. Nonetheless, we do not want to suggest that the cost-benefit framework is always a waste of time, or even a distortion. When the options we face are to a substantial degree commensurable, or nearly so, as in deciding whether to spend the day with your mother or your daughter, discussed in the introduction, then cost-benefit analysis may play a useful role. Similarly, in deciding how much of your income to save for the future, cost-benefit analysis may be helpful. It may be helpful as you contemplate emphasizing flexibility versus usability in software you are designing. It may even be helpful as you decide how much time and attention to allocate to each of your children. Cost-benefit analysis can certainly be of value when you face decisions for which it is appropriate, or when you can reshape more challenging decisions so as to make cost-benefit analysis appropriate. But in using it, it is always sensible to appreciate its limits and not overestimate what it can accomplish.

Chapter 5

RATIONAL CHOICE THEORY AND THE FRAMING OF DECISIONS

We have made frequent reference to "framing" in our discussion thus far, but we have barely scratched the surface given the prominence of framing and its effects in empirical research on decision-making. Let us further explore the significance of framing by examining some classic examples from lab research.

Consider the following hypothetical situations:

1. Imagine that the United States is preparing for the outbreak of an unusual disease, which is expected to kill six hundred people. Two alternative programs to combat the disease have been proposed. Assume that the exact scientific estimates of the consequences are as follows:

> Option A. If Program A is adopted, two hundred people will be saved.
> Option B. If Program B is adopted, there is a one-third probability that six hundred people will be saved and a two-thirds probability that no people will be saved.

2. Imagine that the United States is preparing for the outbreak of an unusual disease, which is expected to kill six hundred people. Two alternative programs to combat the disease have been proposed. Assume that the exact scientific estimates of the consequences are as follows:

> Option C. If Program C is adopted, four hundred people will die.
> Option D. If Program D is adopted, there is a one-third probability that nobody will die and a two-thirds probability that six hundred people will die.

3. You travel into the city by train to see a concert, and when you get to the box office and reach into your pocket for money with which to buy a $20 ticket, you discover that you lost a $20 bill. Assuming that you have enough money to cover the costs, do you

> A. Buy a ticket anyway
> B. Go home without seeing the concert

4. You travel into the city by train to see a concert, and when you get to the box office and reach into your pocket for the $20 ticket you purchased earlier, you discover that you lost it somewhere en route to the concert. When you explain your predicament the box office attendant is very sympathetic but explains that since there is no way of proving that you had a ticket, and seats are unreserved, if you want to see the concert, you will have to buy another ticket. Assuming that you have enough money to cover the costs, do you

> C. Buy another ticket
> D. Go home without seeing the concert

According to RCT, there is a right way and a wrong way to answer these questions. In RCT terms, Example 2 is identical to Example 1, and Example 4 is identical to Example 3 in all relevant respects, though the situations have been "reframed" so that some superficial details differ. Options C and D are essentially the same as options A and B in each pair of questions, so anyone who gives answers A and D, or answers B and C to consecutive questions is acting in violation of the normative principles of rationality. But determining which changes to a situation are relevant to a decision and which are merely superficial "reframing" is not a simple task, and in scenarios like these, an apparently trivial change can have real consequences for the life of the decision maker.

The disease problem, presented here in Examples 1 and 2, was devised and discussed by Kahneman and Tversky as an example of a violation of "invariance." As we mentioned earlier, the principle of invariance states that changes in the descriptions of options and outcomes should not alter one's preference order. Invariance is such an obvious principle that many accounts that attempt to formalize the rules of rational decision-making use it implicitly, without stating it explicitly. It may seem obvious that the two disease problems are identical when they are viewed side by side. However, when answered separately, many people select options A (72%) and D (78%). This pattern of results violates the principle of invariance, but people make these choices because they think in the way that has been elegantly described by Kahneman and Tversky's "prospect theory," published in 1979.

According to that theory, people have diminishing sensitivity to both gains and losses. This leads them to be risk seeking when dealing with losses (deaths) but risk averse when dealing with gains (lives saved). The reason for this pattern, essentially, is that gaining twice as much isn't twice as good, and losing twice as much isn't twice as bad, which makes risk taking in a "gain-framed" situation a bad bet, but risk taking in a "loss-framed" example a good bet. To take a simpler example, winning $20 is not twice as good as winning $10, and losing $20 isn't twice as bad as losing $10, so a fifty-fifty gamble with respect to possible gains is unattractive, whereas a fifty-fifty gamble with respect to possible losses is attractive. Remember that according to RCT, it is the expected *subjective* utility, not the expected *objective* value, that is the key to the decision. The problem posed by Examples 1 and 2 above is that the two problems are actually different descriptions of the *same* problem. This is what makes the pattern of choices typically observed a violation of RCT.

The third and fourth hypothetical situations come from research on mental accounting, a phenomenon studied in detail by Richard Thaler, who published two landmark papers about it. You are in the same financial situation in both cases. Either you could be out $40 and see the show, or you could be out $20 and not see the show. However, people do not take this kind of global perspective on their money. Instead, they group their finances into many narrower mental accounts, and they make decisions based on evaluations of these relevant mental accounts. People who have lost their ticket post both the $20 cost of the first ticket and the $20 that would be necessary to buy a new ticket to the "concert" account, which makes the total cost of attending the show seem to be $40. Since $40 is a lot to pay (please note that this research was done many years ago!), many people who receive this version of the scenario (42%) do not buy another ticket. People who have lost a $20 bill account for that loss in a way that is unrelated to the concert, so most of them (90%) choose to pay for a ticket. Rational choice theorists tend to take the global perspective on people's finances and view the two situations as identical in all relevant respects. Money is fungible — one dollar is the same as any other — so wasting $20 on a lost ticket is the same as wasting $20 on a lost $20 bill. The inconsistency between the two situations caused by mental accounting, then, is another violation of the principles of RCT-defined rationality. And mental accounting — broad or narrow — is just another instance of framing.

That people organize inflows and outputs of money and other resources into a variety of distinct mental accounts helps explain why they are willing to treat themselves to a luxury when they have a windfall, but otherwise not. This also helps explain why people will make deposits into savings accounts that pay 2% interest while at the same time making minimal payments to reduce credit card debt at 18% interest. Since money is fungible (a dollar is a dollar is a dollar), this segmenting of different inflows and outputs into separate mental accounts is viewed as an error in rational decision-making.

And to be clear, often it is an error, the nature of which is sometimes described as "narrow framing." Does it really make sense to pay credit card interest of 18% while earning 2% on savings? Shouldn't you just pay off your credit card bill from savings and then work to rebuild your savings account? And if you're willing to spend $20 to see a concert after having discovered you lost a $20 bill, why aren't you willing to do the same after you lost a $20 ticket? Each is a piece of paper worth $20. One has an image of a president on it while the other has a seat number on it. Thaler's work has highlighted the pitfalls of narrow framing.

But is narrow framing irrational by all reasonable notions of rationality? Imagine getting a $5,000 graduation gift from a wealthy relative. "What should I spend it on?" you ask. As a rational choice devotee, you might first list all the things you can do with $5,000. Then you would assign each possibility a value and a probability that your choice will get you what you are hoping for. Then you would do the math and choose. So, how many things can you do with $5,000? The list of possibilities is very, very long. RCT will *create* a problem, not *solve* it. A way out of this morass would be to organize the possibilities into superordinate categories (begin saving for retirement, save for a down payment on a condo, make a down payment on a car, replace some dying appliances, splurge on a travel adventure, and so on), then choose a category, and then choose within that category. Framing and mental accounting are thus not errors, but essential tools in the sorting process. We argued in chapters 1 and 2 that a process very much like this is needed in order for Mia to use RCT to decide where to apply to college. And we argued similarly in the introduction in contemplating how to answer the question "What should I do today?"

Think about losing your concert ticket versus a $20 bill. Framing and mental accounting can be helpful. Does your expenditure go into a narrow "listen to live music" account, a broader "things to do on a Friday night" account, or a still broader "ways to meet a potential romantic partner at a social event" account? It is not hard to see that your judgment about whether that $20 should be spent will depend on what it is being compared with. And what it is compared with will depend on how your decision is framed. Nor is there anything irrational about this effect. Frames and mental accounts are lifesavers, especially in the modern world.

Let us expand the lost ticket example. Jacob and John have bought tickets to the concert for $20. Jacob discovers he has lost his ticket and decides not to go. John also discovers he has lost his ticket. He decides to go. Is John more rational than Jacob? What else do we know? John is a music fan. He goes to many concerts. He is going to the concert for the entertainment he gets from hearing live music.

"I would get $40 worth of pleasure from hearing this concert." He buys the ticket.

Now consider Jacob. Jacob received a call from his mother, with whom he does not get along very well. She tells him that he never spends any time with her, and that she has an extra ticket to the concert that she needs to get rid of. Would he go to the concert with her tomorrow? Jacob is pretty much indifferent about live music. Nevertheless, he stops by her house and gives her $20 cash in exchange for the ticket. For Jacob the question never was "Should I pay $20 to go to the concert?" Nor was it "Is the concert worth $20?" The question was "Will I spend $20 to please my mother (even if it means going to the concert)?" When he later finds he lost the ticket, he decides not to buy another. We could imagine him thinking, "I am willing to spend $20 to please my mother, but not $40. And the time I spend with her will be even more painful knowing that I have spent $40 for it." Is this an irrational decision?

In a slightly different scenario, Jim's mother calls and asks if he will buy her extra ticket and go with her. He agrees. On his way over to fetch her, he discovers he has just recently lost a $20 bill. "That's too bad," he says to himself, but never thinks to connect it with his mother or the concert. He buys her ticket and goes to the concert. Is Jim rational in this case and Jacob irrational in the previous case? We think not. Was John rational and Jacob not? We think not.

A proponent of RCT might say, "Perhaps you're right, but the situations are completely different. One involves listening to music and the other involves the value (or disvalue) of being with your mother. The value of the concert itself is nil."

The point of this elaboration of the lost ticket scenario is to show that in a sense, the example as originally created depends on disregarding the reasons that our protagonists bought the tickets, consequently making "what they were doing" invisible. Jacob was pleasing his mother. The concert was incidental. John was buying entertainment. The concert was the heart of the matter. John's purchase was a consumer transaction: $40 exchanged for the pleasure of the concert. Jacob's purchase was a social transaction. The consumer exchange aspect of the decision was relatively unimportant. Where John was buying a product (entertainment), Jacob was repairing his relationship with his mother.

The RCT defender might say that objectively, what they are both doing is deciding whether to spend $40 to buy a ticket, and their rationality should be judged on the basis of that. If that is true — that what they were "really," or "objectively," doing was buying a ticket for $40 — then there are vast areas of life, the most important ones, the non-consumer-like ones, to which "what we are really, objectively doing" is irrelevant to our rationality. Indeed, one could argue that describing a lost $20 bill plus $20 spent on a ticket as "spending $40 on a ticket" is itself almost ridiculous. In what sense was the lost $20 bill "spent" on the ticket?

The irrationality revealed in the concert case is an artifact of the selection and construction of the case. Any decisions in which context and meaning are significant factors is inappropriate for the criteria of rationality established by RCT, in part because once you consider context and meaning, you undermine the "closed-world assumption" we discussed earlier. Financial and commercial transactions are least affected by considerations of context and meaning. Billions of transactions take place on the stock exchanges of the world and on e-markets in a day, which is possibly *because* those institutions have been developed precisely to exclude contextual/meaning factors from being relevant. Imagine if buying a stock involved consideration of the name of the company, the city in which its headquarters is located, and the font in which the stock certificate is printed. Or, much more plausible, imagine that your decision involved the moral dimensions of how the company makes its money. In addition, most commercial transactions are "arm's-length," meaning that the buyers don't care who the sellers are, and vice versa. In short, usually money is just money. But mothers are not just mothers. Moreover, imagine that your decision to sell the stock might be influenced by what you thought the buyer would do as a shareholder. Would the buyer be indifferent to or even supportive of practices that exploited workers and polluted the environment? Stock exchanges would grind to a halt if the arm's-length nature of transactions were altered in this way.

We believe, therefore, that RCT is much less useful as a normative standard than JDM researchers have taken it to be. The research tradition of JDM developed by focusing on situations (for example, gambles) that are stylized versions of what RCT was designed to explain. JDM researchers looked where there was quantitative clarity because they framed the goal of the study of decision-making as a rigorous quantitative endeavor, rather than because they thought that mathematical formalization would be where the answers to their questions lay. Instead of the question "How do humans think?," they investigated variants of the question "Are people good intuitive statisticians?" or "Are people good intuitive economists?" The variants of this question never moved very far away from taking statistical thinking of the sort involved in gambling decisions as the paradigm of thinking. Researchers ignored many other kinds of problems that thinking is for: Should I organize my life around the pursuit of pleasure? Money? Accomplishment, like improving our healthcare system? Understanding the universe for its own sake (like Einstein)? What should I want, hold to be important, pursue? Perhaps it is because researchers were so focused on quantitative calculation and RCT that they did not see the really important issues.

Framing as Necessary for Quantification

We have tried to illustrate how important framing is, and should be, in the making of decisions, even with respect to classic demonstrations of framing as rationality gone awry. Our discussion of the lost ticket example was meant to show that the problem as presented blocked several potentially relevant considerations from view. One possible reason why researchers chose to frame the lost ticket example so narrowly is that RCT seeks quantification, and narrow framing may be required if quantification is to proceed effectively. RCT provides us with tools for quantification, both of the value of the options we face and their probability of leading to the outcomes we desire. But for quantification to be possible, framing, rather than (merely) being a source of bias, is essential to close an open system.

To give a concrete sense of the role framing plays in understanding how people do and should make decisions, consider what is perhaps the central example of the importance of framing to decision-making. As we explained in discussing the two versions of the disease problem above, people consistently make risk-*averse* choices when choosing among possible gains (choosing a sure gain over an uncertain larger one) and risk-*seeking* choices when choosing among possible losses (choosing an uncertain large loss over a certain smaller one). Kahneman and Tversky's prospect theory explains this pattern of choice. The pattern is not, in itself, a problem or an error, but it becomes a problem *and* an error when variations in the language of description of the situation induce people to frame two formally identical choice situations as one involving gains while the other involves losses, as was the case in the two versions of the disease problem. In other words, people seem unable to see through the language of description to the underlying reality that is being described. The language "frames" and distorts the decision. Concretely, consider these two examples:

> Gamble 1. Imagine having been given $300 in addition to whatever else you possess. Would you prefer (a) a gain of an additional $100 for sure, or (b) a gain of an additional $200 with a probability of 0.5?
>
> Gamble 2. Imagine having been given $500 in addition to whatever else you possess. Would you prefer (a) a loss of $100 for sure, or (b) a loss of $200 with a probability of 0.5?

Looked at objectively, these two gambles are identical. Given the $300 you start with, Gamble 1 offers you a total of $400 for sure or a 0.5 chance of $500 and a 0.5 chance of $300. And given the $500 you start with, Gamble 2 also offers you $400 for sure or a 0.5 chance of $500 and a 0.5 chance of $300. If you are risk averse, you should choose option (a) in both gambles, ending with $400 for sure in each. If you are risk seeking, you should choose option (b) in both gambles, ending with $500 (p=0.5) or $300 (p=0.5). In short, these gambles are basically two ways of offering the same thing. But people do not see the two gambles as the same. They see Gamble 1 as a choice between two gain options—a sure one and a risky one. And they see Gamble 2 as a choice between two loss options—a sure one and a risky one. And so many choose option (a) in Gamble 1 and option (b) in Gamble 2, just as prospect theory predicts. But crucially, Gamble 1 seems like a choice between gains because you start out with $300, and Gamble 2 seems like a choice between losses because you start out with $500. The two different starting points you are given create two different frames within which the options are evaluated, and these two different frames lead to two different choices.

Moreover, giving people an endowment of $300 or $500 is also intended to put whatever endowments the people actually have outside the frame. The endowments are meant to communicate something like this: forget about whatever financial resources you actually have. Assume or pretend that you start out with $300 ($500). Nothing else you might have matters. Now, pick the sure thing or the gamble. It is striking that this manipulation actually seems to succeed in putting the person's other financial resources outside the frame within which the gambling decision is being considered. But it is plausible to us that this effect of framing is crucial to the results that the study revealed. Without the stipulated initial endowment of $300 ($500), a person might say, before choosing, "My 401(k) has $1.2 million in it. The sums involved in this gamble are pretty trivial. Am I in the mood at this moment for risk or for safety?"

Suppose that over the last decade, a philosophy professor has been changing her teaching of logic, teaching it more rigorously, and she wants to know if the changes improve the results. The professor wants to know the truth about her teaching effectiveness, and that knowledge will serve her goal of improving her performance. She graphs the average final exam results over the years. It turns out there are outliers in several places, but other than the outliers, there seems to be a gradual but substantial increase in the three-year moving average of grades. With the outliers, there is no change overall. Are the results for next year likely to be higher grades?

The data points alone do not imply much about anything else. And the data provide no formal help in determining what other factors need to be considered. Of course, the professor may have hunches (or even well-articulated theories) about what else to include in the analysis. These hunches or theories can be thought of as frames within which the data are evaluated. But they probably will not stand examination by S2 — our deliberative, conscious, rule-governed cognitive system for making decisions — to see if they are justified. Perhaps the grade changes are random. Do we know that they are not random, and that we could find a way of connecting them with a "curve"? Perhaps, but not without appealing to a set of criteria justifying one curve over another. As philosophers like Brian Skyrms have pointed out, for any finite set of data, there are an infinite number of curves that can be drawn connecting the individual data points.

It might seem that we can avoid framing the data with a theory (however formal it may be) if we simply connect the points with the straight lines that fit the data best. We would be sticking very close to the data. As we saw, some data points (the outliers) differ from the others dramatically. Does the graph we get from the straight lines tell us where to expect the next data point to be? But what if by ignoring the outliers and drawing a curve close to the rest we get a pattern that indicates where the next point should be? Should we ignore some data and just come close with our graph of other data, or should we stick very close to all the data?

RCT certainly does not tell us. Framing intelligently does. Looking for data to tell us whether there is an improvement or not makes us notice the outliers, reflect on the data, and, in a sense, reframe them. Puzzlement leads us to go back and look more carefully at the classes we taught in the years of the outliers. It turns out that a high outlier in the early years was a class that consisted of a large number of advanced science majors. A low outlier in the later years was a class that consisted largely of first-semester freshmen intending to be humanities majors. Another outlier in the later years was during a semester in which the campus was distracted by a visiting celebrity humanities professor. These factors make sense. They are in accord with a coherent picture that justifiably puts the professor at cognitive ease, allowing her to draw the curve leaving out the three outliers and get something more like a rising straight line. The professor predicts that next year's grades, if she continues to teach more rigorously, will improve. Framing is not a mistake. Rather than biasing the answer, it has made an answer possible. By helping her to understand the situation, it has enabled the professor to extrapolate usefully. Without the framing, the data would be highly ambiguous, if not silent. With it, the professor is able to come up with a reasonable answer to her question. To be sure, her answer might be wrong. The world is an uncertain place. But the professor may rightly conclude that she has made some progress in evaluating her teaching.

There are, of course, sophisticated statistical techniques, like multiple regression, designed to substitute for intuitions and reflections, including framing, that address and measure potential confounding factors more formally. But even with these tools, one still must decide which factors to include in the statistical analysis. Assessing the effects of a new mode of teaching requires framing the possible causal factors to include the plausible ones and exclude the infinitely many implausible ones. And one strategy that is often used, to just keep adding variables to the regression to account for more and more of the variability, has its own problems. It can lead to what is called "overfitting" – explaining statistical noise by appealing to somewhat plausible variables. It is well known that a price of overfitting is that while it gets better and better at "explaining" the observations we already have, it gets worse and worse at predicting the next observation. Framing in general is not primarily an obstacle to and/or a bias in thinking. It is a necessity for answering many of the questions, even statistical questions, that we ask when we think.

Framing, in addition to being necessary for interpreting data, is important relative to both data collection and statistical evaluation. First, framing influences what S1 (the automatic system that is the supposed source of most errors and biases) and subsequently S2 (the reflective system that uses appropriate cognitive tools to make decisions) will yield. It primes one to notice certain things, which then influences what will even count as "data." Primed to look for improvement, one notices the spikes and treats them as phenomena to investigate, rather than simply the natural result of the randomness of logic grades. Our skill at framing rules out some ways of framing as nonstarters. For example, we ignore the fact that grades are down in even-numbered years or in years in which the New York Yankees baseball team does well. Investigating the spikes yields new data (the professor hadn't noticed that the celebrity professor spent a year on campus) and new insights. Framing offers clues to the relevance of those data to the question at hand (it makes sense that a visiting celebrity humanities professor on campus is likely a cause of lower attention to math/science and logic, and hence lead to lower grades). Framing tells us whether to take the grades of the outlier years as important, or whether they should be ignored or at least taken less seriously as an indicator of the effect of the change in teaching technique, because of this other "extraneous" piece of data.

The examples above were meant to illustrate that several kinds of thinking are involved in the use of statistics and other quantitative methods to solve problems. However, a question comes up as to whether these forms of thinking should be included in RCT. There are arguments on both sides. If, on the one hand, they are not included in RCT, then a great deal of thinking is excluded from an account of what it means to think rationally. If they are included in RCT, then RCT includes a lot of thinking that is not really formal. If these types of thinking are included in RCT, then since several of them can be sources of bias, RCT itself includes sources of bias. This implication seems like something that RCT enthusiasts would find hard to accept.

As we have said, JDM researchers focus on framing as primarily a source of bias, one that interferes with the accurate calculation of utilities. Rational choosers should be able to see through the language of description to the underlying reality being described. In contrast, we believe that it is the framing, not the calculation, that does the heavy lifting in coming to understanding and good decisions. It is framing in a particular way that turns the decision about what to do with your family on a Saturday into the equivalent of a choice between two uncertain monetary gambles.

Let us say again that we do not want to suggest that framing effects like these are never an error. People's choices can certainly be manipulated by changing frames, and people will typically be unaware that they are being manipulated. Nonetheless, without framing, an RCT analysis cannot get off the ground. Framing is essential. Without the help of framing, the person we described in the introduction trying to decide "What should I do on this beautiful Saturday?" might spend the entire day, and the next one, just trying to decide. Framing is a lifesaver.

Chapter 6

FRAMING, LEAKAGE, AND SUBSTANTIVE RATIONALITY

We have discussed how the kind of quantification that RCT aspires to demands closed-world assumptions as well as the assumption that all values are commensurable. There is one further problem we want to address — the problem that Daniel Keys and Barry termed "leakage" in a paper they published in 2007.

Imagine this. You've just gotten a big promotion, and friends have taken you to an elegant, very expensive restaurant to celebrate. The menu has more than a dozen entrées, and as you read it, each option sounds more exquisite than the last. You know you can't go wrong, no matter what you choose, but you also know that you may never have another similar opportunity again. So you study the menu. On and on it goes: each dish enticing, but no clear winner.

Eventually you will choose, and a sumptuous, inviting dish will be placed before you. Will you put your anguished decision-making behind you and enjoy what you've chosen thoroughly and completely, or will your decision conflict linger, diminishing the satisfaction you ought to be getting from your delicious meal? In other words, do the processes by which people make decisions "leak" into their experience of those decisions? Keys and Schwartz argued that the answer to this question is often yes, that the decision phase leaks into the experience phase, and that an appreciation of this fact has profound implications when we try to evaluate the decisions people make against the demanding standards of normative rationality.

The field of judgment and decision-making knows this. Kahneman and Tversky said as much forty years ago:

> In [some] cases, the framing of decisions affects not only decision but experience as well. . . . In such cases, the evaluation of outcomes in the context of decisions not only anticipates experience but also molds it.[1]

Nonetheless, insufficient attention has been paid to the empirical dimensions and theoretical implications of leakage. When frames leak into the experience of decisions, we can't really say that two descriptions — two frames — are "really" descriptions of the same situation.

The pattern of responses in the disease and lost ticket examples discussed in the last chapter seems obviously to violate the principles of RCT, in particular the principle that different descriptions of the same situation should not result in different rational decisions. Simple as this statement seems, it raises very complicated questions, because *when* two descriptions are descriptions of the same situation, in the relevant sense, is not obvious. As a result, people can believe two descriptions are descriptions of the same thing without its being true, and vice versa. Consider a presidential election. Here are some

---

1. Kahneman and Tversky, "Choices, Values, and Frames," 341.

descriptions of events: (1) the election of a successful businessman, (2) the election of the most corrupt president in history, (3) the election of the most straight-talking president in history, (4) the election of the least well prepared president in history. Are people likely to agree about which of those descriptions describe the same situation?

From this example we can see that what may have seemed to be a mere "semantic" question is at least in part an empirical one. And given the nature of the descriptions, it is a "subjective" question — subjective in the sense of involving varying feelings and opinions, and subjective in the sense of involving unresolvable disagreement. It will not surprise us then that Kahneman has written, "The question of how to determine whether two decision problems are the same or different does not have a general answer. To avoid this issue, Tversky and I restricted the definition of framing effects to discrepancies between choice problems that decision makers, upon reflection, consider effectively identical."[2] Kahneman's approach implies that the framing effects he and Tversky studied meet the standard of reflection that he gives for identifying equivalent scenarios. Do they?

Psychologist Deborah Frisch, in one of the few studies that systematically investigated this question, found that participants who reflect on these types of problems often insist that there are real differences between the two versions of a scenario. Frisch presented participants with pairs of scenarios like those described in the last chapter (in her study, the members of each pair were not presented side by side). After participants had chosen their responses to all the questions (two versions of each scenario), they were shown both versions of each scenario side by side and asked a yes or no question:

---

2. Kahneman, "A Perspective on Judgment and Choice," 708.

"Do you think the difference in these two situations warrants treating them differently?"

In all but one of the problems, a majority of the participants who showed the expected framing effect answered that yes, the situations do warrant different treatment. Only on the disease problem did a majority of participants favor treating the two scenarios the same, but even on this seemingly straightforward violation of invariance only 53% of participants took this position. Among the scenarios that people, on reflection, thought were different included how much people were willing to pay for a good bottle of wine and how much they would have to be paid to sell the same wine, and paying a $5 markup for a bottle of wine in a restaurant versus paying a $5 corkage fee for a bottle you brought yourself to a restaurant. So, even though from an RCT perspective the two versions of each problem are equivalent, most participants don't see it that way.

Frisch argued that her results should be taken as evidence that people who are subject to framing effects are not always acting irrationally. She presented her empirical studies as a way of deciding between two accounts of framing effects. The first account is that framing effects are like perceptual illusions that trick decision makers, with framing affecting decisions but not subsequent experiences. The alternative account, which she attempted to defend, is that framing has an effect on decisions because it has an effect on experience. She used participants' reflective judgments about the scenarios as an indirect means to investigate whether framing effects influence people's subsequent experiences. When participants were asked to justify their reflective judgment, she found, for every type of scenario, that many of their justifications were assertions that there *is* a subjective difference between the two versions of a given scenario. In an earlier study done by decision researchers Irwin P. Levin and Gary J.

Gaeth, people were asked whether they preferred a burger that was 75% lean or one that was 25% fat. They preferred the first, lean option, and then, when they tasted the two burgers (which of course were made with the same meat) they thought the "lean" one tasted better than the "fat" one.

Frisch's research makes a simple but profound point. Changes to the description of a set of options should not be ignored if they affect people's experiences, and almost any change to a situation that a decision maker faces, even a change that seems superficial and irrelevant, may end up having some effect on the decision maker's experiences. Even in scenarios that are designed to manipulate the decision maker's choice without changing the objective outcomes, the alterations to the situation may end up changing the outcomes *subjectively* because they leak into the decision maker's experience of the decision.

The key idea in this argument is not that framing exerts effects on a decision, as is well known, but that its effects do not *stop* there. They can continue after the decision is made, when its results are being experienced. When these framing effects persist, the experience of the result of the decision can be consistent with the experience of the decision itself, and such consistency undermines the claim that the framing effect on the decision is irrational. If beef that is "75% lean" tastes better than beef that is "25% fat," where is the mistake in choosing the former over the latter?

Belief in the importance of subjective experiences is widely shared by psychologists, economists, and many, many others. RCT is itself deeply subjective, in that its aim is to give people a tool for maximizing their utility, or preference. As economists have proudly told us for years, money (or almost anything else) has diminishing marginal utility, and in deciding whether to spend money or bet money, it should be the expected utility, not the expected objective value, that drives the decision. So, the *subjectivity* of framing, per se, is on familiar turf in RCT.

And much of Kahneman's later work was focused on subjective experience. But it is interesting to note here that despite Kahneman's attention to the nature of the experience of decisions, he did not combine this line of work with the work he and Tversky did for twenty-five years on the determinants of the decisions themselves. It is as if heuristics, biases, and other System 1 processes exert their effects while a decision is being contemplated, but once the decision is made, experiencing the results of the decision will be "path independent." The object of a decision will be experienced on its own, carrying no trace of how the decision was arrived at. It is this notion of path independence that Frisch's findings challenge.

There is another way to see the workings of this leakage and why they are not obvious from the research literature. Let's return to the concert ticket example we discussed in the last chapter. John "buys a ticket to an event." Why? Does he want to go to "an event," regardless of what it is? Or is he just a ticket buyer, and likes to buy tickets? Possible, but unlikely. More likely is that there is something specific that will happen at the event, and that he bought the ticket to experience that specific something. What is that specific thing? It could be one of a million things. Let's say it is a concert. Did he buy the ticket to go to a concert, regardless of what kind of concert it was? No, he wanted to hear popular music. Any popular music? No, he wanted to hear the Rolling Stones.

So John decides to go hear the Rolling Stones, does so (by buying a ticket and going to the concert), and enjoys himself. A rational choice that pays off. But suppose John had made (framed) his decision differently: John decides to go hear the Rolling Stones perform as they had performed on his recordings of them that were made many years ago, and does so (again by buying a ticket and going to the concert). He does not enjoy himself. They have changed their style and did not perform as they had on his recordings but in a new way that was quite enjoyable, but that he did not enjoy because he had gone to the concert hoping and expecting to hear them sing in the style he was familiar with. Because of those hopes and expectations, he did not enjoy the performance he would otherwise have enjoyed. If someone had told him that the Rolling Stones had changed their style, and he had gone because he simply wanted to hear the Rolling Stones, and had made the decision that way, on that basis, he would have enjoyed himself. His actual decision, to hear the Stones perform as they have all these years and on his recordings, has "leaked" into the outcome, for the worse.

This example is another illustration of how the way a decision or choice is "framed" has, under ordinary circumstances, a significant impact on how the outcome of the decision is experienced. Also, the case as presented shows that the presence of this phenomenon is much more evident when the choice is framed concretely. If we describe the case at a very high level of abstraction — "someone buys a ticket to something in advance" — the possibility of the decision influencing the outcome is more or less hidden. As the description becomes more concrete and specific — "John bought a ticket in advance in order to hear the Rolling Stones play the music of theirs that was familiar to him" — the likelihood of the decision affecting the experience of the outcome is clearer.

It is easy to accept the importance of subjective experience and still fail to apply this view in a thoroughgoing way when thinking about decision-making. What leakage shows is that our experience of the results of a decision is often dependent on the path we take to making that decision. Lost tickets and lost money put us on different paths when it comes to deciding whether to buy a ticket, and potentially how much we enjoy the event we bought a ticket to. Path dependence is often hidden by a way of thinking that treats experiences as if they were caused directly by objects and episodes in the world, rather than as an interaction between the thing that is experienced and the person who is experiencing it. Daniel Gilbert and Jane Ebert compared this "illusion of intrinsic satisfaction" to the perceptual illusion of direct access to the world, writing, "Ordinary decision makers ignore the complexities of psychology and act instead as though their hedonic experiences were due entirely to the enduring intrinsic properties of their outcomes, as though the wonderfulness or awfulness they are experiencing was always there 'in the outcome' waiting to be experienced and none of these properties was altered or induced by the mere act of making the outcome their own."[3] But this variant of what is called "naïve realism" is mistaken: the value of an evening at a concert depends on how the person who is attending that concert construes and experiences the outcome.

Leakage, Formalization, and Closedness

What we are calling "leakage" implies that there are limits to what formal principles of rationality (whether RCT or some other framework) can tell us, since there are surprisingly few cases where the formal principles apply in their strictest forms. Even seemingly inconsequential changes to the situation may leak into experience, affecting one's subjective outcomes and hence the reasonableness of

---

3. Gilbert and Ebert, "Decisions and Revisions," 511.

different choices. Formal rules of rationality may allow researchers to draw important normative conclusions based on minimal, widely accepted structural claims about rationality. However, once the importance of subjective experiences and the prevalence of leakage are taken into account, it becomes clear that much more needs to be known before anything approaching a satisfactory theory of rationality is in hand. For this and other reasons, we believe that what is needed is a *substantive* theory of rationality. The theory we think is needed will not be formal or closed. It is a theory that considers the content and not just the structure of decisions, implying that it will evaluate the decider's preferences and goals. It would also consider each decision in light of the decision maker's goals in life as a whole. What is needed, in the words of decision scientists J. Evans, D. Over, and K. Manktelow, is a theory of rationality of *purpose* to augment the formal theory of rationality of *process*. A formal theory like that of RCT as it stands would describe Hitler as rational, as long as he maximized his utility.

Is there any role left for formal, closed, micro-oriented rationality? Yes, there is. It is most relevant when subjectivity plays or should play a small role for one reason or another. For example, in some cases, formal principles may apply well to a situation because of the overriding objective importance of the decision. When deciding between radiation and surgery as a treatment for cancer, the obvious target factor—the influence of the treatment on survival—is so important that it seems wrong for decisions to change when the survival rates are reframed as mortality rates.

Another factor that can minimize the role of subjectivity is the involvement of other people. In the disease examples described earlier (problems 1 and 2 in the last chapter), letting your particular frame influence a decision seems frivolous because other people's lives are at stake. Consistent with this speculation that leakage should be less important when making decisions for others, there is evidence that people are sometimes more resistant to framing effects when they are making decisions for other people. A judge who is deciding which divorcing parent should be granted custody of a child may make a different choice if the question is framed as which parent should be *denied* custody. But the important consequences here are for the child and the parents, so the effects of the decision frame on the judge's subjective experience should be irrelevant. Indeed, the judge's job demands that his or her subjective experience of the decision be irrelevant to the making of the decision, just as a doctor guiding a patient through the choice of surgery or radiation should be sensitive to the patient's utility, but insensitive to his or her own. These examples combine highly important target factors with a separation between the decision maker and the people who experience the consequence of the decision, as does the disease scenario, which also multiplies the importance of the target factor by putting hundreds of people's lives at stake.

Choosing the Right Frame

We have been suggesting that our task when we make decisions is not to avoid being influenced by frames, but to choose the *right* frames—frames that help us to evaluate all that is relevant. And judging what is the right frame will depend on the purposes of our evaluation and impending decision. A striking example of the framing challenge was described by journalist Michael Pollan in an article that asks us to consider the "true" cost of a pound of beef. We know what we pay for it in the market, but is that a broad enough frame for assessing its cost? What about other costs—what economists call "externalities" — that are not reflected in the market price? Beef is fairly inexpensive because the growth of the corn that is used to feed the cows is government subsidized. So, we pay for beef with our taxes. Cows eat corn rather than grass because it's cheaper to feed them corn. But the cow's digestive system can't handle corn, so cows must be dosed prophylactically with antibiotics to keep them healthy long enough to get them to market. The cost to the farmer of the antibiotics is reflected in the market price of beef, but we also "pay" for this antibiotic prophylaxis in drug-resistant strains of bacteria that make human illnesses harder and more costly to treat. This cost is *not* reflected in a pound of beef. Corn also changes the acidity of the cow's digestive system, making it compatible with the human digestive system, so that microbes — some of them potentially lethal — can survive the trip from cow to person intact, and then make people sick. Corn-fed beef is fattier than grass-fed beef, and the *kind* of fat is worse for human health. And growing the corn that feeds the cows depends on heavy doses of fertilizer, which depend on petrochemicals. Thus, if one framed the price of a pound of beef more broadly, to include all these externalities, the cost of a pound of beef would have to include some fraction of the cost of bacterial infection and cardiovascular disease. That, in turn, would have to include the costs of treatment, the costs in mortality and morbidity, workdays lost, and quality-of-life decreases. And it would have to include some fraction of the cost — in money and in lives — of a foreign policy that is partly driven by the need for reliable access to petrochemicals.

Where does this accounting for the price of a pound of beef stop? How much do we want to include in what might be called the "social" price as opposed to the "market" price?" The narrow frame of the supermarket price puts all these other considerations off-screen. The broad frame suggested by Pollan turns our grocery shopping into a matter of geopolitics. Each of these frames is useful, but they induce us to think about very different things. Using narrow frames may miss various important factors not captured by market-price framing, but using very broad frames may create an "accounting problem" that is simply unmanageable. Deciding on an appropriate accounting frame requires deliberation, and any frame you choose will provoke disagreement, and thus to this extent, it is subjective. But the process of rational discourse may yield a frame that is broad enough to capture some externalities but narrow enough to enable your deliberations to come to a reasonable conclusion in a reasonable amount of time. This is not the sort of job that RCT is equipped for.

Some recent research (not yet published) by Walter Sinnott-Armstrong and Deborah Cesarini Banhos resonates with our discussion of Pollan's work. Pollan's broad framing of the cost of a pound of beef calls our attention to various externalities. But it is important to note that at least some of those externalities have distinct moral dimensions, whereas moral dimensions are absent from the more narrowly framed calculation of the cost of a pound of beef. This point raises a question about whether, when, and how people consider the moral dimensions of the decisions they are facing. Doing the right thing requires that one make the right moral judgments leading to the right moral actions. But before either judgment or action, one must recognize that the decision *has* moral dimensions. One can't do the right thing, except by accident, unless one recognizes that there is a "right thing" that must be sought. Sinnott-Armstrong and Cesarini Banhos studied the factors that encourage people to engage in moral reflection. They discovered that asking people to reflect on a "day in the life" to identify decisions they made and things they did that had moral content encourages people to engage in moral reflection going forward, which in turn substantially increases their sensitivity to the moral content of what they do. So, it is possible that engaging in broad framing of the sort that Pollan did may similarly encourage people to notice and act on the moral dimensions of their decisions.

Many issues similar to those raised by Pollan in his discussion of the "true" cost of beef arose more recently and saliently in connection with the COVID pandemic. What was the right health policy to follow? There were complex issues to consider even when the problem was narrowly framed. How serious was the disease? How, and how easily, did it spread? What were the chances that treatment and a vaccine would be developed, and when? Could we determine whether certain sectors of the population were especially vulnerable and thus tailor health policy with that in mind? As our understanding of COVID grew, it became possible to develop answers to these narrow questions, though none of them were unequivocal.

But as things turned out, the issues were much broader than just medical. COVID killed, and it was easily transmitted. Should we shut down all public gatherings, including schools and businesses? What would be the health effects of a shutdown? What would be the economic effects? What would be the intellectual and psychological effects on our children? Again, these were all relevant questions — and they were all impossible to answer with any certainty. In addition, answering these questions would require trade-offs among very different valuable things. Any relaxation of shutdown rules would surely result in more illness and death. How much more, and was it worth it?

We rehearse here complexities of which you are surely aware. Policies were enacted, or recommended, and they varied from state to state and from country to country. Were they the right policies? More than a million Americans died. Could we have done better?

FRAMING, LEAKAGE, AND RATIONALITY

Millions of jobs were lost. Could we have done better? Massive government financial aid was provided to both individuals and businesses to help mitigate the financial consequences of shutdown. Were such measures adequate or should the government have done more? Over time, the combination of extra money in people's pockets, supply-chain breakdowns that limited the availability of a wide variety of goods, and massive amounts of extra time for consumption by people who weren't working led to significant inflation. In addition, school kids regressed substantially in their educational attainments, and also developed a host of psychological challenges. Were the lives that were saved worth these costs to the well-being of children?

As the epidemic subsided and some of the long-term effects of the health policies appeared, it became fairly clear that policy makers had not accounted accurately and adequately for all of the costs, short- and long-term, associated with their policies. Given the complexity, novelty, and urgency of the problems they were facing, it would have been a miracle if the policies adopted were judged in hindsight to be the best that could have been done. Some costs of the policies were clearly (in retrospect) underestimated. Some benefits of the policies were clearly (in retrospect) overestimated. We say this not to criticize the policies that were actually adopted, but to indicate how incredibly difficult the problem was. Closing the system so that only health effects were considered might have made the problem easier, but it could have led to adverse economic and social consequences from which it might take generations to recover. Fully opening the system so that all potential economic and social consequences were given due consideration might have made formulating a policy unacceptably slow, if not downright impossible. RCT would have helped policy makers decide, but perhaps only at the cost of ignoring major potential consequences, and only if their judgments in balancing incommensurables like adult health, children's education, and the economy in general were well made. What was needed, and arguably what we got, was good thinking and good judgment. Perhaps we did well under the circumstances. And we can hope that should another, similar crisis appear, policy makers will have learned from the COVID crisis how to improve their thinking, their judgment, and their policies.

To review one more, very consequential example, Robert McNamara, who served as the secretary of defense under Presidents John F. Kennedy and Lyndon B. Johnson, played a significant role in the U.S. involvement in the Vietnam War. He was known and praised for his analytical approach and reliance on cost-benefit analysis in decision-making. Using these analytical techniques, McNamara and his "whiz kid" colleagues successfully brought the struggling Ford Motor Company back to prominence. His approach to government service was quite similar to his approach at Ford. However, the effectiveness of McNamara's use of cost-benefit analysis in the context of the Vietnam War has long been a subject of debate and criticism.

Implementation of the "whiz kids" approach involved applying quantitative methods, statistical analysis, and cost-benefit analysis to military decision-making. McNamara sought to manage the war effort efficiently and believed that rigorous analysis could provide solutions to the problems that arose. McNamara's reliance on metrics, including body counts and bombing statistics, reflected this approach.

However, the Vietnam War proved to be a complex and unconventional conflict, with challenges that went beyond the scope of traditional quantitative analysis. McNamara's overreliance on statistical metrics led to a narrow and flawed understanding of the war.

The analytical tools did not adequately account for the political, cultural, and historical complexities of the conflict in Vietnam, and the human cost and strategic implications were often underestimated.

Furthermore, elements of McNamara's management style, which involved little input from military commanders on the ground, perhaps because he did not trust that they would embrace his analytical methods, were seen as contributing factors to the shortcomings of the U.S. strategy in Vietnam. There was a mismatch between the results of his analyses and the realities of the conflict.

In retrospect, many historians and analysts view McNamara's use of cost-benefit analysis in the Vietnam War as flawed and ultimately tragically ineffective. The war's outcome highlighted the limitations of relying solely on quantitative methods in the face of a multifaceted and dynamic conflict. McNamara himself later acknowledged the inadequacy of purely analytical approaches in understanding the complexities of war, partly attributing this inadequacy to the "fog of war." The Vietnam War, probably like most wars, was an open system. Closing the system made the analysis more precise. More than a million people died. Perhaps systems of assessment that work well for the production and sale of automobiles won't work so well for the production and prosecution of wars.

RCT Is Neither Sufficient nor Necessary for Rationality

Is the proper use of RCT sufficient for rationality? No.

1. Suppose you are buying a car. You specify your options as a Dodge Durango and a Chevy Yukon. The attributes you are concerned with are the normal ones, but gas mileage is of greatest concern. After you do an RCT analysis, you pick the Durango. It maximizes

your utility because even though it gets terrible mileage, it gets slightly better gas mileage than the Yukon. (We made this up.) You have never considered a Prius or an electric vehicle. When asked afterward why, you answer, "I should have. They would have suited me fine, but I just didn't think of them as options." Was your decision rational?

2. Once again, suppose you are buying a car. Even though you are very concerned about the environment, so that in considering each option, you carefully estimate the environmental costs of manufacturing it, transporting it, and disposing of it, you never take into account the gas mileage it gives. You use RCT to analyze all the data you have, excluding gas mileage, and you pick a car with terrible gas mileage. Was your decision rational?

3. Again, suppose you are buying a car. When quantifying the value of your options, you give the precise color of the car ten times the weight of all the other normal factors like miles per gallon, reliability and longevity, resale value, handling, safety, and so on combined. Then you run an RCT analysis and pick the car that will maximize your utility according to it. Since values are subjective, there is no obvious stance from which to say that this is not a rational decision. Does this mean that it *is* a rational decision?

4. You are choosing a college to go to. Many factors are relevant here, but it is important to you to go to the best college you can get into. "Best college" is vague. Looking at the *U.S. News* college rankings, you see that they rank colleges largely by graduation rates, faculty publications, and endowment size. So you determine the best college based on those factors, and then run an RCT analysis comparing "best colleges" as defined by *U.S. News*. Did you make a rational decision?

If an RCT decision is a rational decision, then all of the above examples were rational decisions. But they were all terribly made. Can a rational decision be terribly made, or is an RCT decision not necessarily rational?

What actually made these decisions so terrible? Bad specification, bad clarification, and bad valuation. (There is such a thing as bad valuation. Valuation may be subjective, but it can still be done badly if it is arbitrary or inconsistent with higher-level values you hold.) Doing those things well is required for "rationality." Thus, RCT is not sufficient for rational decisions.

Is RCT necessary for rational decisions? Again, no.

1. You are choosing a car to buy. Deliberating, you read that one of your two remaining options is made with underpaid child labor in a Southeast Asian country. "I will not buy a car made with child labor," you decide. The discovery of a new attribute has made your choice. No RCT calculation was involved.

2. You want to go to one of the "best" colleges. *U.S. News* calls Princeton the best. You like Ursinus, but it is not one of the "best." But what does "best" really mean? For *U.S. News*, it is determined (defined) by graduation rates, faculty publications, and endowment size. When you think about "best," you realize those features don't define it—at least not for you. Learning, student attitudes, campus culture, focus on teaching rather than research, small size, and things like that define "best" for you. You choose Ursinus over Princeton. The meaning of "best college" has made your choice for you. RCT plays little if any role.

So RCT is neither necessary nor sufficient for rationality. Is RCT typical of rationality? No. Many decision problems can be forced into RCT-appropriate form with suitable framing, but that is not in general required—and often it is not even helpful. Thus, RCT is not necessary or sufficient for rationality, nor is it typical of rational decision-making. Bad specification (of options or relevant considerations), bad clarification, and bad valuation can make a decision a bad one, even if it meets the specifications of RCT. Good specification, clarification, and valuation can make the decision a good one without RCT. They are as important as quantification and calculation. That is, the relative importance of RCT in making a good (rational?) decision is not all that large. It is not the primary factor in rational decision-making. Why should we connect RCT (quantification and maximization) in any special way with rational decision-making if it is no more important than framing the decision well, picking the options thoughtfully, considering the important attributes, clarifying the concepts we are using, and good valuation?

Chapter 7

INTERIM SUMMARY OF THE ARGUMENT

We have made some complicated arguments in the foregoing chapters, intended to show that RCT has serious defects as a normative model of rationality, and that most of what is required to make rational decisions occurs before RCT can even come into play. Before we proceed, it might be useful to summarize what we have suggested thus far.

RCT as Normative and Descriptive

1. RCT is taken to be the normative framework for rational decision-making, that is, how decisions *should* be made.

2. Kahneman, Tversky, and many who have followed them have shown that whatever its merits as a normative theory, RCT is inadequate as a descriptive theory. People are prone to errors and biases as they violate the norms of RCT when they make decisions.

3. Nonetheless, this line of research on errors and biases has relied on RCT to provide the normative standard against which empirical work is assessed.

INTERIM SUMMARY OF THE ARGUMENT

Transforming Everyday Decisions into RCT-Appropriate Decisions

4. RCT treats the gamble as the canonical paradigm for studying decision-making, with the value and the probability of the outcomes as the key parameters.

5. But almost no everyday decisions take this canonical form.

6. It takes a lot to turn an everyday decision (What should we do today?) into a version of the canonical gamble.

7. The various steps required to turn decisions into gambles all function to turn an open system into a closed one. They include processes we called specification, clarification, disentanglement, and quantification. These processes serve to prepare a decision for specifically RCT-type thinking. These processes eliminate vagueness and overlap, a step that RCT requires, but everyday decision-making typically does not.

8. By overemphasizing quantification, RCT distracts from equally important aspects of decision-making, like specifying the right options and attributes, and clarifying in the best ways which attributes are the most important and why.

9. Much of the apparent success of RCT is actually the result of oversimplification and a measure of arbitrariness in the assignment of both values and probabilities to options under consideration.

Framing

10. To a very large degree, closing an open system means imposing frames around a decision that render many important contextual factors both invisible and irrelevant.

11. Thus framing is essential in order for RCT to apply.

INTERIM SUMMARY OF THE ARGUMENT

12. Yet framing has been taken in decision-making research to be a paradigm case of how errors and biases can intrude on rationality.

13. And RCT has nothing to tell us about how decisions *should* be framed, which makes its status as a comprehensive normative theory of decision-making highly suspect.

An Example: How to Light Up a Room

To put a little flesh on the bones of this summary list, consider the following. A young child, having received a playhouse as a gift and finding its interior too dark, asks her mother how she makes their house so light. "By flipping a switch," says the mother. The child finds a spare switch in the basement, hangs it on the playhouse wall, and flips it, but gets no light. How charming is the innocence of young children! And how oblivious can adults be to the background conditions that are necessary to make "flipping the light switch" give us light!

We believe that someone who asks how to make a good decision and is told to use RCT – to quantify the options and attributes, the probabilities and values, and to calculate – is like the child who is told that light comes from flipping a switch. The switch works only if it is connected to the house wiring system, which in turn is connected to the utility's wiring system, which in turn is connected to an extremely complicated electricity-generating system, which in turn is energized by some sort of fuel. Similarly, RCT works rationally and well only if the decision problem is framed well; if the options and attributes are specified well, formulated in quantifiable terms, disentangled adequately; and if the probabilities and values

INTERIM SUMMARY OF THE ARGUMENT

are quantified well. Typical decision problems do not come in that form. They need to be put in that form by a series of substitutions for the original amorphous form (What shall I do today?). These substitutions replace the original problem, step by step, with a version that RCT can handle. These substitutions crucially involve framing and closure, and the decisions we make, with or without RCT, will only be as rational and good as those processes are.

Our argument is that RCT has little to contribute to that process of framing and closure. RCT is, for explicit and implicit reasons, more or less limited to the kind of methods used in resolving a typical gambling problem. That sort of problem is the paradigm of RCT, in the normal everyday sense of being an exemplary case. It is also a paradigm in the sense used by philosopher Thomas Kuhn in his landmark book, *The Structure of Scientific Revolutions*, in which he suggests that scientific paradigms establish both the problems to be solved and the methods of inquiry to be used in formulating a solution to those problems. The gambling paradigm strongly determines a form of process that is largely formal and quantitative. But framing and closure decisions cannot be accomplished by quantitative and formal methods. Formal methods do not — and more important, cannot — tell us how to frame a problem well, how to specify options and attributes, how to formulate the options and attributes as measurable, how to disentangle various options and their attributes, or how to quantify the relevant probabilities and values. Nor can formal methods provide a criterion for when we have framed and closed a problem well. And the decision is no better than the framing and closure of the problem allows. Of course, once all that is done, solving the problem requires only mathematical calculation, just as bringing light to the house requires only flipping the switch, but to credit flipping the switch with lighting the house is extremely

INTERIM SUMMARY OF THE ARGUMENT

misleading. Framing and closing a problem requires deliberation, a decidedly nonformal process, just as generating and transmitting electricity has little in common with flipping a switch.

To light a room, the light switch must be connected to the power grid. Most of what we have tried to do in the preceding chapters was to spell out how the power grid of rationality works, and what it requires.

Chapter 8

WHY RATIONAL CHOICE THEORY IS DANGEROUS

One way of interpreting our line of argument is that we are criticizing RCT for oversimplifying what most decisions entail. You squeeze every decision into the gambling paradigm and see how far that can take you. But every scientific endeavor oversimplifies. Ideally, as a science matures, various complexities can be introduced, and the account it offers becomes a closer and closer approximation to the reality it is trying to describe and explain. It seems unfair to criticize a developing science for its immaturity. In this chapter, we will suggest that RCT's oversimplification is not merely inaccurate, it is dangerous. It is dangerous because it holds up as a model of rationality a framework that excludes from consideration the most important aspects of thinking and decision-making. And RCT is not merely a theoretical research project. It is more and more often used in practice and threatens to permeate our lives. If people actually adopted RCT as their model of decision-making, their decisions would be worse — much worse — which would result in bad decisions not just for them but for others who are affected by those decisions. And when RCT is exalted as the model for decision-making in public policy, these worse decisions can exert powerful effects on society more generally. In addition, as people rely on RCT for decision-making, the various other approaches we use in making decisions may atrophy, so that we become less and less skilled at using them.

The example we cited at the end of chapter 6, about Defense Secretary Robert McNamara's approach to fighting the Vietnam War, is an example of how RCT (and its various cousins) can be dangerous. We don't mean to suggest that the *only* thing wrong with U.S. policy in Vietnam was McNamara's analytical approach. By no means. But we do mean to suggest that his approach may have blinded him to considerations that lay outside his analytical frame. The outcome was not just wrong, but dangerously wrong. And there are many other examples of this type. Here are some of them.

Where to Locate Pollution

We suggested earlier that finding a basis of comparison for moral and practical objectives is extremely complicated. The complication encourages framing a decision in a way that diminishes or ignores moral considerations. An excellent example of this is a famous memo by the former assistant secretary of the treasury and president of Harvard, written when he was chief economist for the World Bank, that a good way to deal with pollution would be to ship polluted material to countries with the lowest wages, because "the measurement of the costs of health impairing pollution depends on the forgone earning from increased morbidity and mortality."[1] That is to say, when people earning low wages get sick and miss work or even

---

1. Summers, World Bank Memo, 1.

die from pollution, there is less total income loss than when people with high wages get sick and die. Thus, it is cost effective to export pollution to low-income countries.

Where to begin criticizing this argument? His reasoning about siting sources of pollution seemed to involve treating people as things — things that earn money and whose value is equal to the money they earn. To criticize this proposal is to dignify it in a way that is itself contemptible. We limit the criticism then to expressing horror that this way of approaching the decision of what to do with pollution treats people as nothing more than a source of income, and noting that RCT-type thinking encourages such solutions because it simplifies specification in the service of quantification. In fairness, we should say that the source of this argument, Lawrence Summers, did not actually write the memo (an associate did), and that his defense of it was that it was meant as a satire of strict economic logic, not a serious policy recommendation. Analogous suggestions have been proposed to defend the argument made by Judge Richard Posner and Elisabeth Landes about the virtues of creating a market for babies as a way to improve the efficiency of adoptions. Perhaps so. But one of the lessons we have learned from contemporary American politics is that "just kidding" is not an adequate defense of an outrageous claim.

Fare-Shirking Insurance

Steven Levitt and Stephen Dubner have published a series of books, starting with *Freakonomics*, where this sort of simplification is glorified. Their works are full of examples like this:

> How to cheat the Mumbai train system. A blogger named
> Ganesh Kulkarni discovered that the commuter trains of

Mumbai serve six million passengers daily, but the system isn't equipped to check everyone's ticket. Instead, Kulkarni writes, ticket agents conduct random ticket checks. This has given rise to a form of cheating that is elegantly called "ticketless travel." Although it's probably not very common to get busted for traveling ticketlessly, there is a significant fine if you are. And so, Kulkarni writes, one clever traveler has devised an insurance policy to make sure that ticketless travelers who are caught can lay off some of the expense. Here is how it works. You pay five hundred rupees . . . to join an organization of fellow ticketless travelers. If you do get caught traveling without a ticket, you pay the fine and turn in your receipt to the ticketless-traveler organization, which refunds you 100 percent of the fine. Don't you wish that everyone in society was as creative as the cheaters?[2]

What makes this work? At the very least, it seems to require that the "ticketless travelers" have no qualms about being such, at least not enough to induce them to buy a ticket. Somehow that goes unmentioned.

Voting

It is a cliché of RCT that voting is irrational. Levitt and Dubner discuss this in *Freakonomics*. The probability that your vote will affect the outcome of an election with a lot of people voting is approximately zero, so the effort involved in voting, however small, is virtually for naught. Hence it is not rational to vote. The argument

---

2. Levitt and Dubner, *When to Rob a Bank*, 140–41.

assumes that the only reason a person can have, or most people do have, for voting is to affect the outcome. But there are people who vote because they think it is their duty, because it strengthens democracy to have a good turnout, because seeing them vote encourages their neighbors to vote, and other reasons of that kind. There is a lovely example of two political scientists who were both on sabbatical in the same small Italian town when a presidential election day in the United States occurred. To vote, they had to drive about three hours to the nearest U.S. embassy. So they drove together: one to vote for the Democrat and the other the Republican.

The claim that voting is irrational is a result of drastic oversimplification. It reflects the form that RCT often actually takes when applied to situations with any moral content or complexity. Perhaps strengthening democracy and the other considerations mentioned are not strong motives for voting. Still, neglecting nuances and moral considerations to suggest that voters are irrational fools is at least a little reprehensible. And RCT opens the door to a slippery slope down to more serious forms of reprehensibility, like sending polluting industries to poorer countries or widespread cheating when the painful consequences of getting caught can be minimized.

Other People

Another deplorable form of oversimplification that we have mentioned elsewhere but that calls for elaboration in this context is the neglect of people other than the decider. This kind of simplification is almost defined out of any place in the formulation of decision problems, it is neglected in the process of making the decision, and it is neglected in enumerating and evaluating the outcomes of decisions.

WHY RATIONAL CHOICE THEORY IS DANGEROUS

As we saw in chapter 5, a classic case in the literature concerns a person who buys a ticket in advance to a concert and finds when they arrive at the venue that the ticket has been lost: the choice in question is whether to buy another ticket. It is virtually never considered that it is quite unusual for people to go to concerts alone, and if they are not going alone, the impact on their companions' feelings and thoughts needs to be taken into account. By framing the choice as between buying another ticket or not, the consideration of disappointing their friends is defined out of the problem, or marginalized. We should acknowledge that the main point of this example, from the perspective of mental accounting, is the difference in willingness to replace a lost ticket versus willingness to buy a ticket in the face of a lost $20 bill. Nonetheless, framing concert attendance as a social activity changes the stakes considerably, perhaps making a lost ticket feel even more different from a lost $20 bill than it otherwise would.

Neglect of other people is common and obvious in the literature. Normally problems are defined or treated as one-person problems, but our everyday situations are frequently not of this kind. We saw this in connection with the beach/museum example we discussed earlier. The decision grows much more complex when the feelings and desires of all interested parties are considered. Similarly, consider the decision of what to give your mother for her birthday. The meaning of the gift can be great, even if the cost is inconsequential, and for that reason her feelings and beliefs will be crucial. The significance of the gift will be determined largely by "nonobjective" factors, the kind of factors that stop people from giving knives, no matter how valuable, as wedding gifts. Yet consideration of the thoughts and feelings of others is largely ignored in practice by RCT.

Beyond the neglect of other people, oversimplification disregards multiple facets of possible outcomes and their consequences.

WHY RATIONAL CHOICE THEORY IS DANGEROUS

If I am deciding whether to surf the internet or to visit my mother, RCT would suggest that the relevant fact about visiting my mother is how much utility it yields. If I choose to visit her because I think she is lonely, my visit will take a form that reflects that reason. Compare a visit based on the belief that she is lonely with one based on the belief that she misses me, even though she has plenty of company. The visit based on the belief in her loneliness will be futile, resulting in very little utility, if there is company there when I arrive. The visit based on her missing me will be productive of utility whether or not she has company. Moreover, my subjective experience of the visit when it turns out she actually has company will be one thing if it is motivated by my intention to keep her company, but my experience based on her missing me will be another. Subjectively speaking, they will be different visits. Some would say that the decision has leaked into the outcome, but this terminology suggests that "non-leakage" is the norm when, as we suggested earlier, that is not true.

In certain ways RCT is very flexible. In principle it is possible to take everything into account in calculating probabilities and values, so that the feelings and intentions of other people *can* be considered. Still, the structure of RCT points to ignoring feelings and intentions and treating people the way we treat things. Treating people in that way, which leads to engaging with them largely in terms of how they affect us, how much utility they provide us, is a harmful thing—to us and to them. That the rise of so-called "transactional" social relationships has paralleled the rise in RCT-type thinking is, we think, no accident.

In our personal dealings with people, perhaps the single most important factor in how those interactions go is attunement of our own feelings and beliefs and the feelings and beliefs of others. This attunement is, in Kahneman's language, an S1 process. It tells us, without explicit and effortful thought, what people are thinking and feeling. We read tones of voice and bodily cues. This process is, of course, quite fallible, but nonetheless it is the best we have — and absolutely essential to our interactions with others. Mentally healthy and socially competent people rely on such attunement in their personal dealings with others, and it is essential to good decision-making in those important contexts. RCT cannot contribute significantly to that attunement. Moreover, RCT can conflict directly with it because it is very difficult to be attuned to the feelings and beliefs of yourself and others while thinking about these things quantitatively, which is how RCT would have us think. Imagine attempting to appreciate a painting while thinking of it primarily as reflecting patterns of different wavelengths of light rather than focusing on the colors as experienced. While it is true that RCT can marginally improve our decision-making in certain respects in certain conditions, it is, more important, bad for our mental health and our relations with others when it is made habitual or primary and interferes with attunement.

Ranking Colleges

The spirit of RCT is formalization and quantification, so that every difficulty RCT confronts creates a temptation for oversimplification and arbitrariness. To see why this can be not only mistaken but dangerous, let's examine in more detail something we have already discussed — the procedures of the preeminent ranker of colleges and universities, *U.S. News*, which is widely consulted to find out how good colleges and universities are relative to one another.

U.S. News makes public what its criteria are, and what weight they are given. It lists many criteria used in 2024, and they are quite diverse: six, with a total weight of 42%, are concerned with various graduation rates; three, with a total weight of 18%, are financial factors (amount of borrowing, financial resources per student, student earnings after graduation, and so on); nine, with a weight of 15%, are concerned with the faculty (publication, salaries, full/part time, and more); standardized tests of admitted students are weighted 5%; and one category, weighted 20%, is "peer assessment."

Peer assessment, the single most heavily weighted attribute, is a measure of how a school is regarded by top administrators at other institutions. It accounts for qualitative attributes of schools that may not be fully captured by the other rating factors. A school's peer assessment score is calculated from the weighted, two-year rolling average of ratings on academic quality that it receives from presidents, provosts, and deans of admissions — or officials in equivalent positions — at institutions submitting a peer-assessment survey administered by *U.S. News*. Each survey respondent is asked to rate the overall academic quality of peer schools' undergraduate academic programs on a scale from 1 (marginal) to 5 (distinguished). This is an example of something we discussed earlier, an attempt to get objective quantification by formulaic measurement of subjective opinions.

Consider the *U.S. News* criteria as a definition of what a good college is. In effect, it defines a good college as one that students are likely to graduate from, one with a well-paid, publishing faculty, one that is highly thought of by administrators at similar types of colleges, and one with good financial resources and whose graduates earn more after graduating than they otherwise would.

If you were evaluating a college without the constraint of limiting yourself to quantifiable features, you might think that the most important factor to assess should be academic quality itself. But academic quality is a difficult thing to judge precisely. No doubt, *U.S. News* takes the factors it *does* evaluate as proxies or indices of academic quality. This is not unreasonable. It is plausible that schools with better financial resources will use them to create and maintain better programs, and perhaps teach students in smaller classes. It is plausible that higher-quality faculty will create higher-quality academic programs, and that higher salaries will attract better faculty, and that active programs of research and publication will make for a more knowledgeable faculty. It is also plausible that higher graduation rates are a sign of greater academic quality, since high graduation rates may be a reflection of the care and attention that faculty devote to students. Though *U.S. News* makes no *direct* attempt to assess academic quality, it is trying to do so indirectly, with measures that are objective and quantifiable. And the evaluation of schools by experts at peer institutions is a way to catch aspects of academic quality that the objective measures may miss.

But let's take a closer look. This is what Sonia Cardenas, a senior administrator at Trinity College in Connecticut, had to say about peer evaluation, which she is routinely asked to do:

> The peer reputation survey asks respondents — such as presidents, provosts and deans of admissions — to rate the academic quality of hundreds of colleges nationwide. In the case of a liberal arts college, where I work, you're presented with a list of more than 200 other liberal arts institutions. When rating each college, you're supposed to consider the quality of its curriculum, faculty and graduates....
>
> Judging the quality of an institution at which I've never worked, studied or conducted an accreditation review is like asking a culinary expert to rate the signature dishes at hun-

dreds of restaurants where they've never eaten. No person—no matter how informed they are—has sufficient knowledge of the academic quality of all other colleges in the country to rate them responsibly on a five-point scale. That's absurd.[3]

Cardenas's point is that "peer assessment" of quality is really an assessment of reputation for quality, not of quality itself. The relation between reputation for quality and actual quality is anyone's guess, since if we knew how to measure actual quality, so that we could compare it with reputation, we wouldn't need to assess reputation at all.

You might also think that graduation and retention rates are closely related to the academic quality and the acquisition of knowledge. But actually, often the relation is not that close. When one of us (Richard) was an academic dean at a highly rated, small, liberal arts college, it was all but impossible for a student to fail to graduate. One way or another, professors and administrators adjusted their standards in a way that saw the students through to graduation. As for the quality of the faculty, that is surely important, but using publication records to index that quality is highly problematic. It is well known that, in general, the best research faculty teach so little that their knowledge is not reflected in what students learn. This may be why publication is actively discouraged at some colleges that are explicitly focused on teaching.

Financial factors raise a different issue. Increasingly, higher education is seen as a financial investment. A person pays for college in order to earn more money, based on the plausible idea that earn-

---

3. Cardenas, "*U.S. News and World Report*'s College Rankings."

ing will be a significant function of learning (academic quality). In college, you learn more than you knew in high school, and that should lead to greater earnings over the course of your working life. If this were true, earnings might be taken to be an indication of academic quality. Is this a reasonable assumption? Does a social worker learn a tenth (or less) of what an investment banker learns? Does a corporate lawyer learn ten times as much as a public defender? Earning as an index of learning ignores all the other personal factors that affect earnings (intelligence, previous knowledge, character, connections, looks, height, and so on). And, of course, earnings are significant at all only in fields of study in which success is more or less directly reflected in salaries.

The focus on earning potential as a measure of institutional quality may reflect the increased materialism of American society. It certainly reflects how much it now costs to get a college degree, especially from a prestigious institution. These factors may explain why students or their parents are interested in the earning potential of graduates of various institutions. But why is *U.S. News* so interested? Why is *U.S. News* looking for dropped car keys at midnight under a streetlamp when they dropped the keys fifty yards away? Why are they relying on criteria so distantly related to what they should be measuring? Our answer to this question is that the streetlamp is where the light is — which is to say that earning potential can be quantified in a way that academic quality cannot. Earning potential may not reveal much about academic quality, but it can be fed into RCT-type formulas.

U.S. News might defend itself by saying that sure, earning potential is not the most direct measure of school quality, but at least it *is* quantitative, as are virtually all the indices that *U.S. News* relies on. It is surely better than some vague assessment of academic quality, which may be nothing more than an assessment of reputation. And it's the best we can do.

However, consider the drawbacks. By ranking colleges as they do, *U.S. News* is encouraging students to apply to colleges with the best graduation rates, the most published faculty, and the best prospects for financial yield. It is, in effect, teaching the public that those are the best colleges. Students groom themselves to be admitted to those colleges, rather than the ones at which they can learn the most, and colleges groom themselves to rise up in the rankings, not to teach better. At an earlier time, when one of the *U.S. News* criteria was the percentage of faculty with PhDs, colleges were tempted to take their physical education teachers, who did not typically have PhDs, off the faculty and call them "staff." Would that have made them better colleges?

At one time, "yield" was one of the measures used by *U.S. News*. The yield is the percentage of admitted students who accept the admissions offer. To raise their yield, some colleges rejected well-qualified students if they thought the applicants would not accept admissions offers. They would look at an applicant's folder, see that GPA, test scores, and recommendations were much better than those of a typical applicant, and conclude that this applicant viewed their institution as a "safety school." "She'll never come," they would think. "If we accept her, it will hurt our yield. So let's reject her." Similarly, when *U.S. News* uses a school's acceptance rate as an index of quality (acceptance rate is simply the percentage of applicants who are accepted), it puts a premium on schools to encourage applications. Stanford, Harvard, or Yale can each boast that it rejects up to 95% of applicants. To induce more applications, schools may devote financial resources to amenities (such as student centers, athletic facilities, dining options) that will contribute little to education but a lot to whether students apply. Even wealthy schools, whose bank accounts seem to be bottomless, find themselves having to say no to new academic programs, enlarging faculty, financing summer student internships, and the like, in part because of the money spent attracting excess applicants. It is hardly a badge of honor that you reject nine of every ten applicants, knowing that many of those you reject meet your standards and are perfectly capable of doing the work.

Let us turn from the school's point of view to the potential applicant's. Imagine the *U.S. News* way of evaluating colleges as part of a prospective student's attempt to pick a set of colleges to apply to. Suppose the student wants to go to a college that is close by, that is not too expensive, and that is good. The student uses *U.S. News* to figure out what the "good" colleges are. Is there anything about this process that would encourage the student to ask, "What is a college education for?" "What does it mean to be educated?" "What is the point of the knowledge higher education gives?" "How does learning happen?" The point here is that encouraging the student to put effort into coming up with quantifiable criteria does not point the student to the right questions. Furthermore, it also likely affects how the student operates, and what the student learns, in high school. Having come up with a set of target schools, the student checks out their admissions criteria. The focus then becomes less on learning what the high school has to offer and more on getting a high GPA, raising SAT scores (by taking SAT prep courses), and getting involved in a large number of extracurricular activities, while participating minimally in each. In other words, students focus on looking better at the cost of learning less. Even if the student picks the right schools to apply to, engineers high school activities to look like an attractive candidate, gains admission, and ultimately attends a fine school, the student will not have done it for the best reasons and will not come to college as the best version of him- or herself.

There are several things that *U.S. News* or a similar rating system might say in response to our concerns. They might admit that their system is imperfect, but argue that any such system would be imperfect, and they keep working on making it better. They might argue that their rating system encourages schools to raise more money, improve academic programs and living conditions, hire better faculty, and pay more attention to helping students succeed after graduation. There may be some truth to these responses, but not enough. For one of the features of ratings systems, whatever they are, is that they can be "gamed." Raising your rejection rate by building a new gym to encourage applications makes rejection rate a less useful index of quality than it was before. Rejecting talented students because you think they won't come to improve yield makes yield a less reliable index of quality than it was before. Using research productivity as a criterion for hiring faculty makes faculty "quality" a less reliable index of education quality than it was before. Raising the SAT and GPA standards for admitting students makes these measures a less reliable index of quality (because of what the students will do to make their credentials more impressive) than it was before.

The general point here is this: *U.S. News* measures what it measures as a quantitative index of qualities that are much harder to quantify. Of course the index is imperfect. But as schools find ways to improve their scores on the index without doing anything to improve academic quality, the index gets more and more imperfect. SAT scores are an index of what students have already learned and what their potential for further learning is. They are meant to be a predictor of how well students will do in college (and evidence suggests they are not a great predictor beyond first-year grades). SAT scores, too, are imperfect. But as students find ways to improve SAT scores (by learning how to take the test rather than by learning more in the classroom), the index gets more and more imperfect. Almost any index can be gamed. Anything that starts to matter (like *U.S. News* ratings and SATs) will be gamed. And as it is gamed, its usefulness as an index is diminished.

There are other examples of this process, many with serious consequences. One example, again from education, is the growth of insistence on "rubrics" in the classroom that explain criteria for grading individual assignments and for grading performance in the course as a whole. One feature of student performance that matters in many rubrics is "class participation." How often does the student contribute and how worthwhile are the contributions? So, suppose you are a student and you see in the course-grading rubric that participation will determine 20% of the grade. What do you do? You make damn sure that you participate and that you say clever things. You invent questions that you don't really have. When other students are speaking you are not listening to them but formulating your own contribution. For sure, class participation goes up. But the quality of that participation likely goes down. And students spend their time showing off rather than listening to one another.

Another, much more tragic, example is historical. There was a great deal of protest in the United States over the country's involvement in the Vietnam War. Part of the protest stemmed from the sense that the United States wasn't winning—that people kept dying but no progress was being made. In a war of this type, what has come to be called "asymmetric warfare," it is often hard to tell which side is gaining. As economist Fred Hirsch pointed out in his book *Social Limits to Growth*, leaders of the U.S. war efforts came to the conclusion that they needed to show Americans evidence that they were making progress. They came up with an index of success—body counts. If the enemy was suffering more casualties than we were, we must be winning. Are body counts a good index of military success? Perhaps they are, though they are surely imperfect. But what this move resulted in was a change in U.S. strategy to maximize body counts. That way, the military could show citizens that the war effort was successful. Body counts went up. But at the same time, adopting enhanced body counts as a deliberate strategy made them a far worse index of success. Many people died as a result of this strategy.

We think this kind of process is essentially inevitable. To quantify, you create an index. People find ways to improve how they look on the index. They succeed in looking better, but the index gets worse. No index is bulletproof. The more you feel the pressure to quantify, the more you rely on indices, the more your performance is distorted by the gaming of the indices. And as we have seen, quantification is at the heart of RCT; you can't use the latter unless you can do the former. The solution to this dynamic problem, we think, is to avoid the use of indices, by resisting the pressure to quantify. Talking to people who have had direct experience at the schools you are thinking of applying to, or reading what they have to say online about their academic experience, without feeling compelled to attach numbers to what they have to say, may give you much useful information about the schools under consideration. And there would be no quantitative index to game. There is no assurance that doing this will lead prospective students to ask themselves the right questions and do the right things, and no assurance that it will lead institutions to direct resources in the right directions. Errors of judgment are inevitable. But at least both students and the institutions they are considering will be *trying* to do the right thing, for the right reasons.

How to Assess Well-Being

After many years studying decision-making and its errors, Kahneman turned his attention to studying happiness, or well-being. This was, perhaps, a natural development since so many people think the goal of their lives and thus their decisions is to enhance well-being. His aim was to come up with objective, scientific tools for measuring an inherently subjective phenomenon. Perhaps success in this enterprise would ultimately lead to substantive, objective measures that would replace "utility" in RCT calculations. Being able to measure happiness objectively could have tremendous potential importance. An objective measure of happiness would enable people, and policy-making institutions, to make better decisions when it came to allocating their time and resources. Having something like a "pleasure thermometer" would be better than just guessing about how good a decision would make you (or the people on whose behalf you're deciding) feel.

Kahneman developed an approach to the question of how good life is by measuring people's reported well-being in living that life. To understand his approach, it is helpful to apprehend how he approached another, smaller problem — how unpleasant is a colonoscopy. He measured that in two ways: First he asked patients undergoing a diagnostic colonoscopy procedure how much discomfort they were experiencing, moment by moment, during the procedure (at this time, colonoscopies were not performed under general anesthetic, as they are now). Then he added up the quantities to come up with a measure of how bad the procedure had felt overall. He also asked the patients at the end of the procedure how uncomfortable it had been. The moment-by-moment measures were different from the after-the-fact measures, and Kahneman was convinced that the sum of the moment-to-moment assessments of discomfort was the right "objective" measure of how unpleasant the procedure was.

When it came to measuring "how satisfied" people are with their lives more generally, Kahneman's experience with the colonoscopy patients (and other studies of people subjected to having their hands immersed briefly in hot or cold water, or listening to bursts of loud white noise through headphones) taught him that overall retrospective judgments were not really as reliable as "online," short-duration reports. So in *Thinking, Fast and Slow*, he observed, "I proposed to measure . . . objective happiness precisely as we assessed the experience of the two colonoscopy patients, by evaluating a profile of the well-being experienced over successive moments of . . . life."[4] He could ask the colonoscopy patients how they felt at short intervals during the procedure. That was obviously impossible in evaluating well-being over a longer period of normal life, so Kahneman devised a method relying on people's memory in a way that seemed to avoid the memory bias he had discovered in the colonoscopy case. In this way, we might say that Kahneman was looking for the "atoms" of happiness:

> The experience of a moment or an episode is not easily represented by a single happiness value. There are many variants

---

4. Kahneman, *Thinking, Fast and Slow*, 392.

of positive feelings, including love, joy, engagement, hope, amusement, and many others. Negative emotions also come in many varieties, including anger, shame, depression, and loneliness. Although positive and negative emotions exist at the same time, it is possible to classify most moments of life as ultimately positive or negative. We could identify unpleasant episodes by comparing the ratings of positive or negative adjectives. We called an episode unpleasant if a negative feeling was assigned a higher rating than all of the positive feelings. . . . We called the percentage of time that an individual spends in a pleasant state the U-index."[5]

This procedure, together with certain others, he called collectively the "Day Reconstruction Method" (DRM). "We used the DRM to study the determinants of emotional well-being."[6] A high U-index was taken as an indicator of emotional well-being. In the final analysis, this approach measured emotional well-being at a given period based on the amount of time that people recollected experiencing a negative feeling greater than all the positive feelings they had at that same time, or a positive feeling greater than all the negative feelings they had at that same time.

In the case of the colonoscopy, the units, or episodes, could be defined simply by duration, since the whole experience was more or less homogenous, without major differences except for amounts of discomfort over the course of the procedure. In other words, the colonoscopy comes neatly framed, in the same way that a bet at the roulette table is neatly framed. Daily life is different in that respect.

---

5. Kahneman, *Thinking, Fast and Slow*, 393.
6. Kahneman, *Thinking, Fast and Slow*, 393.

The units, or atoms, that will be measured have to be defined in a way that respects various aspects of a changing life. Kahneman addressed this problem. These are the instructions he gave to his participants for defining episodes:

> Think of your day as a continuous series of scenes or episodes in a film. Give each episode a brief name that will help you remember it (for example, "commuting to work," or "at lunch with B"). The episodes people identify usually last between 15 minutes and 2 hours. Indications of the end of an episode might be going to a different location, ending one activity and starting another, or a change in the people you are interacting with.[7]

Kahneman used this method to identify eighteen different types of episodes that his participants positively evaluated, including intimate relations (presumably sex), relaxing, eating, watching TV, shopping, using the phone, napping, and computer/email/internet, as well as episodes they negatively evaluated (commuting, cleaning house, and, perhaps surprisingly, caring for children). Though there was variation between people, there was also consistency, and for a given person, similar activities usually produced similar evaluations. Moreover, Kahneman and his collaborators found that there were real differences between the well-being people experience as they are *living* their lives and the judgments they make when they are asked to *evaluate* their lives. For example, educational attainment affects life evaluation a good deal more than it affects experienced well-being, whereas the reverse is true of physical illness.

7. Kahneman, *Thinking, Fast and Slow*, 392.

WHY RATIONAL CHOICE THEORY IS DANGEROUS

The results of Kahneman's pathbreaking studies drew much attention and have been adopted in one form or another throughout the world, as societies and their governments try to improve the lives of their citizens and measure whether their efforts are working. But from our perspective, a serious question arises as to whether the DRM is measuring the right thing. We think the DRM reflects several forms of impoverishment of experience. It oversimplifies and decontextualizes experience. It takes away the meaning of experience, as well as the intention behind it. It eliminates the connection of the experience to other experiences in both the short and long term—the "story" of which the episode is a part. And it eliminates the potential moral significance of the experience. In other words, stripping the momentary experience away from these complicating factors—imposing a very narrow frame—distorts the experience. It leaves much that is significant about the experience out, in the same way that treating everyday decisions as gambles leaves much about the decisions out.

Imagine a participant in a DRM study is having an argument with her child about going to bed. On the surface, the argument is about bedtime, but there are other important issues that are not as explicitly articulated, such as how parental authority is to be used, how much of the child's life will and should be under her own control at this particular age, and the child's relation to her siblings. More generally, how are disputes going to be settled—rationally, or on the basis of power? The mother feels a whole range of emotions: anger (at the child's stubbornness), shame (at her own impatience), pride (at her child's independence), determination (because of the importance of what is at stake), fear (that she is being authoritarian), and others.

Kahneman's DRM portrays this episode simply as either positive or negative. The mother's feelings about this episode will be strongly influenced by several things that are not taken into account. One of these is what preceded the episode. Has the child been reasonable or excessively demanding before being asked to go to bed? Another is the broader temporal context. Is the child slightly spoiled, or perhaps too unassertive? The mother's understanding of the child's intentions is also relevant. Is the child testing limits, or simply wanting to stay up? Is the child jealous of her older siblings, or too excited to be willing to go to sleep? If the mother has been impatient, then a negative assessment of the episode, reflecting a judgment of the absence of well-being, is inappropriate. On the contrary, negative feeling as a response to impatience *reflects* well-being. A positive feeling in response to her own impatience would indicate the opposite of well-being. And if the mother should strike the child, the episode exemplifies anything but well-being no matter how happy it made the mother to vent her anger. In fact, the happier it made the mother, the more she enjoyed it, the less it exemplifies well-being and the closer it comes to exemplifying immorality. What these various hypothetical complexities we have introduced in describing this mother's attempt to get her child to sleep are meant to reveal is just how complex an incident can be, and how heterogeneous the collection of such incidents can be. Homogenizing such incidents, in the aid of quantification, leaves most of the action on the cutting-room floor.

We should make clear that capturing these complexities was not Kahneman's objective. His objective was to find a way to measure the "atoms" of happiness, not the "molecules" of which they are a part. Our concern is that this may have been the wrong objective.

In discussing the DRM, Kahneman lists the "positive emotions" that contribute to well-being—happiness, warm/friendly feeling, enjoyment. Perhaps these feelings are easier to measure than other aspects (like context, meaning, and intention) of the sorts of episodes Kahneman had in mind, but measuring well-being by measuring feelings cuts it off from reality. Is the happiness one feels or the enjoyment one gets from playing violent video games, or from pornography, indicative of well-being? Shall we credit a person who has cancer with a high level of well-being because he does not know he has cancer and does not yet "feel" any untoward symptoms? How about the warmth and friendliness one feels in the company of a salesperson who sees you wholly as a source of income? Is that feeling indicative of the customer's well-being? It should be clear that the significance of these feelings for well-being is much too complicated to be dealt with in a context-free, quantitative way.

It is significant that in the discussion of well-being, the terms *satisfaction, enjoyment, happiness,* and *experienced utility* are used, perhaps interchangeably, with *well-being,* and there is no discussion of their relation to one another. One problem with this is that while it makes perfect sense to ask how happy someone was at an instant, the notion of measuring well-being at an instant makes much less sense. Can we meaningfully ask what a person's level of well-being was while they ate their Big Mac? If we can, it is only with reference to the broader context of their lives and longer time horizons. What do we say about the life of a person who has thrived for a long time believing she was on the way to finding a cure for a horrible disease, but spent the last one-third of her life regretting that she had been completely wrong and had "wasted" her life? Does the genuine happiness of the first two-thirds of her life outweigh the unhappiness of the last one-third? Or is it perhaps more complicated than that? Is her life a more satisfying one than that of a person who struggled painfully at the same project for two-thirds of his life, but eventually succeeded and basked in that success for the last one-third of his life? Are these cases importantly different? If so, what does this say about well-being in life as the mere sum of the happiness of the times of one's life? Doesn't the relationship among the times — the trajectory, the story — make a crucial difference?

It is not clear to us that any of the activities identified and evaluated by the DRM contribute significantly to well-being, but treated, as they have been, in the way we just discussed, it seems even less likely. The context and meaning of these activities can make all the difference. Are adulterous, promiscuous, casual, or cruel forms of sex unequivocally contributions to well-being? Are all or most forms of relaxation contributions to well-being? Is the way that many members of this society eat or shop a sign of a contribution to well-being? Is not much of it escapism, the very opposite of well-being? Watching TV? Compulsively? Using the phone? Compulsively?

Presumably, with his eye on measurement and calculation, Kahneman avoided these considerations. But they are important. This is partly because in a way somewhat similar to how the overemphasis on measurement and calculation has deformed this approach to well-being, an overemphasis on material features of life has distorted the way we get happiness, enjoyment, and even a feeling of warmth and friendliness.

The key underlying point here is that the factors that Kahneman's analytic method claims increase well-being as they themselves increase actually do so only for certain kinds of people in certain kinds of situations. To define what that kind of person is (a person with good values?) and what kind of a situation that person is in (a healthy and free society?) in quantifiable terms is a heroic task, and perhaps even a fool's errand. So, it is no wonder that in attempting to define well-being, Kahneman and others ignored those considerations. But they are ignored at a very high price, a price that will be paid when the argument is made that we should not worry about giving up freedom or the struggle for justice or aspirations to live a more constructive and creative life because not worrying about such things will make us happier, enable us to enjoy ourselves more — perhaps even to feel more warmth and friendliness from our neighbors.

How is it that these factors can be minimized by distinguished researchers? We don't know, but one reasonable conjecture is that they are so focused on quantification and calculation in the service of "objectivity" that they have not paid enough attention to what has been lost in the process. Are we, for the sake of quantification, going to rank high on the scale of well-being a society where people are happy because they nap, shop, eat, use their computers (perhaps to play games), relax and watch TV, and hook up?

To assess well-being requires depth of understanding, but RCT will not provide the depth of understanding of our situation that we need. And if we deploy other ways of thinking about our lives and our decisions, they might provide just such a deeper understanding on their own, making RCT superfluous. Broadening our notions about how we should think about decisions increases our reflectiveness. One can and should, if the decision is important enough, ask, "Is there some aspect of my outlook on the world that is interfering with making a good decision here? Am I being selfish? Lazy? Am I oversimplifying? Am I framing the situation too broadly? Too narrowly? Do I see this decision through a scientific lens? A pragmatic lens? A traditional lens?" Reflecting on questions like these can yield not only a perspective on a looming decision, but the decision itself.

In the earlier chapters of the book, we discussed RCT and what we take to be its serious limitations. In this chapter, we suggested that RCT is not merely an oversimplification, it is potentially a dangerous oversimplification. Decisions could be made perilously worse by the use of RCT. The appropriate conclusion from this, we believe, is that RCT is misguided because its deepest underlying assumption, as reflected in the gambling paradigm, is that decision problems are quantitative problems. That assumption is true, or true enough, in connection with many financial, gambling, and consumer problems. But those problems are not similar in relevant respects to the many other kinds of decision problems we face in normal life. Most of the issues of everyday life are not, and should not be turned into, closed, quantitative problems. In the next chapter we will sketch out alternative guidelines for making good decisions — guidelines that we think will lead not only to better decisions, but to a better society in which to make decisions.

Chapter 9

AN ALTERNATIVE TO RATIONAL CHOICE THEORY

Our aim in proposing an alternative to RCT is to present a different understanding of what it means to be rational than RCT provides. Our conception of rationality certainly has implications when it comes to choices and decisions, but it is about thinking more generally, not just about choosing. It encompasses many aspects of our lives that RCT leaves out. We think that being human entails a much richer understanding of rationality than RCT does. As we have argued in the book thus far, many transformations of a decision problem are required to frame the decision in a closed way that RCT can handle. These processes are part of what it means to be rational, but are not themselves comprehensible through the lens of RCT. Thus, what follows is not just intended to replace RCT as a theory of decision-making, but to replace it as a theory of rationality more generally.

RCT contains three core elements: quantified probability, quantified value, and maximization. These elements are connected by an algorithm: multiplying value by probability and choosing the option with the highest result is the algorithm, with the aim of maximizing utility. Our alternative minimizes the role of all these factors, substituting understanding for probability, virtues and nonquantitative values for utility, moderation for maximization, and judgment for the algorithm. We present our alternative in contrast to RCT as an outgrowth of our criticisms of RCT. And our alternative and its elements will not be as rigorously defined as the elements of RCT are. We believe that wisdom tells a person not to expect more rigor than the subject matter at hand allows.

In our criticisms of RCT, we have suggested that many processes that are taken as errors or biases within RCT, most especially framing, are not always "errors" but sometimes essential preconditions for serious inquiry and for RCT-type analysis even to get off the ground. And we have suggested that while RCT may have a place in an account of thinking and rationality, most of what we think of as "thinking" cannot be incorporated into RCT, and much of what we think of as the hallmark of being rational bears little relation to RCT. Let us, then, (incompletely) specify aspects of thinking that are largely excluded from RCT. What should the thinking and the decisions of a mature, rational human being look like?

Predicting versus Understanding

As we have said, a key reason why probability calculation is a central part of RCT is that the world is uncertain, and almost every decision we make is a prediction about how the results of that decision will turn out. Thus, being able to predict is important. But there is a big difference between prediction and understanding. For example, from the time of the emergence of Homo sapiens, our species was able to predict that the sun would reappear regularly, but people certainly did not understand the phenomenon. The difference between understanding and lack of it that we have in mind is nicely illustrated by Steven Sloman and Philip Fernbach in their book *The Knowledge Illusion*. As an example of the many demonstrations of the knowledge illusion they discuss, if you ask someone, "Do you know how a flush toilet works?," most people say yes. If you then ask them to explain how a toilet works, almost no one can. Being confronted by their inability to explain the operation of a toilet (what psychologists Leonid Rozenblit and Frank Keil called "the illusion of explanatory depth"), people realize that though they obviously know how to *use* a toilet, and can *predict* what will happen when they depress the handle, they do not understand it.

Within the JDM research tradition, decision scientist Paul Slovic, in collaboration with Kahneman's research partner Amos Tversky, proposed what they called the "Understanding/Acceptance" principle: the better people understood the formal principles of RCT, the more likely they were to accept RCT. The evidence for this principle came from research in which people who made errors in judgment were exposed to arguments for and against one or another formal principle, and presumably came to understand the principle better. We want to highlight this notion of better understanding. We also want to make clear that better understanding of the formal principles of RCT does not necessarily mean better understanding of the decisions to which RCT is being applied. Understanding the rules of RCT may enable people to engage in and accept the results of RCT-type deliberations, but whether that leads to better — more rational — decisions is an entirely open question.

One crucial aspect of understanding is putting a phenomenon into a coherent and relatively parsimonious framework. Both science and everyday inquiry attempt to do this. Copernicus's heliocentric theory of planetary motion did not actually predict any better than its predecessor, but it was appealing because it was simpler and more coherent. Newton's theory amazed people not because it made better predictions, but because it synthesized terrestrial physics and astronomy in a simple and coherent framework. One of the sharpest contrasts between RCT and our alternative is in the fact that while decision researchers typically assert or imply that the construction of coherent frameworks (what we have discussed as "framing") is mostly a source of bias, we believe that the formulation of coherent frameworks is the heart of understanding. The neglect of the importance of understanding and coherence is connected, we think, to the neglect of the importance of framing. We might say that "well framed is half solved."

Understanding in terms of coherent frameworks certainly contains the possibility of distorted and inaccurate statistical predictions, but it contributes more than enough to knowledge to make up for that problem. It puts the phenomenon of interest in context, relating it to other phenomena. It helps to explain the successes and failures of statistical prediction. We may know that a certain car is statistically more likely to roll over than another, and that is useful. But if we understand the principles that explain that statistical fact, it can help us to understand why it rolls over in some circumstances and not others, what changes (in design of the car or in our behavior in driving it) might decrease the chances of it rolling over, why seemingly similar models do not have a similar tendency, and so on. So framing the choice of a car as involving an understanding of its operating characteristics is likely to lead to a better choice and better driving than an RCT analysis that proceeds without understanding.

We hypothesize that in general, people who seek understanding of a subject—who consider arguments about it—will make very different responses to the real-life situation they eventually face than people who have not—often more effective ones. This mental exploration enables people to understand the situation they will face in a way that they previously would not. We believe we cannot understand rationality without understanding how understanding changes the way people approach decisions. And the process of framing contributes to the process of understanding (as well, of course, as misunderstanding). But understanding has no obvious place in RCT.

Understanding depends on classification. If we classify the Earth and its surroundings as unique and different from other celestial objects, we will not connect falling objects in our experience with the motion of planets, when in fact falling objects are operating according to the same principles as the orbiting planets. Classification can bias predictions in the same way that coherent theories can, but it is inconceivable that any serious thinking at all, including any kind of rational decision-making, could proceed without classification.

Suppose our car navigation software suggests one route over another because the latter has heavy traffic. If we know the area and understand traffic patterns along the latter route, we may know that the heavy traffic is due to a special event drawing a large crowd, and will have dissipated by the time we arrive. Of course, some version of this knowledge can be formulated as statistical knowledge ("whenever there is this sort of event, the traffic dissipates by the start of the event"), but no statistical inquiry is required. This judgment depends on the correct classification of the episode in question and, relatedly, to the understanding of the cause. If the cause were a collapsed overpass, the traffic would not likely disperse anywhere nearly as soon. Classification is part of framing, and as we have pointed out, RCT provides no help in framing. Our alternative involves close attention to framing/classification and understanding.

AN ALTERNATIVE TO RATIONAL CHOICE THEORY

Understanding Other People

The understanding of human beings is to an important extent a very different matter from the understanding of other things. If we want to understand people, how they feel and think, how they act, what they say, write, and otherwise create, we need to use our capacity to determine people's intentions, motives, meanings, and purposes, another capacity that decision researchers often treat as a source of bias. That it may sometimes be, but it is hard to imagine living as a member of society without it. We illustrated the importance of purpose and meaning in our earlier discussions of *why* you visit your mother, and *why* you purchase a concert ticket. The days are behind us when we could confidently assert, as behaviorists did, that all we needed to do to understand human beings was to observe their behavior. And neurobiological explanation of how human beings function is far from mature enough to allow us to dispense with purposes and intentions. Thus, at present, we continue to rely on what philosopher Daniel Dennett called "the intentional stance" when we try to understand and explain the actions of ourselves and others. Moreover, considering the purposes and intentions of others is essential if we want to act in the world in a way that takes other people's needs and desires into account. A satisfying life includes the enjoyment and fulfillment provided by the company of other people, cooperation with other people, and concern with the well-being of other people. Someone who cannot or does not treat people as purposive, intentional creatures is closer to being a defective person than a fully rational one.

This last concern for the good of other people is the mark of genuinely human relationship, as opposed to the sort of relationship we typically have with things. Affection for others based on enjoyment or usefulness in getting things done is a kind of selfish affection. A life in which a person's relationships with others are totally based on what they can provide for her (what we might call instrumental or transactional relationships) is a life lacking something very important. These kinds of relationships, based wholly on mutual gain or mutual enjoyment, are generally superficial and fleeting. It is not enough *that* you want relationships with other people; it is also important *why* you want such relationships. Purposes always matter, but they matter especially in our relationships with others. We think it is a hallmark of modern society that transactional relationships are increasingly replacing deeper relationships based on concern for the good of the other person.

As we saw in discussing whether to take the family to the beach or the museum, even simple decisions get much more complicated when we consider the effects of what we do on relevant other people. How wide the circle of relevant others should be (and who should count as a relevant other) is itself complicated, but even if we finesse that issue and focus only on people we are close to, balancing diverse needs, interests, and desires is hard. To do so well requires the ability to understand the intentions of others. It requires empathy for others and perspective-taking about how others see the world. Many see this concern for other people as a potential source of bias that can distort the "rational" methods of RCT. Nonetheless, others have argued that social sensitivity, though very imperfectly realized, is a natural inclination of people, and necessary for a fully human life.

In a remarkable paper written almost fifty years ago, "The Social Function of Intellect," Nicholas Humphrey argued persuasively that managing social relations is what human intelligence evolved *for*. Finding food and protecting oneself from predators were not major challenges in prehistoric times. Big brains and slow cognitive maturation were not needed to keep people alive. What *was* needed was group coordination and harmony. And maintaining that, in the face of individual differences in needs, perspectives, and power, was what required big brains. Note that the evolutionary "price" of big brains was quite high. Big brains required big, hard heads, which made childbirth a dangerous adventure. Big brains demanded a great deal of caloric energy, which made food seeking more significant. And slow maturation, which built up the flexibility of human intelligence that other species lacked, meant a long period of helpless dependence of offspring on adults. These costs, Humphrey argued, were worth paying, as it was this intelligence that enabled groups to stay together, work together, and learn from their members.

Of course humans, like other "things," are subject to principles of causation, but when human beings act, they are expressing intentions; they are acting for reasons — with purpose. If we are to be social beings, we will need to understand these intentions and purposes. It is this capacity that enables us to speak seriously with people or read books about people and understand their actions.

Reflectiveness

Part of what enables us to discern, if imperfectly, the purposes and intentions of others is reflectiveness. We don't just live and act in the world, we think about our living and acting, and about how the other people in our lives live and act. Reflectiveness is often effortful and perhaps even unpleasant. But it can also occur somewhat automatically. We can, as it were, develop a habit of reflection.

People who develop the *habit* of thinking about situations come to a greater understanding of those situations, and their choices are often, though not always, better ones. Good poker players do this. They know that they need to understand the people they are playing against as well as the way that the cards dealt so far have changed the odds that they will end up with the winning hand. This thinking is of little help in playing roulette. In playing roulette, and even in deciding whether to play roulette, RCT is probably the best tool. Skilled poker players probably relish the chance to play against people who know nothing about probability, but they understand that knowledge of probability is the beginning, not the end, of their poker education.

If this sort of thinking is so habitual that it does not require conscious focus or effort, then it is by definition not something that S2 does. And if it does not in itself deliver a specific kind of choice or decision, then it is either not something that S1 does, or it is different from the other things that characterize S1. So, what is it, and what bin of mental operation does it belong in? Barry is an enthusiastic, if inexpert, contract bridge player. Bridge is a very complicated game. Almost every hand offers plenty to think about. Nonetheless, when you watch world-class players, it is surprising how long they think early in a hand. You would expect such experts to be extremely facile – even automatic – in playing a hand. But they think far longer than an inexpert player would think. What they typically are *not* doing is *thinking about what to think about.* The kinds of things that matter to playing a bridge hand are habitual or automatic to bridge experts. But knowing what to think *about* does not tell you what to think. And so expert bridge players seem to combine S1-like automaticity regarding what to think about with S2-like deep thought about what to think in the play of every hand. We have no category for what we are inclined to call automatic reflectiveness, and it is typically ignored by RCT.

AN ALTERNATIVE TO RATIONAL CHOICE THEORY

In a different context, researcher Gary Klein has studied how experts in various fields make high-stakes, high-pressure decisions. He went into his research assuming that, say, an experienced firefighter will go to a fire with the advantage of being able to prune many options for fighting the fire from her list of possibilities (just as a chess master prunes many possible moves from her set of possibilities), and then gather information on site to choose among the two or three possible strategies that remain. On this model, something like S1 does the pruning and then S2 does the deciding. What Klein found, in contrast, is that firefighters rarely reported entertaining possibilities. They mostly knew, by gathering data and reflecting on the data automatically, which strategy was called for. It was only after the fire had been stopped that firefighters took the time to review the evidence from the scene to see if there were considerations that they had overlooked.

In choosing where to apply to college, Mia recognized that she was more inclined to involvement with social issues than she was with preparing herself for a well-paying career. The capacity for reflection and self-knowledge that this insight indicates would have been no less true had she decided that a well-paying career was important to her, perhaps so she could pay off student debt and begin an independent life away from her parents' house. Neither insight is inconsistent with RCT, but there is nothing about RCT that encourages an insight like this. If everyone were motivated by the desire for physical pleasure, money, and things comparable to them, such reflection would not be as important as it was for Mia, and perhaps for other people.

One might say that the attribute we are pointing to here is "thoughtfulness," but "thoughtfulness" is sometimes used to mean being nice in ways that exceed expectations. We want to use it here to mean the habit of thinking, consciously and unconsciously, in the way we have been discussing. Whether we call it thoughtfulness or reflectiveness, a life that has it normally makes better decisions, and is probably a better life than a life without it.

Substitution and Self-Knowledge

As we've said, much of the discussion in Kahneman's *Thinking, Fast and Slow*, as in much of the empirical research on judgment and decision-making, is devoted to what are regarded as mistakes, or biases, that lead to mistaken, inconsistent, and sometimes irrational choices. Often, a general feature of those mistakes is the substitution of a simpler and more accessible question for a complex and less accessible one. As Kahneman describes it, people often answer a simpler question than the one they were asked (or have asked themselves), without realizing that they have substituted one question for another. They may be giving the right answer, but to the wrong question. We have just suggested that a very important kind of thinking is reflection, and that it does not — and perhaps cannot — be included in Kahneman's framework, in part because it is neither choosing nor deciding, but something closer to understanding. By substituting the notions of choice and decision in quantifiable contexts for the much more complicated notion of thinking — reflection and understanding included — most decision-making researchers are making one of the mistakes Kahneman emphasized. We want to know what it means to be rational — what it means to think well — and instead we are learning what it means to choose and decide. This raises the question, for JDM researchers and for all of us, of how we can avoid making this mistake. One way that we can and should do so is to know which mistakes we in particular are prone to — and in which ways and which contexts. Kahneman's work can be understood as helping us to understand ourselves in just this way with respect to choosing and deciding. But in addition, we have the capacity to understand ourselves as individuals outside the realm of decision, narrowly construed.

Suppose, then, that we begin to treat ourselves as the participants in Kahneman's experiments have been treated (and we focus on Kahneman as the leading representative of a very large collection of researchers). Suppose we pay attention to our choice behavior and look for patterns. We could also add additional helpful information by trying to introspect about our would-be S1 responses, as they are suppressed and replaced with the results of S2 thinking. We might, for example, find that we are quite risk averse, as decision researchers might say. In ordinary language we might say that we are timid. If we find that we are extremely risk averse, we might be inclined to say that we are cowardly. And this characteristic is not simply applicable to abstract or artificial decision problems. We would likely exhibit it in ordinary life.

If we scrutinize our own actions as we might scrutinize those of others, then we are doing what Kahneman is doing, except that we are both experimenter and participant. If we introspect about our would-be S1 responses, and test them against "arguments" in favor, for example, of courageous behavior, we are being reflective, in this case in regard to ourselves as opposed to some external matter. However rarely exercised, we have some capacity to know ourselves. No doubt, as countless studies have shown, we also have the capacity to deceive ourselves, but the processes through which such self-deception is corrected are surely an essential part of thinking and rationality.

AN ALTERNATIVE TO RATIONAL CHOICE THEORY

Value

The RCT model for rational decision-making treats values as given. Our alternative to RCT, in contrast, is as much about what values are worth pursuing as it is about how to pursue them. RCT evaluates decisions largely in isolation from one another. The rationality of each decision is evaluated on its own. Our alternative regards rationality as crucial to judging how a particular value fits in with other values a person may hold. The focus in our alternative is a good deal broader than that of RCT. We focus on using rationality to help us live good lives, not just to make good (useful or satisfying) individual decisions. We think individual decisions should be evaluated with respect to whether and how they contribute to living good lives. We think that what makes a life a good one are worthwhile goals and the means to work constructively toward them. And these goals, in addition to being worthwhile in themselves, are also integrated enough to give our lives a kind of narrative unity. Our decisions should ultimately shape those goals and be shaped by them. RCT cannot help us to formulate such goals. RCT is the tool for making decisions to achieve goals that come from somewhere else and are present before an RCT analysis even begins.

What is a good life? One reason that RCT is so attractive to people may be that it avoids this question, letting each of us decide for ourselves. And avoiding this question is tempting because it is so difficult to answer. We certainly cannot do so. The best we can do is to put some constraints on notions of what a good life is. A good life is one that does not involve inflicting unnecessary cruelty, being unfair, being greedy, and basic evils like those. These things are incompatible with choosing well and living well. The ability to recognize, and the inclination to avoid, basic evils is a prerequisite for rational choosing in our nonformal sense.

AN ALTERNATIVE TO RATIONAL CHOICE THEORY

Beyond this, perhaps the most important element of living and choosing well is meaning, and an ideally meaningful life is one of organic unity organized around purpose. A musician's life, for example, may be organized around the enhancement and exhibition of his musical ability. Of course there is a limit to how much unity should be sought and can be achieved. An emotionally healthy person will be involved in life in other ways as well, and will be flexible. But at any given time, the person's life will be largely unified in that music will be an aspect of most of it — career, family life, social life, and so on. This person might teach his children to play music together as a family. Many of this person's friends might be musicians. And life will be unified over time by a narrative that organizes the history of this person's life — learning, performing, perfecting skills, recognition of accomplishments — each phase of life an outgrowth and continuation of the previous phases. In a paper written some years ago with psychologists Amy Wrzesniewski, Paul Rozin, and Clark McCauley, Barry suggested that people who lived lives like this did work that was a "calling" — and they did better work and had more satisfying lives than people whose work was a "job" or a "career."

Living a life of this kind is obviously a luxury. It depends on life circumstances that enable this musician to study music, to own an instrument, and to belong to a cultural or racial group whose members are not oppressed and unwelcome in the music community. So, the ideally meaningful life of the musician may be available only to the few. Nonetheless, to approximate a unified life to the extent that one can will make life more meaningful, whatever one's material and cultural circumstances. We think narrative unity organized around purpose is necessary for the most worthwhile kind of life, and particular choices (for example, "Should I live where the night life is good or near my music teacher?") should be made largely on the basis of how to sustain and enrich the meaning of life. We do not want to minimize the obstacles to creating and living this kind of life. Indeed, on the contrary, we want to suggest that public policy should be paying attention to providing the means for living this kind of life, alongside the attention it pays to meeting basic material needs. This is one valuable thing that so-called "rich" countries should use their riches for.

With regard to meaning and purpose, there is room for enormous diversity. A worthy goal may be to continue operating the family business successfully and supporting the community in which it is located. It could be to help find a cure for cancer. It could be to contribute to the world of the humanities, say, by better understanding an episode or character in history, or a work of art. It could be to create such a work of art. It could be to improve the lot of your community, some other community, or some category of people suffering from an oppressive condition. It could be to prevent the spread of hospital-borne infections by keeping patients' rooms clean. It could be to protect your community by committing to military service or to domestic uniformed protective service. It could be to help solve whatever "problem" brings customers into your retail store. It could be to raise strong and virtuous children who enter adulthood with a sense of who they are and what they are after in life. It could be creating a healthy family and raising children who have good values, good families themselves, and good relationships to the community, culminating in the ability to see grandchildren thrive. There may be no more worthwhile goal. In many cases it may be less a matter of *what* is done (for example, retail sales) than *how* it is done (meeting people's needs rather than just making money), insofar as the two can be separated. The ability to identify meaningful purposes in life and to choose between them is a peculiarly human one, perhaps the most important one of all. We think rationality has no higher purpose than this.

Meaningful lives, in the sense suggested above, are very different from lives of mere accumulation, whether of money, pleasure, or experience. If one's purpose in life is to accumulate as much as possible of such things, then the purpose will not help unify that life. The things a person does will be unified in the sense that each is an example of accumulation, but that is like the unity of the contents of a basket that contains variously shaped rocks. It is a unity of similarity rather than of integration. And such unity will not be a narrative but a list: first I got this rock (pleasure, money, experience), then this one, then this one.

Both immediate purposes and life goals are relevant here, in addition to the way they fit together. When evaluating how good a life is, Kahneman tried to ignore people's life goals, but he found it impossible as it seemed clear that a life's purposes affected the amount of happiness that given outcomes produced. The inclination to break life into units that are added up was important for Kahneman because it was crucial for the quantification of happiness — "objective happiness," as he called it. We believe, in contrast, that the *story* of a life reveals more of the worth of that life than the sum of the happiness of its constitutive episodes, and that thinking about oneself and others in terms of these stories is essential for a good understanding and assessment, prospectively and retrospectively, of one's own life and the lives of others. This understanding, in turn, is essential to good decision-making. To the extent that a life should be understood in terms of episodes, the episodes should be defined and evaluated in terms of their relationship to one another and to the overall purpose of a life. In the language that Kahneman used in his own work, we think that more emphasis should be placed on how people feel in *evaluating* their lives and less on how they feel in *living* their lives.

The inclination to see life as a purposive, coherent (though not uni-dimensional) narrative is a common and natural one. Relevant to this suggestion is the recent book by Nobel Prize-winning economist Robert Shiller called *Narrative Economics*. One of Shiller's main points is that attempts to explain the economic past and predict the economic future with highly formalized quantitative models often run aground. This happens in large part because people — the "atoms" of the economy — do not see their economic lives through a formalistic lens. Instead they see them as narratives — as stories — and the stories often fail to line up with the formal models, leading economists to err in predicting the future. For example, as we write this, a very consequential presidential election has just occurred, and one issue that may have been decisive is the effects of post-COVID inflation on people's ability to make ends meet. High inflation turned out to be short-lived, but as inflation came down, prices did not. On the other hand, real incomes went up, so that on average, people were not worse off after inflation came down than they were before it started to rise. Nonetheless, people's narratives about recent economic events included facts like "gas used to be under $3 a gallon, and now it's over $4" and "eggs used to be less than $3 a dozen and now they are more than $5."

Shiller's argument about the importance of narrative suggests to us that seeing one's life as a narrative is quite natural, and that it will often lead to considerations and decisions that the formalism of RCT can't handle. From the perspective of RCT, the results of these narrative lenses may look like decisions that are "errors," but from the perspective of the person inhabiting the narrative, and us, they will not be errors at all. Rather, they are a part of giving meaning to life.

AN ALTERNATIVE TO RATIONAL CHOICE THEORY

Kahneman implied a lack of interest in coherence, unity, and narrative in several places. As we saw, when he offered a method for determining the well-being of a period of life, he broke life into fragments, evaluating the pleasure of each part. And in looking only at the amount of pleasure, and not the source, the kind (healthy or degraded), or the consequences (useful or trivial), he fragmented the fragments themselves. That he did so is not incidental. This fragmentation was essential to quantification. We discussed Kahneman's rejection of a patient's retrospective assessment of the painfulness of a colonoscopy in favor of the sum of momentary estimates. This can be seen as rejecting the understanding of the colonoscopy in narrative terms and insisting on treating it as a series of separate events, an episode of accumulating pleasure (or in this case pain), not an episode of caring for one's long-term health. The retrospective view, which Kahneman criticized, in all likelihood implicitly treats the colonoscopy as part of the ongoing process and meaningful narrative of keeping healthy.

RCT avoids matters of meaning, purpose, and narrative unity by focusing on utility as the common attribute that all good things share. That is perhaps utility's main virtue as a concept. Various things that people value in different ways and for different reasons can all be compared, quantitatively, for the utility they provide. Utility is thus little more than a placeholder for the hope that the values attached to the things we do and have are quantifiable and comparable. We have suggested that the concept of utility is essentially an empty one. It is not that comparison and quantification are impossible. But they are often done at the expense of obliterating extremely important distinctions, like the difference between the value of a human being and the value of a gold bar, the difference between a luxurious vacation and psychotherapy, and the difference between the value of justice and the value of pleasure.

Historically, the concept of utility has its inspiration in pleasure, but in recent times, it has been best represented by money. The appeal of money as a kind of anchor or reference point in assessing utility is especially attractive to RCT because money is quantifiable in a way that almost no other good things are. And money can be exchanged for many other things, and thus it can be used as a measuring stick for the value of those things, making the things we value comparable to each other in the way that RCT requires. It is perhaps for this reason more than any other that the monetary gamble has become the paradigm frame for RCT research.

But "utility" is a fiction. When it is necessary to actually give meaning to the fiction of utility, stand-ins like money are used, but to say that everything has a monetary value (or even a pleasure value) is not to state a fact, even an unproven fact, but to make a very controversial and dubious claim. We have already pointed to the absurdity of acting as if a quantity of money fully captures the value of a lost leg. And to say that the loss of a life is equal to the loss of some specific amount of money is to make the value of a life a transactional matter, as Lawrence Summers did when he calculated the worth of people's lives in terms of their incomes, and Kenneth Feinberg tried to avoid doing in awarding compensation to the families of 9/11 victims.

One of the functions of the bogus concept of utility is to make RCT and related methods applicable to all values. It is part of making the method formal. Our alternative is not universal in that way. We have no interest, for example, in proposing a way to determine which choice of how to exploit other people provides more utility and thus is more rational. As we said earlier, we are interested in helping people choose and achieve worthwhile purposes—in substantive, not "formal," ways. The capacity for the recognition of and desire for worthwhile goals and purposes is a prerequisite for good decision-making.

In short, instead of its "utility," we propose considering the role and value of a decision as a contribution to meaning in life. And this implies three other differences between RCT and our alternative. First, the focus on formal, quantitative thinking must be replaced by judgment. Second, the concept of rationality must be broadened beyond decision and choice to include the understanding and cultivation of aspects of character, what Aristotle called "virtues." Finally, the goal of maximization must be replaced by the goal of moderation—finding the appropriate amount of any factor in our lives. We turn to these issues now.

Good Judgment

RCT is a systematic, almost algorithmic way to make decisions. We propose to replace RCT-type calculation with judgment—to replace counting with thinking. As we have suggested, deciding which are the right colleges to apply to is not a matter of maximizing something, or a decision that can be made by formula: it is a matter of judging what is a good subset of appropriate schools given a potential student's purposes. The same is true of most other significant decisions in life.

Imagine, for example, that having just graduated from college, you are offered six different jobs in your field as a management consultant. The jobs vary in a host of respects: starting salary and benefits, location, size of the firm, opportunities for advancement, attractiveness of colleagues as potential collaborators and friends, and the nature of the work you will be doing itself. Each of these features of the jobs (and no doubt there are others) can itself be decomposed into sub-features. Take location. What is the cost of living in the area? How close is it to family and friends? What about housing and commuting? Restaurants and nightlife? Which job to take is a complex and consequential decision indeed—one that may cast a long shadow into your future.

As we have seen, RCT offers us a way to make such decisions. You might create a spreadsheet. Across the top are columns for each of the features of prospective jobs that matter to you. Below that are columns for the relevant sub-features that matter. For each of these many columns, you need to assign three numbers. First, how important is this feature or sub-feature to you, say on a 10-point scale? Second, how good or valuable is each job you've been offered on each dimension you care about, again on a 10-point scale? And finally, what is the likelihood that each feature you are evaluating will deliver the goods (or bads) that you are expecting? Every decision is a prediction—not only about what will happen, but also about how what happens will make you feel.

It's a lot of work, but it's an important decision. The virtue of using RCT in this way is that it may encourage more rigorous examination of features of various jobs that are important to you. It may also protect you from allowing preconceptions and biases from putting their fingers on the scale. In any case, if you do your due diligence and fill out this spreadsheet, it becomes a simple matter to calculate which is the best job. Push a key on your computer, let Excel do its calculations, and voilà, you know which job to take.

The same sort of analysis could be done to decide which college to attend, which discipline to major in, which career to pursue, whether (and whom) to marry, and whether (and when) to have children. And it could be done for more trivial decisions, like where to go on vacation, what restaurant to eat in, and the like. It is, one might say, a precise and objective way to calculate what is essentially a subjective quantity—how much satisfaction (utility) each option is likely to deliver.

We believe, however, as we have argued, that the precision apparently offered by RCT is an illusion. Virtually every number you enter into the spreadsheet requires a significant amount of judgment. It is, at best, a rough estimate (perhaps an educated one) about how each job is likely to unfold for you, how important each feature of the jobs will be to you, and how much, in what ways, you will change as you work at the job and mature as a person. And the job you take will have effects on the lives of people who matter to you. How much, and in what ways, should that enter into your calculations? There may also be moral dimensions to your work in that it will have effects on clients and customers. Will you be contributing to social welfare or impairing it? And how much should that matter? Finally (well, not really *finally*, since the dimensions of this decision are endless), the job you choose may affect other aspects of your life that you care about. A great job whose demands leak into other important features of your life won't be such a great job.

And this point illustrates what is perhaps the greatest deficiency in the RCT approach to decisions like this. It claims to substitute calculation for judgment. Remember, for each feature of the jobs you are considering, you have to enter a number that represents how good or valuable that feature is. What, exactly, do "good" and "valuable" mean? Location is not valuable in the same way that salary is. Salary is not valuable in the same way that good colleagues are. Good colleagues are not valuable in the same way that work you care about is. Each of these different dimensions of each job likely provides not just a different *amount* of value but a different *kind* of value. If so, how can you sum scores across columns and arrive at a grand total for each job? You can't. RCT provides an abstract term — utility — to capture value. It thus requires you to translate financial, social, moral, and intellectual values that may be reflected in your spreadsheet into the common currency of utility. Does that make sense? We think not.

Creating an RCT-type spreadsheet has its value. It may force you to think more broadly and carefully about many aspects of a decision than you otherwise would. But that virtue is not quantitative. It exists before you enter a single number estimating value or probability into the spreadsheet. The spreadsheet helps you to avoid overlooking something important. But having done that, it is time to substitute judgment and reflection for calculation and thus avoid the false precision that using a spreadsheet encourages.

Aristotle taught us that many, perhaps most, on-the-ground decisions require judgment — what he called practical wisdom. The particulars of a given situation are crucial: context always matters. Context influences how we should balance our obligations to family and friends with our own opportunities. It influences how differently we should treat each of our kids, or our students, each of whom needs different things. The answer to questions we ask ourselves about issues like these is, almost always, "It depends." The right thing to do with one person at one point in time may be a catastrophe with another person at another point in time. In the book *Practical Wisdom*, Barry and Kenneth Sharpe argued that in almost every part of life we care about — work, education, friendship, parenting, politics —

when we face decisions, the right answer is usually "It depends." No formula substitutes for judgment. A formula, or a rule, is like a road map with enough resolution to distinguish various cities and towns, but not enough to distinguish streets. Such a map may get us to the right city, but not the right address in that city. Finding the city provides a frame within which locating the address becomes possible.

Why does the importance of good judgment constitute a criticism of RCT? We believe that to exercise good judgment reliably, one must cultivate understanding, reflectiveness, self-knowledge, and values. So, when RCT leaves all these attributes of rational thinking out, or simply presupposes them, it discourages the cultivation of exactly those qualities of mind that are most essential to good judgment and good decisions.

The kinds of decision problems people are posed in the laboratory, though they come within frames, come within very limited frames. As we have shown by embellishing several examples, by adding context to the situations, one changes the frames and thus also the character and complexity of the decisions we face. By keeping background information skeletal, researchers make decision problems seem more similar to one another than they really are, and more simple than they really are. In consequence, aspects of thinking like meaning, understanding, reflectiveness, and narrative sink to the background, seemingly irrelevant to the problem at hand.

Our proposed alternative to RCT does not take the form of a formal procedure or anything approximating or modeled on one. Our alternative is based on the notion that acts need to be understood as parts of whole lives, and that a given decision, if it is an important one, has to be made largely on the basis of how it fits into a whole life. Decisions are not, and should not be, made in isolation. We believe the best sort of life is (among other things, and all other things being equal) a life of narrative unity and purpose — a life with worthy goals that, to the best of our ability, we articulate as we make progress toward them. It is a life that is appropriately unified (not obsessively limited) by those goals or purposes. We will abbreviate this desideratum as calling for a *meaningful life*.

We think understanding, reflectiveness, and self-knowledge are essential ingredients in a meaningful life. They help us place perspicuous frames around our experiences, which in turn enables us to assess their current and future significance. They help us appreciate the radical uncertainty of many events in the world, which in turn helps us to maintain a flexible and adaptable stance toward the future. They help us, also, appreciate the inherent ambiguity of many experiences, opening us up to the interpretations and decisions of others. And they help us articulate the values we want to live by, and then to assess how the decisions we face may impact those values. In a world in which framing is unneeded or to be avoided, radical uncertainty does not exist, ambiguity can be eliminated, and diverse values can all be reduced to utilities, understanding, reflectiveness, and self-knowledge may not be needed. But that is not the kind of world we live in — or would want to live in.

And a whole life itself has to be evaluated above and beyond the evaluation of the individual decisions that comprise it. As we said in chapter 1, the judgment of the whole life is not a yes-or-no, good-or-bad matter. But having some ideals in mind can facilitate our assessment of our lives in something like the way that geometry helps us understand the physical world. There are no objects in the world that are perfect geometrical shapes. Nonetheless, models from geometry put us in the right ballpark. It's a great start, but it must be reconciled with the empirical facts on the ground. Thus, the process of thinking we envision is one that shuttles back and forth between the ideal and the real—between the simplified formalisms of a discipline like geometry and the bumps and ridges of lived reality. RCT is missing this back-and-forth. It impoverishes decisions by analogizing them to gambles and stops there, rather than re-normalizing them.

We think a similar point can be made about what we called closure—the narrow framing of decisions so that RCT can be used to make them. In general, what is needed is not the sort of maximum closure that quantification requires, but a balance of openness and closure that allows for full reconsideration of any methodological or theoretical decisions that lead to quantification. In other words, it takes judgment to know when and how much to close the decision context, and when and how much to open it back up. We have seen how the deliberation about a choice between two options can and perhaps often should lead to the realization of a hitherto neglected third option. Perhaps the two original options, on examination, are both inadequate, and that discovery "forces" us to open things up and consider new alternatives.

We can easily imagine something similar happening when the whole RCT process is completed. Suppose the process yields a decision for an option that, looked at freshly, seems simply unacceptable. Is it irrational to simply say, "No. There must have been something wrong with the process that led up to the calculation"? This is similar to rejecting a hypothesis when it leads to a false prediction. Is that not rational? A conclusion like this has no explicit role in RCT, but it should have a role in rational decision-making. Rejecting such reasoning is at least partly the effect of the (false) notion that the real work in deciding is in the calculation, not the thinking that surrounds the calculation.

AN ALTERNATIVE TO RATIONAL CHOICE THEORY

A Constellation of Virtues

Having suggested that living a good life is part of what good individual decisions contribute to, we want to point out that a good life depends on more than just good decisions. There are also traits of character that are essential to making good decisions and living a good life. They provide a kind of "moral geometry" that keeps us on track as we navigate our complex and largely unpredictable worlds. We will elucidate some crucial character traits that we think are essential to pursuing and living a good life. The list is meant to be illustrative, not exhaustive.

Self-Respect

Self-respect may help us to distinguish between what philosophers call "higher" (human) and "lower" pleasures and keep us from allowing the lower pleasures to interfere with our pursuit of the higher ones. This challenge is illustrated by the case of addiction, discussed earlier. Self-respect may help people to discount the pleasure they get from tobacco and other addictive substances—treating them as things beneath their dignity. This distinction between "higher" and "lower" is not and could not be included in the scheme offered by RCT. And though people may differ in judging what is to count as higher or lower, the distinction is still important. It still matters.

Courage

Courage is a necessary trait to deal with the obstacles to what needs to be done. One must defend oneself, one's family, one's friends, one's country, and one's ideals. And standing up to challenges to any of these requires the courage to overcome the fear that is likely, at least sometimes, to arise from those duties.

AN ALTERNATIVE TO RATIONAL CHOICE THEORY

Perseverance

Perseverance is necessary to overcome the obstacles to any achievement—to meet a challenge. Maximizing pleasure or utility does not necessarily involve meeting challenges. And maximizing other values may not either. But a life that does not involve confronting challenges is not a very worthwhile life. As in the case of courage and danger, so in the case of perseverance and challenge. Psychologist Angela Duckworth, in her book *Grit,* highlights the importance of perseverance to accomplishment, at least of many of the goals worth striving for.

Fairness

Treating people fairly, understanding what people need and what they deserve, is not a matter of formulas. It is a matter of delicate balance of judgment and one's own desires. There is no formula with which to calculate what I owe to someone who has done me or someone in my family a favor, or to calculate the relative contributions to a joint project, or how much support I should give to a member of my community whose house has burned down. As we argued before, in discussing the work of Alan Fiske, neither what he calls equality matching ("you scratched my back, I'll scratch yours") nor market pricing are fair in the sense of encouraging us to give other people what they need, not just what we owe them.

Self-Control

Self-control is the ability to resist temptation or distraction, to stay on task even when the going gets tough. This trait is not literally in contradiction with "maximizing utility," since self-control is often needed to attain whatever utility-enhancing outcome one is after.

But it is certainly at odds with utility maximizing in spirit. Without self-control, a sense of fairness, and some sense of proportion, there will be no check on greed and self-indulgence. Despite the widespread explicit belief and implicit sense that "greed is good" – that it motivates the system that produces a larger pot for all – we believe that this is a vice that, to a great extent, has lost its opprobrium.

Practical Wisdom

What we previously described as good judgment (as opposed to quantitative formulas) Aristotle identified as practical wisdom (*phronesis*). With all of these virtues we just described, rules and formulas will not suffice to lead to good decisions, except in very limited circumstances. A life of good choices will require the ability to determine what is relevant to concrete, day-to-day decisions, and how all the relevant circumstances should be related to one another to make decisions in specific circumstances. RCT simplifies these problems by assuming that the only relevant facts are first, what it is you desire and how much you desire it, and second, the probability that you will get what you desire. However, in all but the simplest situations, there are much more varied considerations, and they are related in much more complicated ways. It takes practical wisdom to keep the various virtues aligned, and to determine when, how, and how much to deploy them.

We have touched on the problems of substituting quantifiable factors for moral and social considerations, to allow for calculation. We propose to keep such considerations central to decision-making and confront the complexity that moral factors and social relations raise directly, like the inextricable part of life that they actually are. One of the things we think needs to be seriously reflected on, by all of us, is whether such factors are being given sufficient attention in our contemporary lives.

Virtues and the "Mean"

As we have argued, the problems with RCT extend beyond its efforts to quantify probability and value to assess utility. Also problematic is the goal that utility should be maximized. If some of what we value is good, more of it must be better. If one of the virtues we just enumerated is good, more of it must be better. Aristotle thought otherwise:

> Both excessive and defective exercise destroys the strength, and similarly drink or food which is above or below a certain amount destroys the health, while that which is proportionate both produces and increases and preserves it. So, too is it, then, in the case of temperance and courage and the other virtues. For the man who flies from and fears everything and does not stand his ground against anything becomes a coward, and the man who fears nothing at all but goes to meet every danger becomes rash; and similarly the man who indulges in every pleasure and abstains from none becomes self-indulgent, while the man who shuns every pleasure, as boors do, becomes in a way insensible; temperance and courage, then, are destroyed by excess and defect, and preserved by the mean.[1]

We think Aristotle was right and that we should seek the "mean" — the right amount — of all things we value. For Aristotle,

---

1. Aristotle, *Nicomachean Ethics*, 22.

possession of traits of good character — virtues, like those illustrated above — was a *sine qua non* for rationality and for happiness (*eudaimonia*) as he understood it. In recent years, psychology has begun to pay serious attention to virtues. It is at the heart of a powerful book by Blaine Fowers, *Virtue and Psychology*. And it is central to a relatively new area of psychology spearheaded by Martin Seligman called positive psychology.

Examining Seligman's view will help to bring out some of the problems of using formulas in pursuit of maximization to define a good life. Seligman argues that historically, psychology has focused on easing misery — alleviating pain — but paid scant attention to nurturing flourishing. To flourish, people must be able to develop and deploy virtues like the ones we have just discussed. According to the tenets of positive psychology, one can flourish by cultivating some virtues while ignoring others. Identify your strengths, and make them even stronger. But we think the virtues are not fungible in this way. Excessive engagement and/or accomplishment in one part of one's life — say, work — does not make up for the lack of friendship ("relationships" in Seligman's language). Nor can elements of virtue simply be added up to determine how good a life is.

We think this is what Aristotle was getting at. For him, pretty much all the virtues are necessary. And they have to be related and balanced appropriately, in general and in particular cases, if one is to live a good life and make good decisions. Doing so will reflect judgment, not maximization or application of a formula. Virtues constrain and regulate one another. One can be too self-reflective, too empathic, too courageous; or one can display these virtues in inappropriate contexts. These positive character traits must in some circumstances be reined in. Sometimes, admirable character traits can be in conflict. Consider, for example, two traits we did not mention —

honesty and kindness. Each has a vital role to play in maintaining harmonious social relations. Each will be needed some of the time. But they can also point us in different directions. You might ask, after a fractious group discussion, "Should I be honest with my friend about how destructive her outspokenness can be to group solidarity, or should I be kind in this instance?" We need both honesty *and* kindness, but they need to speak to each other—to be coordinated and regulated. What does the coordinating and regulating, from Aristotle's point of view, is practical wisdom. Whether or not he is right about this, it seems clear to us that people need an ensemble of virtues to live good lives. As the philosopher Amélie Rorty observed, "Virtues hunt in packs." Focusing on some virtues and ignoring others can turn life into a closed system analogous to what the gambling paradigm does for RCT. To lead full lives, people need a full complement of virtues. None of us have this complement, of course. We sometimes make decisions that hurt other people and ourselves. We have imperfect self-control, and we misread what some situations require of us. We are not perfect friends, lovers, or parents. We are not perfect teachers or doctors. But it is largely our effort to cultivate this ensemble of virtues that enables us to make better decisions and to live our lives better.

And in order for these character traits actually to be virtues, they must be deployed in moderation. As mentioned earlier, Barry, along with Adam Grant, asked whether Aristotle's claim that there can be too much of a good thing, turning a virtue into a vice, was consistent with the research literature on human flourishing. After reviewing several different areas of research, they concluded that the evidence that there could be too much of a good thing was pervasive. When Aristotle explored what makes for a happy and successful life, he determined that happiness and success are a function of cultivating virtues that lie at the mean between the extremes of deficiency and excess. For example, in the domain of self-presentation, honesty is the mean between the deficiency of self-deprecation and the excess of boastfulness. In the domain of pleasing others, friendliness is the mean between the deficiency of quarrelsomeness and the excess of ingratiation. Grant and Schwartz showed that there is good reason to believe that many character traits are like this. That some character trait is beneficial to living a good life does not mean that more of that trait is even better. Virtually all "positive" traits, states, goods, and experiences have costs that at high levels may begin to outweigh their benefits. Choosing how kind or honest or courageous to be, when to be kind or honest or courageous, and how to be kind or honest or courageous is not a matter of formula or algorithm, but of judgment.

An appreciation that more is not always better leads us to wonder about the goal of maximization. In place of maximization, we offer moderation, as Aristotle, and Grant and Schwartz suggested. And we mean moderation not in a primarily quantitative sense, but in the sense of appropriateness to the relevant context. What is wanted and should be valued is not as much as one can acquire of whatever it is one seeks, but the right amount.

Rationality

It is common to think of the ways of making decisions as being of two kinds, scientific and intuitive. Our contemporary concept of science derives in large part from Descartes, specifically his emphasis on mathematics and his complete rejection of intuition. Many of us are also inclined to think of science as the paradigm of rationality, so we might think that rational decision-making is mathematical in the way that science is and reject any argument of the sort we've been making in this book. That view would lead to the conclusion that our proposed alternative is not rational—that, rather, it is intuitive. Said another way, our alternative may be viewed as more like System 1 than System 2.

We want to insist that the dichotomy between scientific and intuitive ways of making decisions is a false one, and that our alternative, while not scientific, is anything but based on plain intuition. In this, we are partly inspired by philosopher of science Thomas Kuhn. After the massive attention that his *The Structure of Scientific Revolutions* received, people throughout the intellectual world took his argument that science does not proceed in a rule-governed way to mean that what counts as "scientific progress" in general is mostly arbitrary, largely determined by the power and privilege that some people have and others do not. Kuhn, appalled by this conclusion, wrote a paper trying to explain what the public at large seemed to misunderstand. Scientific progress is not rule governed, but it *is* rational. Science practitioners share a set of what Kuhn called "epistemic values," including simplicity, accuracy, fruitfulness, and comprehensiveness. One scientific theory is better than another to the extent that it possesses more of these epistemic values, even though reasonable and knowledgeable people can disagree about how important each of these values is and how well a given theory embodies them. So rational discourse, rather than arbitrariness or the exercise of power, will determine which scientific theory wins the day.

Our alternative involves a similar kind of rational discourse, sometimes with others and sometimes with ourselves. Moreover, we believe that it is more rational than "scientific" decision-making as embodied in RCT. To exemplify this, we are going to contrast deciding intuitively and deciding using our alternative.

AN ALTERNATIVE TO RATIONAL CHOICE THEORY

Consider someone deciding which car to buy. He sees a macho advertisement for a Jeep that makes the Jeep seem very appealing partly, though he doesn't realize it, because the ad is macho. He goes to a Jeep dealer and, faced with a variety of models and colors, picks out one that appeals to him. His is a thoroughly intuitive decision. He could be a little less intuitive and use some common sense to think about features of the car that come readily to mind, like price, fuel consumption, durability, and resale value — the obvious things. He might also compare the Jeep to models of other brands in all those categories, but the comparison would not seek to quantify probability or utility, or be done by formula or algorithm.

Someone using our method would proceed differently. He would want to understand how the car works. He would find out whether it had normal automatic transmission or a continuously variable transmission; was normally aspirated or turbo charged; six, four, or two cylinders; unibody or body-on-frame construction. He would go seriously beyond the obvious considerations. He might ask himself why he is so drawn to the Jeep, examining whether aspects of the advertising that had nothing to do with the car's quality were influencing him. That is, he would examine not just the car, but his own intuitions and prejudices. And because living as sustainably as he can is a major goal of his life, he would seriously consider the effect of the building and operating of the car on the environment and if he should perhaps be considering an electric or hybrid. That is, he would evaluate how the purchase fits with other important goals that he has. Is the Jeep made in a developing country by underpaid laborers? How will his family feel about the vehicle? He cares about his basic values and the effects of his decisions on the feelings of relevant other people.

He would carefully consider whether he is indulging himself in buying a car that is much more expensive than necessary, knowing that he is inclined to self-indulgence. He might wonder whether he has given too much weight to the impression the car will make on others. And finally, he would think carefully about how to balance these considerations against one another, since they may not all be pointing in the same direction.

While different from intuitive decision-making, our method can be viewed as an enhanced form of common sense. Neither is quantitative, though the commonsense considerations seem more narrowly framed — more "closed" — than those of our alternative. Our method starts not by considering scientifically collected "evidence" against the background of a blank slate, but with the opinions we have. However, it does not take them at face value. It examines them carefully and deeply to decide just how much weight they should have, and what has been left out. Nothing in our proposal is at odds with common sense, but our proposal emphasizes and takes seriously the elements of common sense that are frequently neglected or treated somewhat cavalierly. It is a conscious and deliberate version of what we hope is common sense. It demands going beyond the obvious. Insofar as a commonsense decision suggests naïveté or unreflectiveness, our method could not be further from it, let alone from intuition. Practical wisdom is not formal, but it is not "whim," as the term *intuition* suggests to some people. It is seriously cultivated, and it is supported by other virtues such as understanding and self-knowledge, which have themselves been cultivated carefully.

The difference between our proposal and intuition or unreflective common sense, or formalized RCT, can be made even clearer with another example. Let us revisit one more time Mia's decision about where to apply to college.

AN ALTERNATIVE TO RATIONAL CHOICE THEORY

Example: Choosing a College

Mia might begin with intuitions, focusing on schools she has heard about (from fellow students, on social media, and the like), putting together a list rather uncritically. Then, as she considers how to evaluate such schools, she might start with obvious features (cost, location, available majors), but then decide to let the experts tell her what is important to think about, so she buys a college guide. It seems like common sense to buy the guide and trust the experts. If she stops here, rearranging the list of recommended schools a little to take things like cost, location, and chances of admission into account, we might say she is supplementing her intuitions with some common sense. The list she ends up with, let's say, includes NYU, Boston University, Ursinus, and Rutgers.

Now let us envision Mia using the alternative that we outlined in this chapter. Rather than accepting the obvious and stopping there, Mia scrutinizes what she has been hearing from other students and what the "experts" (college guides) are telling her. She asks herself why she is planning to go to college, and whether her reasons for going are like those of her friends. She asks whether the college guides were put together with her kinds of purposes in mind. She asks herself about the strain her college choice might put on her parents, both financially and socially. She considers the potential long-term consequences of her college choice with respect to finances, career opportunities, and relationships with people she feels close to. Finally, she asks herself whether she knows herself well enough to be making such an important decision. She may be wrong about herself, or she may change as her education proceeds. She considers the possibility, given the uncertainty of her future, that maybe she should be looking not for the best college for her but for the college that will be good enough for her in the face of various changes she may undergo. Mia creates no spreadsheet and does no calculations. She reflects on her goals, her opportunities, and her uncertainties to come up with a list. The list she arrives at includes NYU, Boston University, Ursinus, and Rutgers.

Thus, Mia's reflections about both college and herself lead to the same result that intuition and common sense had led to. What, then, is the difference between the two methods if they yield the same result? The answer is everything — everything of importance except the answer to the question "Where did Mia apply to college?" But what else is there? There is why she applied, how she feels about her decisions, and perhaps how she will experience the results of her decisions when she starts college. There is, in the end, the meaning of it all. And if done in the right way, the process will have yielded a deeper knowledge of who she is. And she will have made a better, more thoughtful and reflective decision, even if the simple question "Where did you apply?" is finally answered in the same way. The "betterness" of the decision in the second case is perhaps to a large degree the difference between the way an animal makes a decision and the way a human being makes, or can make, one.

Chapter 10

RATIONAL CHOICE THEORY AND HISTORY

Rational choice theory is a part of a project, shared by psychology and other social sciences, of trying to understand what humans think and do, part of trying to understand human nature more generally. One of the things that humans think about and do is psychology (and other social sciences) itself. It is a social enterprise. It is done in groups. It is done in institutions (universities, professional associations, granting agencies, scientific journals). And it is done in social history — at particular times and in particular places. Aspiring to achieve maximum power and generality of the principles psychology discovers, psychologists often try to separate psychological inquiry from the social and historical context in which it actually goes on. But there are limits to how well we can separate psychology from that context, and in some cases it is important to acknowledge those limits and examine their significance.

More than forty years ago, in collaboration with philosopher Hugh Lacey, we explored those limits in connection with the theory of behavior developed by B. F. Skinner. Skinner's view was that a thorough understanding of human nature, or at least human behavior, could be achieved by understanding the contingencies of reward and punishment that were present in the environment, as well as the dynamic processes by which they changed behavior. This approach, often known as reinforcement theory (RT), was dominant in psychology from the 1940s to the 1970s and continues to have committed adherents today. Skinner's paradigmatic research methods involved studying rats or pigeons in simple environments (which came to be known as "Skinner boxes") in which they could make simple, easily repeated responses to get food. These methods were "paradigmatic" in the sense that Skinnerians believed that they exemplified virtually all of the voluntary behavior of virtually all organisms, including people.

In our discussion of Skinner's approach, we tried to show that the activities RT best applied to were, in important respects, similar to factory work. As discussed in detail below, we traced the development of the factory from Adam Smith's era in the eighteenth century to "scientific management" in the early twentieth, to Skinner. Relying on the work of economic historian Karl Polanyi, we tried to point out various ways in which factory work was anomalous in the history of human economic activity. By modeling a general theory of behavior on a form of historically and culturally specific behavior, RT was mistaking a phenomenon limited in time and place for one that was universal and eternal. Insofar as RT was claiming to have discovered eternal features of human life, it was reifying—that is, treating a dynamic historical human phenomenon as a natural object. Moreover, we suggested, this was not merely a benign instance of overgeneralizing a significant empirical finding. Our worry was that more and more aspects of social and cultural life could be transformed into extensions of the factory (for example, classrooms, athletic fields, hospitals, courtrooms, friendships, and marriages). As that happened, RT would come to look better and better as a general theory of behavior, not because it had discovered broad and powerful principles but because it had transformed society by applying what were once rather narrow and specific principles.

This process of reification is dangerous to the extent that it implies that at a basic level, human behavior always has been and always will be what we see it to be now. This view distorts understanding of the past and limits possibilities for the future. It can also generalize what seems true of the way people act in one kind of context, the economic, to serve as an explanation of their behavior in other, perhaps even all, contexts. How people choose their friends and partners, how they act in politics and social matters, how they engage in the arts, and the like can all be understood in the same terms as their economic behavior.

In what follows, we will elaborate on the history of the workplace, and then suggest that a very similar dynamic may be at play with respect to RCT. As it stands, RCT is a powerful but limited model of what it means to make rational decisions, true of some but not all thinking and rationality. But as its features are valorized, and its influence grows and spreads to aspects of life where it does not belong, it can become the only game in town.

"Human Nature" as a Battle between Metaphors

In Barry's book *Why We Work*, he illustrated the problem of reification with a few stories. On the campus where Richard and Barry once taught, every time a new building is built or an old one is substantially renovated, an issue arises about where to locate the asphalt walkways that go between that building and other campus locations. One school of thought suggests that the placement of walkways should be part of the building plan. But a second school, no doubt having observed many asphalt paths that lie unused near trails of dirt where once there had been grass, has the view that you build the building, watch where people walk, and then put the asphalt where the grass has been worn thin. Proponents of the first view are folks we might call "theory driven." Guided by some sense of efficient movement, aesthetics, or both, they are inclined to do the "ideal" thing and have people conform to it. Proponents of the second view are folks we might call "data driven." They let the users of the space tell them, with their behavior, what the "ideal" thing is.

When done right, almost all inquiry is an ongoing conversation between theory and data. The point of theories is to organize and explain the facts. Facts without organizing theories are close to useless. But theories must ultimately be accountable to, and conform to, the facts. And new facts force us to modify or discard inadequate theories.

That's the ideal. But in real life, things don't always work out this way. At least in the social sciences, proposed theories, rather than being beholden to facts, can shape facts in a way that strengthens the theories. You build that path and then force people to walk on it, perhaps by roping off the grass.

"If you build it, they will come." This is the mantra the main character in the movie *Field of Dreams* keeps hearing as he turns his farmland into a baseball park in the middle of nowhere. He builds it, and they *do* come. In what follows, we will try to show that at least sometimes when social scientists build theories, people *do* come. That is, people are nudged into behaving in ways that support the theories. The discussion to follow, then, is an attempt to resolve a battle between these metaphors. The "watch where they walk, then pave it" metaphor argues that empirical data shape the theories people develop. The "if you build it, they will come" metaphor argues that theories shape data, in part, as Thomas Kuhn famously noted, by telling us what will count as data and how such data should be collected. We will attempt to defend this second metaphor in connection to RCT, and draw out some of its implications for social and cultural life going forward.

Thus far, we have suggested that RCT is heavily theory driven, treating consistency with its norms as "rational" and calling deviation errors. We have also suggested that the empirical methods that have grown out of RCT systematically exclude from consideration most of the activities that people regard as thinking, most of the values that people pursue in their lives, and most of the decisions that people regard as rational. Constrained in these ways by theory and methods that exclude most human activities, RCT presents a model of thinking and deciding that seems exotic at best. In contrast to RCT, inspired by a different theoretical perspective, we have tried to be data driven, presenting many examples of everyday rationality, largely invisible to RCT, that we hope people will recognize. Ours is meant to be a "see where they walk and then build the path" approach to thinking and rationality.

In a sense, the distinction we are making is between discovery and invention. Discoveries tell us things about how the world works. Inventions use those discoveries to create objects or processes that make the world work differently. The discovery of pathogens leads to the invention of antibiotics. The discovery of nuclear energy leads to the invention of bombs, power plants, and medical procedures. The discovery of the genome leads, or will lead, to untold technological changes in almost every part of our lives. Of course, discoveries also change the world, by changing how we understand it and live in it, but they rarely change the world by themselves.

The distinction between discovery and invention is crucial. When a scientist, or anyone else, discovers something, it probably doesn't occur to us to ask whether that discovery *should* exist. In other words, though discoveries often have moral implications, they do not, by themselves, have moral dimensions. If someone were to suggest that the Higgs boson shouldn't exist, we'd wonder what mind-altering substance he'd ingested. Inventions, in contrast, are a whole other story. Inventions characteristically have moral dimensions. We routinely ask whether they should exist. We wonder what's good (life improving) about them, and what the drawbacks are. We debate whether their wide distribution should go forward, and if so, with what kind of regulation. At present, such a debate is raging about the development and use of general artificial intelligence. Should it be developed? Should it be regulated? If so, in what ways?

So, is a theory about human nature a discovery, or is it an invention? We believe that often it is more invention than discovery. Ideas about human nature — about what people care about and what they aspire to — are significantly influenced by the context in which people live. And like fish that don't know they live in water, we live with ideas about human nature that are so pervasive we may not even realize there's another way to look at ourselves. The core ideas of Skinnerian theory were not an invention; they were a discovery. But the use of those ideas to shape the factory, the classroom, and other social settings *was* an invention. And this invention changed how people behaved in these social settings. In effect, social science has created a "technology" of ideas about human nature. Let us explore this technology of ideas with respect to RT, and then turn to a potential similar case going forward in connection to RCT.

The Destruction of Values and the Creation of New Means-Ends Relations

The part of experimental psychology most closely associated with the work of Skinner (see his *Science and Human Behavior, Beyond Freedom and Dignity,* and *Walden Two*) has focused historically on how instrumental, voluntary behavior is controlled by its consequences. This approach has had built into it the presumption that means and ends — responses and rewards — are both conceptually and empirically distinct. The relation between the particular response one requires an organism to make and the rewarding consequence of that response is arbitrary. Whether it is a rat pressing a lever for food in an experiment or a worker pressing slacks for a paycheck in a factory, the relation between these means and ends does not exist until the experimenter (or factory owner) creates it. Various possible means to reward are essentially interchangeable with one another, and they have no value apart from their relation to the rewarding consequences they produce. The reason these kinds of arbitrary response-outcome relations were studied in the laboratory is that they were thought to be paradigmatic of means-ends relations that characterize most human behavior more generally, analogous to how the gamble was taken to be paradigmatic of decision-making more generally. The automobile assembly line worker can perform anywhere on the line for his or her weekly wage. Which particular task is required is presumed, minor considerations aside, to be a matter of indifference to the worker, as long as the compensation is held constant.

It is undeniable that some human activities reflect this kind of means-ends relation. However, the relation need not have this arbitrary form. For some activities, means and ends are interconnected.

To see the point, consider the example of a person who works as an automobile mechanic from nine to five each day, and then goes home to pursue her hobby—restoring old cars to running order. On the job, fixing cars is instrumental. The weekly paycheck is the reward. The mechanic would not be fixing cars were it not for the paycheck, and she would just as soon do some other kind of work for an equivalent or greater paycheck. Thus, the job is a means, and the paycheck is an end, and there is no special relation between the means and the end that could not be duplicated by substituting some other job for her current one.

The situation is quite different when the mechanic gets home. Now, fixing cars is both means and end. While it is true that she does not tinker with cars just for the sake of tinkering—achieving the goal of a good-looking, smooth-functioning automobile is an important influence on her activity—it is also true that she wouldn't be satisfied with any old means of achieving that end. She would not, for example, be satisfied with hiring someone else to restore the old cars for her. The rewarding consequences of the activity are intimately tied to the activity itself, and other kinds of activity are not interchangeable with it in the service of the same reward. Indeed, we might even say that "owning old cars that run well" is not even properly a reward, for it will not support any behavior except for "fixing old cars." Similarly, the activity of "fixing old cars" is not properly instrumental, since it will not be rewarded by anything except "having old cars that run well."

The distinction between this mechanic's job and her hobby should be familiar. Some people have jobs that are like this mechanic's; they are simply means to an end. Other people have jobs that are more like this mechanic's hobby. While the wage is certainly significant, and without it people wouldn't do the job (just as for the hobbyist, having a finished working automobile is crucial, and without it, she would abandon her hobby), it isn't everything. There are aspects of the job itself that make it more than just a means and make people unwilling to substitute other jobs that pay just as well or better. We are characterizing this mechanic's hobby in the way that we think Aristotle might, in discussing the proper *telos*, or goal, of activities.

The importance of the distinction we are making between different kinds of relations between means and ends is this: the connection of people's activities to the ends they produce depends upon how those activities are organized. And the way in which activities are organized is subject to historical and cultural change. Thus, whether and why activities are valuable is a matter not of natural law but of cultural and historical contingency. Does the student work hard to master algebra or to do well on tests and win the class a pizza party? Does the financial advisor work to assure the financial future of clients or to get a hefty year-end bonus? Does the professional athlete stay in shape during the off season so as to be ready for excellent performance in the next one, or is it because there is a half-million-dollar bonus awaiting him if he shows up at training camp below a target weight? This distinction between arbitrary and nonarbitrary means-ends relations is everywhere. But nowhere is this more clearly in evidence than in the history of the workplace.

Centuries ago, what came to be modern industrial society was feudal. Large portions of land were controlled by lords. The majority of the population worked the lord's land as serfs. These serfs had no legal alternative to the work they did. In return for the lord's protection, serfs were required to work his land and to turn over a fixed proportion of their yield to him. They had no choice of the terms they would work under, or of the conditions of their work. They could not hire themselves out to the highest bidder. Nor could the lord sell off his land. The details of the relation between serf and lord were part of a long-standing set of political and social practices that was neither based strictly on economic considerations nor changed strictly on the basis of these considerations. This network of political and social practices is what economic historian Karl Polanyi had in mind when he said, "Man's economy, as a rule, is submerged in his social relationships."[1]

If the factors operative in the choice of work were different in feudal than in modern times, so also was the nature of the work itself. Serfs and other premodern workers engaged in a wide variety of different activities in the course of a day. Their work required flexibility and decision-making. The rhythm and pace of their work changed with the seasons. In addition, the work they did for the lord was integrated into the rest of their daily activities. They didn't leave home for the shop, work from nine to five, then return home to engage in personal pursuits. This pattern of work is in sharp contrast to the modern factory worker, or call-center employee, who does the same thing all day, every day, with little flexibility or decision-making required. Over a period of several hundred years after feudalism ended, the descendants of serfs eventually became wage-laborers. This change coincided with other changes in work that resulted in the emergence of the factory system. By the end of the eighteenth century in England, masses of people were not only working for wages but were free to hire themselves out to the highest bidder. Moreover, with increasing mechanization and division of labor, work became less and less varied and flexible. When the factory system was

---

1. Polanyi, *The Great Transformation*, 46.

fully in place, behavior in the workplace seemed a perfect exemplification of the laws of means-ends relations observed in the reinforcement theorist's laboratory. Indeed, it may have provided the real-life model for what was studied in the laboratory.

Industrialization, as we now know it, did not come all at once. For a time, even when masses of people were working for a wage, the wage they received and the way they did the work were largely determined by social custom, not by the competitive market. As industrialization proceeded, however, wages came completely to dominate the work people chose and the way they performed it. And the reason is that custom, its principal competitor for control, had been systematically and intentionally eliminated. A central component of the final stages of development of the workplace, in its modern form, was a movement explicitly designed to eliminate custom as an influence on behavior. The movement was one of the earliest examples of what is now called "human engineering." It went by the name "scientific management," and its founder and leader was Frederick Winslow Taylor.

Early in the twentieth century, Taylor argued that custom interfered with efficiency and productivity. What industry needed was a set of techniques for controlling the behavior of the worker that was as effective as the techniques used for controlling the operation of machines. Accomplishing this control involved two distinct lines of human engineering. First, one would need to break up customary ways of doing work, substituting for them minutely specialized and routinized tasks that could be accomplished mechanically and automatically. Second, one would need to discover the rates and schedules of pay that resulted in maximal output. The idea was to strip work down to its simplest possible elements: to eliminate the need for judgment and intelligence, and to wrench work free of its customary past. With this done, there would be no possible source of influence on work except for the arrangement of pay—and that was something the boss could control. Thus, work as pure means is a relatively recent human invention, an invention that took all value out of work itself, locating it instead in the wage, the consequence. And it is an invention that was abhorrent to most of the workers subjected to it. As economist Stephen Marglin pointed out, bosses had enormous difficulty harnessing the efforts of their workers. Workers chafed at the confining discipline of the factory. They malingered, they failed to appear, they quit altogether. When employers raised wages to induce workers to show up for work, the workers showed up even less, since they could now earn enough to live on in fewer hours.

Harnessing the worker was difficult, and for the successful boss, it was a singular achievement. But eventually, the problem of inducing workers to put up with the conditions of the factory disappeared. Eventually, what for one generation was the wrenching out of a complex network of customs and social relations was for another "only natural." So it was that scientific managers could see themselves as merely increasing the efficiency of work rather than transforming its very character. And so it might have been that the reinforcement theorist, looking around at this "natural" order of things, could see the principles of the discipline as reflecting an eternal feature of human nature rather than a historical peculiarity.

John Kay and Mervyn King discuss this sort of process in their book *Radical Uncertainty*. They call it "reflexivity," borrowing the term from the distinguished sociologist Robert K. Merton, whose work we will discuss later. Reflexivity refers to the fact that the social system we live in is itself influenced by our ideas about it. And not merely our ideas, but the social and institutional practices these ideas give rise to. The concept of reflexivity is also prominent in the work of philosopher of science Karl Popper, and in the theoretical writings of a student of Popper's, financier George Soros. The central point is that the social systems and institutions within which we live are not static or stationary; they are dynamic. And a significant influence on this dynamic is the ideas we have about ourselves and our social institutions.

We are suggesting here that the historical transformation of the nature of work provides evidence that values in work can be altered dramatically, or even destroyed. Supporting evidence can be found in several lines of experimental research. One such line can be summarized as showing how rewards can have the effect of "turning play into work." People are given the opportunity to engage in a variety of activities that might be regarded as pleasurable: solving various puzzles, for example. These are activities people would happily engage in even in the absence of any reward. The twist in these demonstrations is that even though no reward is necessary to keep people at the activities, they get it anyway, typically in the form of money. And the reward has two effects. First, it gains control of the activity, increasing its frequency, as Skinner would predict. Second, and more significant for our purposes, when reward is later withdrawn, people engage in the activity less than they did before reward was introduced. That is, "play" has been turned into "work."

These experiments illustrate how rewards can alter motivation. Another series of studies, done by Barry, shows how beyond this, rewards can also affect the form behavior takes. Participants sat in front of a matrix of lightbulbs, five across by five down. Beside them were two buttons and a counter to keep track of their score. Periodically, the top left bulb in the matrix lit up, signaling the start of a trial. "This is a game," participants were told. "By pushing the two buttons, you can change the position of the illuminated light in the matrix of lights. If you do it right, you get a point. What I want you to do is to figure out the rules of the game; figure out what you have to do to earn a point."

When participants succeeded in discovering a rule, it was changed, and the procedure started again. They were given no instructions about how one might most effectively tackle the problem. Sometimes the participants were told they would get a few cents for each point they earned in the process of discovering the rule. Sometimes they were told they would get a dollar for each rule they discovered. Sometimes they were able to get a few cents for every point *and* a dollar bonus for every rule. Finally, sometimes no monetary rewards were offered at all.

When participants played the game, these varying conditions of reward made no difference. In almost all cases, they varied their responses from trial to trial with great efficiency. They behaved much as an experimental scientist might, varying what they did – their "experiment" – from one trial to the next in an effort to discover the rules. Almost every one of them discovered each of the rules, and they did so quite rapidly. The reward contingencies failed to have any impact.

But there is more to the story. Another group of participants was exposed to the same set of problems with the same contingencies of reward as the first set. What distinguished the two groups was that this second group had had prior experience playing the game. The prior experience was this: they were brought into the laboratory, shown the game, and told that every point they scored would earn them 2 cents. They were then given one thousand opportunities (trials) to play the game. Each participant settled on a particular sequence of responses that occurred in about 90% of all trials. The little game and the payoffs had turned the participants into assembly-line workers, engaged in the same task, done the same way, over and over again, completely controlled by the reward.

What happened, then, when these newly formed factory workers were instructed to discover the rules? Compared to the first, inexperienced group, they were much less effective. They discovered fewer of the rules and took longer to discover those they did when they were successful. And unlike the first group, what they did was powerfully influenced by the prevailing contingency of monetary reward. They were especially ineffective at discovering rules if each point they got earned them money.

This experiment can be thought of as a simulation of the historical process suggested above. Exposure to means-ends contingencies of reward creates an efficient, stereotyped pattern of behavior that can be executed with effortless and mechanical precision, just like work on the assembly line. The contingency makes it possible for people to do the right thing, over and over again. Lapses of attention have no cost, because attention is not required. Lack of intelligence has no cost, because intelligence is not required. That this automatization is achieved at the expense of another potential influence on the nature of the activity becomes apparent when these participants are later asked to discover rules. Participants without pre-training know what rule discovery means. As students, they have been engaging in a tradition of rule discovery or problem solving for years, and it is a relatively simple matter to plug this new challenge into the wisdom they have acquired from previous experience. The pre-trained participants are a part of this same tradition. But they have been induced, by their pre-training, to place this particular task outside it.

The debilitating effect of this pre-training is modest. But one can imagine that if the participants were required to engage in this task for eight or more hours a day, day after day, week after week, year after year, the effect might be considerably more dramatic. And if everyone around them was engaged in a similarly repetitive activity, the effect might be more dramatic still. For instead of participants simply failing to locate this task in the problem-solving tradition, that tradition might erode and disappear altogether. Adam Smith captured this possibility most forcefully. He had this concern about the side effects of factory work: "The man whose life is spent in performing a few simple operations . . . has no occasion to exert his understanding, or to exercise his invention in finding out expedients for difficulties which never occur. He naturally loses, therefore, the habit of such exertion and generally becomes as stupid and ignorant as it is possible for a human creature to become."[2] Exactly so.

Practices and Their Contamination

The research just described is merely an example of how activities that are valuable in themselves, or intimately tied to specific ends, can be transformed into activities that are simply means to ends that could be attained in other ways. To appreciate better the general character and significance of the transformation reflected in this research, we need a clearer idea of what it means for a domain of activity to be valuable and tied to specific ends. What is it that participants strive for when they engage in activities that are not purely instrumental? This question has been illuminated by philosopher Alasdair MacIntyre in his attempt to reconstruct a moral philosophy. Central to

---

2. Smith, *The Wealth of Nations*, 734–35.

that attempt is the concept of a *practice*. Practices are certain forms of complex and coherent, socially based, cooperative human activities. Among their characteristics are these:

1. They establish their own standards of excellence, and indeed are partly defined by those standards.
2. They are teleological, that is, goal directed. Each practice establishes a set of "goods" or ends that are internal or specific to it, and inextricably connected to engaging in the practice itself. In other words, to engage in the practice is to pursue these internal goods.
3. They are organic. In the course of engaging in a practice, people change it, systematically extending both their own powers to achieve its goods and their conception of what its goods are.

Thus, practices are established and developing social traditions, traditions that are kept on course by a conception of their purpose that is shared by the practitioners. And most important, the goals or purposes of the practices are specific or peculiar to them. There is no common denominator of what is good, what is valuable, like utility maximization, by which all practices can be assessed. We can illustrate the concept of a practice and its significance by considering an example in some detail. The collection of activities referred to as "science" is a practice. Sciences are certainly complex, social activities. They establish their own standards of excellence. They have a set of "goods," the pursuit of which partly defines them. And they develop. The goal of science is to discover generalizations that describe and explain the phenomena of nature. Different scientific disciplines develop traditions that provide guidance as to which generalizations are worth going after, which methods are best suited for going after them, and which standards should be used for determining whether one has succeeded. Now, not all people who do what looks like scientific work are engaged in the practice of science. People who do experiments to achieve impressive publication records are not engaged in the practice. The goods they seek—status, promotion, financial success, fame—are not internal to science. Science is just one means to those goods among many. It is certainly true that people who are pursuing such external goods may do good science—that is, they may contribute to the development of the practice. But they are not themselves practitioners. And if everyone engaged in science were to start pursuing these external goods, the practice of science would cease to exist as we know it. The core of the practice of science—the thread that keeps it going as a coherent and developing activity—lies in the actions of those whose goals are internal to the practice.

And these internal goals are not commensurable with other kinds of goals. The scientist does not choose from among a variety of market baskets, each containing some amount of truth and some amount of status and money, the one that maximizes her or his preferences. One does not bargain away portions of truth for portions of something else, at least not if one is working within the practice of science. But in the experiments with the light matrix just described, some of the participants did precisely this. They bargained away truth—or, more accurately, the best techniques for discovering truth—in return for money. For participants who were pre-trained to perform a particular task for monetary reward, the problem-solving task was not "pure" science. It was an amalgam of truth seeking and money seeking, of doing what will yield a general principle and doing what works. These participants struck a compromise between two competing masters when they faced the problem-solving task. Their compromise was not necessarily deliberate, but it was there nonetheless. They forsook the traditional methods of doing good science that their untrained colleagues followed, so that they could earn more money.

One doesn't need a laboratory demonstration to see this compromise between scientific and more material objectives. Material considerations have been affecting the behavior of real scientists, doing real science, for years, and continue increasingly to do so. It is not good science to do the same experiment again and again — to repeat what works. Yet with research success, promotion, and the granting of tenure largely determined by rate of publication, many scientists effectively do so. Each experiment is a minor variant on the preceding one, because such mechanical and unimaginative variation is the quickest road to print. It is not good science to decide what to study on the basis of what people are willing to pay for. Yet government agencies are able to manipulate fields of inquiry by shifting funding from one domain to another. It is not good science to keep one's results a secret, keeping others in the dark, or even intentionally misleading them. Yet in areas that are hot, scientists often do this as a way of protecting claims to priority, even at the cost of scientific progress. Above all, it is not good science to lie — to misrepresent results willfully, or to invent results of experiments that were never conducted. But such misrepresentations litter the history of most sciences, and they seem to have increased in frequency in recent years. This last perversion of science, presumably in the interest of self-aggrandizement, is especially crippling. Science must proceed on the presumption that its practitioners always tell the truth, even if they aren't always successful at finding it. Were this presumption seriously undermined, science would grind to a halt. All experiments would have to be repeated by all interested parties to make sure of the veracity of published reports.

Economic Imperialism and the Destruction of Value

The distinction between internal and external goods and the concept of a practice more generally are illuminated by the notion of "economic imperialism." Economic imperialism is the spread of economic calculations to domains that were once regarded as noneconomic. It is the infusion of a practice with the pursuit of external goods. This pursuit pushes a practice in directions it would not otherwise take, and in so doing undercuts the traditions that comprise it. Economic imperialism evaluates practices by a common, material denominator, abandoning the ones that fall short and encouraging the ones that do not, without regard to the internal goods that each practice possesses uniquely. And whenever internal and external goods conflict, economic imperialism moves in the direction of maximizing the latter, sometimes at the cost of eliminating the former. This is arguably what happened in the factory, as indicated above. It may also be reflected, as pointed out by management scientist Jeffrey Pfeffer in his book *The Human Equation*, in the growing rate at which the CEOs of large companies are drawn from the area of finance rather than from the areas of design or production, presumably in the belief that the goal of these companies is to maximize profits and stock prices, which people from finance are best equipped to manage.

For MacIntyre, the concept of a practice has a central place in a theory of what it is to be a good person. Good people possess just

RATIONAL CHOICE THEORY AND HISTORY

those characteristics, or virtues, that permit them to engage successfully in practices. The list of these virtues, some of which we discussed briefly in the last chapter, is fairly traditional—justice, honesty, courage, wisdom, respect, determination, and so on. And the continued existence and development of practices depends upon the continued existence of people who possess these virtues. Thus, our judgment of moral worth is bound up with our judgment of the set of practices to which that worth contributes. What, then, happens to moral worth if the practices disappear, if economic imperialism transforms them into simply means to external goods? If that happens, there is only one practice—the practice of utility maximization. And the good person will be the good utility maximizer. Virtuous moral people will be indistinguishable from rational economic agents. By penetrating and transforming the set of practices that comprise human social life, economic imperialism will have created the conditions under which its conception of human nature is true.

There are many aspects of modern life that once were largely independent of material considerations but are now increasingly pervaded by them. One example is education. With increasing competition among members of society for good jobs, employers keep erecting new hurdles that must be jumped before job entry is possible. First high school degrees were required, then college degrees, then special training programs, then master's degrees, then doctoral degrees, then doctoral degrees at only a handful of select, prestigious institutions. These hurdles have a profound effect on the way people view education. With education so closely tied to job entry and job training, it becomes an "investment" in one's future. The money spent on school is expected to be returned—in kind and with interest—later on. One can put a dollar value on a college degree by surveying the wages paid for the jobs to which it gives access. It is easy to see how thinking of education as an economic investment can affect what people want out of education, and thus how they evaluate what they get. We saw some of this in our discussion of Mia's efforts to determine where to apply to college.

If enough people assessed their education in these terms, what actually went on in the college classroom would surely change — as indeed it has. Colleges and universities would have to be sensitive to market demand; they would have to provide what students wanted, or the students would go elsewhere. The goal of education would shift from creating well-informed, sensitive, and enlightened citizens to creating skilled workers. To the claim that one can't put a dollar value on having an educated citizenry comes the reply, of course one can. One simply looks at how much extra salary the education makes possible. Extra salary becomes the yardstick for evaluating the effectiveness of an educational institution. Before long, the institution changes what it does, so that the creation of extra salary potential becomes the goal itself, instead of just a measuring stick. And it should be said, parenthetically, that colleges and universities have not been innocent victims in this transformation. As the costs of higher education head toward the stratosphere, it seems increasingly sensible for people to be asking whether the cost of such education is "worth it."

Another example of economic imperialism is that our everyday social relations — as friends, neighbors, spouses, and parents — are taking on an economic component. In part this comes from the fact that consumption takes time. If one has money only for the essentials of life, finding the time in which to consume them is not an issue. But if there is money for dinners in nice restaurants, the theater, and vacations, one must find the time to decide which restaurant, play, or resort to partake of. In addition, one must find the time actually to partake of it. The pressure for time to consume has real costs. It produces what economist Fred Hirsch calls "the economics of bad neighbors." Time spent being sociable is time taken away from consumption. Whether we like it or not, the decision to be sociable becomes an economic decision, another example of the spread of economic considerations to traditionally noneconomic domains. Many people have experienced how much harder it has become to find the time to spend a quiet evening sipping beer and chatting with a few friends. It is becoming increasingly rare for such occasions to develop spontaneously; they must be planned days, or even weeks, in advance. And of course, it seems ludicrous to "plan" an evening of casual conversation. So instead it becomes a dinner party. This in turn only adds to the time pressure, since now food must be purchased, and an impressive meal must be prepared.

In the economic world, people get what they pay for. Certainly, they get nothing more, and vigilance is required to see that they don't get less. So presumably, when social "goods" become economic, people start getting only what they pay for in social relations as well as economic ones. In the economic world, people are prepared to operate on this assumption. Products come with explicit guarantees, services are provided in accordance with detailed and specific contracts. People enter into exchanges with their eyes open, expecting, and guarding against, the worst. They are not so prepared in the social world. People assume that friends, lovers, families, doctors, and teachers will act with good will, doing, insofar as is possible, what is best for them. As a result, they ask no guarantees and write no contracts. People trust that part of what it means to be a spouse, lover, parent, doctor, or teacher ensures that people close to them will behave honorably, truthfully, courageously, and dutifully in social interactions.

As social relations become commercialized, however, this assumption grows more and more suspect. Increasingly, people feel the need to have things written down in contracts. Increasingly, they feel the need to be able to hold others legally accountable – whether doctors, lawyers, teachers, or even friends or lovers – to assure that they are getting what they pay for out of their social relations. To appeal to the distinctions among modes of social life developed by Alan Fiske, discussed earlier, it is as if all social relations become governed by the norms of market pricing. One might argue that this shift from a dependency on what is implicit in various social relations to what is explicit and contractual is merely a recognition of cold, hard reality. But what the person who makes this argument fails to realize is that the process of commercializing social relations affects the product. By treating the services of doctors and teachers as commodities being offered to the wary consumer, we change the way doctors doctor and teachers teach. Doctors practice defensively, doing not what they regard as the best medicine but what they regard as the best hedge against malpractice suits. Medical costs soar, but medical care does not improve. Teachers teach defensively, making sure their students will perform well on whatever tests will be used to evaluate their progress, at the expense of genuine education. Test scores go up, but students are no wiser than before.

There is, in short, a self-fulfilling character to the commercialization of social relations. The more we treat such relations as economic goods, to be purchased with care, the more they become economic goods about which we must be careful. The more that an assumption of self-interest on the part of others governs social relations, the truer that assumption becomes. Probably not even the most committed economist or RCT theorist is sanguine about this vision of the world. If it is true that moral traditions depend on practices, and practices can be corrupted by the pursuit of external goods, and the pursuit of external goods is encouraged by economic imperialism, then all we have to do is be vigilant and keep economic considerations from penetrating all our practices. By keeping practices relatively pure, we can preserve a proper place for morality in a highly industrialized, productive, and affluent culture. But choosing to keep practices pure, to maintain a distinction between economic and noneconomic goods, is not a decision that can effectively be made individually. If few others make that choice, and instead enter practices with instrumental orientations, the practices themselves will change so that the pursuit of previously internal goods will no longer be possible. The logic of "if we build it, they will come" will triumph.

Chapter 11

RATIONAL CHOICE THEORY AND IDEOLOGY

The previous discussion of the evolution of work and the spread of economic ideas to parts of life that were once not thought of as "economic" illustrates the process that Barry has called "idea technology" in his book *Why We Work*. What is "idea technology"? We live in a culture and an age in which the influence of scientific technology is obvious and overwhelming. Whether it's laptops, smart phones, and tablets, or MRI scans, gene modifications, and designer drugs, adjusting to technology is a brute and insistent fact of daily life. The technology of smart phones and MRIs — the technology of things — is what most of us think of when we consider the modern impact of science. But in addition to creating things, science creates concepts, ways of understanding the world and our place in it, that have an enormous effect on how we think and act. If we understand birth defects as acts of God, we pray. If we understand them as acts of chance, we grit our teeth and roll the dice. If we understand them as the product of prenatal neglect, we take better care of pregnant women.

RATIONAL CHOICE THEORY AND IDEOLOGY

It hardly needs to be said that people are profoundly affected by the material conditions of their lives. The availability of necessities like food and shelter and the means by which individuals may obtain them makes all other influences on life seem insignificant. And yet it is clear, as we argued in the last chapter, that ideas also matter, and they matter a lot, even in the case of obvious material conditions like how we earn our livelihoods.

If we understand the concept of "technology" broadly, as the use of human intelligence to create objects or processes that change the conditions of daily life, then it seems clear that ideas are no less products of technology than computers are. However, there are two things about idea technology that make it different from most "thing technology." First, because ideas are not objects that can be seen, purchased, and touched, they can suffuse through the culture and have profound effects on people before they are even noticed. Second, ideas, unlike things, can have profound effects on people *even if the ideas are untrue.* Smart phones, designer drugs, and the like generally don't affect people's lives unless they do what they were designed to do. Companies can't sell technological objects that fail — at least not for very long. Technological objects may do bad things that people don't want them to do, but at least there is little reason to worry about them unless they can also do the things they were designed to do in the first place. In contrast, false ideas can affect how people act, just as long as people believe them. Following philosopher Karl Marx, let's call instances of idea technology based on untrue ideas "ideology."

You might think that the methods of science protect against ideology. The hallmark of science is that it operates in the world of testable hypotheses. That is, if you have an idea, you test it, and if it fails the test, it disappears, just as failed thing technology does. If so, there's no need to worry about a technology of false ideas. False ideas will simply die of "natural causes." Right?

Alas, not necessarily, as our discussion of the evolution of work and of practices and their contamination was meant to illustrate. Ideology bears a large measure of the responsibility for the nature of our work. As we pointed out in the last chapter, Adam Smith says of the man who works on the assembly lines that "he naturally loses, therefore, the habit of such exertion and generally becomes as stupid and ignorant as it is possible for a human creature to be." The key things to notice about this statement are the words *loses* and *becomes*: Smith is saying that work in a factory will cause people to "lose" something and "become" something. So, what is it that they *had* before entering the factory that they *lost?* And what is it that they *were* before entering the factory that was different from what they *became?* Right here in this quote we see evidence that Smith believed that what people were like as workers depended on the conditions of their work. And yet, over the years, this nuanced understanding of human nature as the product of the human environment got lost. As a result of this lost subtlety, the creation of soulless, dehumanizing workplaces needed no justification except for productive effectiveness. It wasn't changing people. It wasn't depriving people of anything. It was simply taking people as they were and using their labor with maximum efficiency.

We now know that it *was* changing people, as our discussion of the development of factory work was meant to exemplify. Much more recently, Sanford DeVoe and Jeffrey Pfeffer have shown that even the way in which people are compensated changes them. Professionals who bill by the hour, like lawyers and consultants, start putting a price on their time, even when they aren't at work. An evening spent with friends watching a ball game has "costs" in legal fees and consulting fees that are forgone. So, a person who bills by the hour becomes a different person than she was before she started working in that way.

How does ideology happen? In the scientific, big-data age in which we live, good data ought to eventually drive out bad ideas. Well, sometimes it does. Psychologists have made much progress over the years in understanding perception, memory, thinking, language use and comprehension, cognitive and social development, learning, and various types of emotional and cognitive disorders in exactly the same way that natural sciences make progress in their domains. Good data drive out bad theories. But there's a crucial difference between theories about planets, atoms, genes, and diseases and theories about at least some aspects of human nature. Planets don't care what scientists say about their behavior. They move around the sun with complete indifference to how physicists and astronomers theorize about them. Genes are also indifferent to our theories about them. But this is not true of people. Theories about human nature can actually produce changes in how people behave. A theory that is false can *become* true simply by people believing it's true. The result is that, instead of good data driving out bad data and theories, bad data change social practices until the data become good data, and the theories are validated. This is what our discussion of the evolution of factory work was meant to illustrate.

There are at least three basic mechanisms by which ideology can become true. The first is by changing how people think about their own actions. For example, someone who volunteered every week in a homeless shelter might one day read a book that tells him it is human nature to be selfish. He might then say to himself, "I thought I was acting altruistically. Now social scientists are telling me that I work in a homeless shelter for ego gratification." Or someone on her way to work might say, "I thought I showed up for work every day eager to be challenged and do a good job that improves someone's life. Now social scientists are telling me it's all about the money." If this kind of reconstrual mechanism is in operation, nothing outside the person necessarily changes; she simply understands her actions differently. And of course, how we understand our past actions is likely to affect how we act in the future.

The second mechanism by which ideology becomes true is via what is called the "self-fulfilling prophesy." Here, ideology changes how other people respond to the actor, which in turn changes what the actor does in the future. A classic demonstration of this self-fulfilling mechanism in action was reported by Mark Snyder and Elizabeth Tanke. In this study, groups of men were shown a photo of either an attractive or an unattractive woman. They then had a ten-minute phone interview with a woman they were led to believe was the woman in the photo (she was not). After the interview, those who thought they were talking to the attractive woman rated her as more likeable than those who thought they were talking to the unattractive woman. No surprise here perhaps. The surprise came next. Audiotapes of the interviews were played for other participants who had not seen photographs of the woman or been told anything about her attractiveness. They, too, judged the "attractive" woman as more likeable, friendly, and sociable than the unattractive one.

Think about this result. Somehow, thinking their interview partner was attractive led participants to conduct their interviews in a way that led third parties who listened to the interview to come to the same conclusion. In effect, the interviewers collected "data" in a way that was biased by their initial beliefs.

The phrase "self-fulfilling prophecy" was coined by sociologist

Robert Merton in 1948. He discussed examples of how theories that initially do not describe the world accurately can become descriptive if they are acted upon. In essence, a self-fulfilling prophesy is an initially *false* conception of the situation that evokes a new behavior, making the originally false conception come *true*.

The parallel of this kind of process in the workplace is clear. You start out believing that people are basically lazy, don't want to work, and care only about their pay when they do. Based on this belief, you create a workplace that is focused only on efficiency, with jobs that are mindlessly repetitive, counting on the paycheck to motivate your workers. Lo and behold, in an environment like that, all that matters to workers is their pay.

Another notable example of this process is the teacher who pays more attention and works harder with children identified as "smart" than those identified as "slow," thereby making the "smart" ones smarter. Being labeled as "smart" or "slow" does not in itself make kids smarter or slower; it is the teacher's behavior that makes the difference. Perhaps the best-known demonstration of the self-fulfilling prophesy in education is shown in the research conducted by Robert Rosenthal and Lenore Jacobson on the effects of teacher expectations on student performance. Unbeknownst to the teachers in the study, the researchers randomly assigned certain students in elementary school classrooms the designation "spurter." These students supposedly had taken a diagnostic test at the end of the preceding school year that identified them as having the potential for impressive academic gains. No such test actually existed. Nonetheless, the students who'd been labeled as "spurters" *did* manifest more impressive gains than average by the end of the school year. High expectations from the teacher somehow resulted in high student achievement. In short, Rosenthal and Jacobson argued, the labeling of certain students as promising became a self-fulfilling prophecy by changing the way teachers taught. This finding has been highly influential in the fields of both psychology and education.

Some years later, Lee Jussim and colleagues followed up on this line of inquiry by assessing specific ways in which teacher expectations affect student performance and the specific contexts in which such expectations have the most marked effects. Though they found evidence supporting the self-fulfilling prophecy framework laid out by Rosenthal and Jacobson, they also identified bounds to the pervasiveness and power of the self-fulfilling prophecy. Such prophecies are not all-pervading, and the magnitude of the effects, though significant, is often modest.

It is perhaps not surprising that these effects are not large. After all, kids may get one subtle message about their ability in school but quite a different one at home from their doting—or denigrating—parents. But if the message were delivered more consistently, across all the domains of a child's experience, then the effects might be very large indeed.

To some degree, the effects of ideology on how people act will depend on how broadly, how pervasively, and how saliently it is disseminated in a culture. When it lives in isolated places, its effects will likely be small and correctable. But when it's in the water supply—when it is everywhere—its effects will likely be much more profound.

This brings us to the final mechanism—the one that we believe has the most significant effects. This is when institutional structures are changed in a way that is consistent with the ideology. The industrialist, believing that workers are motivated to work only by wages, then constructs an assembly line that reduces work to such meaningless bits that there is no reason to work aside from the wages. The politician believes that self-interest motivates all behavior, that people are entitled to keep the spoils of their labor, and that people deserve what they get and get what they deserve. Therefore said politician helps enact policies that erode or destroy the social safety net. As a result, people start acting exclusively as self-interested individuals. "If it's up to me to put a roof over our heads, put food on the table, and make sure there's money to pay the doctor and the kids' college tuition bills, then I'd better make sure I take care of myself and mine." When social structures are shaped by ideology, ideology can change the world.

The concept of ideology, and the self-fulfilling feedback loops that ideology can give rise to, helps explain why it is that most human workplaces have come to be dominated by excessive reliance on close supervision, routinized work, and incentives. If you think that people lack the skill for wise judgment on the job, you impose detailed rules of conduct. As a consequence, people never get the opportunity to develop wise judgment. Your lack of faith in the skills of the people you oversee is vindicated, leading you to impose still more rules and still greater oversight. And if you think that people lack the will to do their work in pursuit of the right aims, you create incentives that enable people to do well by doing good. In so doing, you undermine whatever motivation people might have to do the right thing *because* it is the right thing. Once again, your lack of confidence is vindicated. Instead of putting in place procedures that nurture people's desire to do meaningful work, the manager, convinced that such attributes are a very slender reed on which to build and run an organization, puts practices in place that undermine this desire. Before long, meaningful work disappears — from the factory, from the call center, from the classroom, from the courtroom, and from the examination room.

Within broad limits, we are what society expects us to be. If society asks little from us, it gets little. It is clear that, under these circumstances, we must be sure that we have arranged rules and incentives such that they induce people to act in ways that serve the objectives of the rule makers and the incentive setters. If society asks more of us, and arranges its social institutions appropriately, it will get more. As anthropologist Clifford Geertz observed, human beings are "unfinished animals." What we can reasonably expect of people depends on how our social institutions "finish" them.

Let us apply our arguments about ideology to RCT. The word *rational* is used to describe not only decisions and the processes that lead to them, but also people. And it is an honorific; people *want* to be rational and are celebrated for their rationality. But where and how do people learn what "rational" means? In our characterization of RCT, we have identified several attributes that may serve us well in limited circumstances but are potentially disastrous if meant to capture all that rationality means. It assumes that people have, or should have, well-articulated values that exist largely independent of context. These values, no matter how disparate, can be compared — even quantitatively. It assumes that the probabilities of possible outcomes can be specified with precision. Given the precise nature of both value and probability, it regards decisions themselves, if made rationally, as the output of a largely mechanical process. A rational person enters values and probabilities of options into a mental spreadsheet, and then just does the math. RCT treats decisions as isolated in time, so that individual decisions can be assessed for rationality, and the rationality of a person is just the sum of the rationality of that person's individual decisions. It regards phenomena like framing and mental accounting as errors — as significant departures from rationality that we should endeavor to correct.

We have argued that a view like this of rationality fails to capture most of what we typically mean by rationality. It ignores our long-term aspirations to be good people and live good lives, whether pleasant or not. It ignores the reasons we have for making the decisions we make. It ignores the life narrative in which individual decisions are embedded. It ignores how different frames give decisions different meaning, and that the meaning of what we choose and do can be at least as important as the concrete result of a decision. It ignores our belief that not all values can be compared to one another. It ignores the fact that because of the complexity and often incommensurability of values, it usually requires wise judgment, and not a mechanical procedure, to make rational decisions.

Shane Frederick, a leading decision-making researcher, has argued that RCT is a tool like an ice cream scoop, and we shouldn't expect it to open cans, sweep floors, or do our taxes. But rationality is not an ice cream scoop. It is more like a Swiss Army knife. It takes many different forms and serves many different functions. It is chameleon-like in its ability to take on different appearances in different contexts. This analogy, like all analogies, is imperfect, of course, since the components of a Swiss Army knife do not interact; each component has a specific function. In contrast, the different facets of rationality, as we described them in chapter 9, will interact most of the time. A person who ignores the multifaceted nature of rationality and slavishly follows the dictates of RCT, wedging every decision situation into the framework that RCT creates, will be, as Nobel economist Amartya Sen says, a "rational fool," if not a moral monster.

You might believe that rational people learn when to follow the dictates of RCT and when not to. A rational person uses RCT only when it is appropriate and relies on other manifestations of rationality when a situation calls for them. In other words, the applicability of RCT ought to be self-limiting. But we have tried to suggest that it is a mistake to be so sanguine that people will discover both the usefulness and the limits of RCT in the course of their empirical experience in the world. Just as the means-ends understanding of work has come historically to pervade our modern understanding of work and shaped our institutions so that that understanding is the only game in town for most of us, RCT may come to be regarded as the only "rational" way to make decisions. Government agencies may (some already have) come to regard RCT as the only rational way to make public policy. Schools may come to regard (many already have) RCT as the only rational way to make decisions about resource allocation and pedagogical practice. And individuals may be taught that if they aspire to be rational, they must commit themselves to framing their decisions as RCT problems. Such an influence on individual decisions, on public policies, and on social norms will make it increasingly hard for people to imagine another way to think about themselves, their lives, their social relations, and their world. And ideology will have triumphed again. It is largely with an eye on this sort of transformation of how we decide and even of who we are that we came to characterize RTC as dangerous in chapter 8.

Though they are quite different in detail, RCT is similar to RT in crucial respects. Like RT, it is applied most effectively to certain aspects of behavior, specifically consumer behavior, commercial behavior, and financial behavior, especially when these behaviors can be modeled on gambling behavior. Again, like RT, it generalizes its model to apply to all behavior in all situations. It also assumes that it applies to all historical periods since the emergence of "rational man," prior to ancient Greece, thus reifying the concepts it articulates. It is also a kind of intellectual technology, one that tends to increase the kind of behavior it describes, which makes it less vulnerable to empirical refutation. Finally, like RT, it has seriously undesirable consequences. And even more than RT, RCT pushes people to adopt its practices. After all, as we said, the word *rational* in RCT is an honorific, implying that failure to use RCT is a failure to be rational.

In the nineteenth century, the focus of economic life was industry and production. The growth of mass production, innovative manufacturing techniques, and transportation were characteristic features of that century. During the twentieth century, consumption and finance dramatically increased in significance for the economy. After World War II, we experienced another jump in consumerism and another jump in the significance of finance, with ordinary people rather than just financiers and speculators investing in the stock market.

Choice under uncertainty plays a bigger role in consumerism and investment than it does in manufacturing, where technology and organization of business play a bigger role. "Should I buy this product?" "Should I buy this brand or that?" "Should I invest in stocks or bonds, and which ones?" were the kind of questions that began to loom much larger than they had in the nineteenth century. So it should not surprise us that RCT, which is most at home in connection with these sorts of questions, should get much more attention.

And why is RCT so comfortable with these questions? Starting with finance, it is obvious that investment decisions will be made best if they are made rationally rather than emotionally. And such investments, perhaps in the stock market, are relatively free of the kinds of subtleties that characterize decisions about, say, where to go to college or friendship or social life generally. Success can easily be measured because it normally comes down to increases in wealth.

Consumption has some of the same advantages with regard to the application of RCT. Price is easily measured, and in many cases so is value. "Should I buy one pound of apples for $1 a pound or five pounds at 75 cents a pound?" The parameters are easily defined in cases like this. Choosing between brands is less clear cut, since differences in character and quality complicate the measurement of outcomes, but RCT still seems an appropriate tool, more so than for the decision about having another child. And in addition to consumption and finance, societal change itself, which was accelerating, forced choice into the forefront as issues that had previously been constrained by technological limits or tradition became matters of individual decision. As domains for individual decision proliferated, the appeal of RCT as the tool for making such decisions grew.

One significant sign of the growth in importance of RCT and similar systems for rational decision-making is the explosive growth of the business consulting industry in the last seventy-five years or so. Outside consultants, who may know next to nothing about your business and its subtleties, are brought in to provide fresh eyes, bringing with them a powerful set of analytical, formal tools. The power of these tools may enable them to discover ways you can change your standard operating procedures to make your enterprise more efficient and more profitable. Having solved your problems in this way, by "rationalizing" your operations, they pack up their computers and move on to another enterprise about which they might know little but to which the same tools can be applied.

While there is no doubt that having fresh eyes examine a problem may be helpful, it would probably have seemed bizarre a century ago to imagine that these fresh eyes could be almost completely ignorant as to what you do. One of the features that makes RCT and other, similar formal systems seem so powerful is the abstractness of their tools. They can be applied to anything. Factories, retail establishments, hospitals, educational institutions – all can be subjected to the same type of analysis. What counts as utility will be different from one setting to the next, though generally the aim of consultation is to improve efficiency and profitability. The factors that influence the achievement of utility will also differ from one setting to the next. But the promised power and generality of the tools make it plausible that consulting "guns for hire" can provide guidance that is almost independent of detailed knowledge of any particular domain. The popularity of consultants for hire is testimony to our collective willingness to accept RCT as the model of rational decision-making.

The mention of efficiency is a good occasion to raise another question about RCT. RCT is almost wholly devoted to efficiency and maximizing utility. Do we want to make these the most important values in our lives? To do that is to bring us dangerously close to making selfish, heartless accumulation the center of our lives. Of course, the formal framework of rational decision-making can always add in considerations of justice, ecological harmony, moderation, tradition, and so on. All we need is to include them in our preference ratings. But there are important problems here. Can we efficiently maximize the satisfaction of our desire not to maximize? Perhaps there is a technical solution here (maximize satisficing?), but there is something about the idea that gives one vertigo. Also, there is an important sense in which the form of our reasoning sets the tone of our lives, overshadowing the content. The preferences we "insert" will at an important level never be as important as the framing of all our preferences as things to be maximized. We will be maximizers in a world that calls for moderation (can one maximize moderation?). We will be devotees of progress in which we are not at all sure what progress is, and where the default is maximizing in the form of accumulation. It will be within that framework that we will be trying to moderate our accumulation and define progress before we wholeheartedly pursue it.

There are two dimensions to "rationality" that are often thought of as completely separate but that are connected, at least to the extent that "rationality" connects them: the descriptive and the prescriptive, or fact and value. Each raises considerations that need to be thought about in this context. As a descriptive/factual notion, a theory of rationality is a theory of how rational people actually behave. And in certain respects, humans are thought to be rational beings. In the late nineteenth century, the articulation of classical economic theory partly took the form of treating people as though their economic behavior was basically, though certainly not always, rational. People were known to be careless, emotional, and fallacy prone, but for the purposes of theory, the ideal type of an economic actor was rational. To that extent, the rationality of an economic actor was an "empirical" law, comparable to the law of gravity. As such, it would be thought to be an eternal law.

The rationality that late nineteenth-century economists attributed to people was very similar to the rationality that is central to RCT. However, the kind of rationality that Aristotle was thinking of when he famously defined "man" as a "rational animal" is a very different thing. What RCT defines as rational Aristotle thought of as "clever." Plato's admiration for reason was not approval of anything closely resembling rationality as defined by RCT. Both of these thinkers established traditions of thought that were built around very different notions of rationality than RCT espouses, so it is certainly controversial, at the least, to take the fact that RCT's particular notion of rationality explains the behavior of people at a particular

RATIONAL CHOICE THEORY AND IDEOLOGY

time, who are rational in a particular sense, and infer from that that people at all times were rational in that particular sense.

The prescriptive dimension of the particular form of rationality cultivated by RCT also has important consequences. By now, decision theory is a standard component of the curricula of business schools, which are themselves a more common and important part of university life. In a sense, as we said, the techniques of RCT can be looked at as a form of intellectual technology. If its use is persuasively prescribed and seems effective, it will be more widely used. So the use of RCT as an explanatory device and a technology can spread both by natural means and by prescriptive encouragement. This raises a problem. As the use of RCT spreads, it, like RT, can become a self-verifying theory.

We believe that the widespread use of RCT in life can and will have serious unfortunate consequences. We can describe these by returning to Mia's decision about where to go to college. We presented Mia as having two alternatives: RCT and the alternative we sketched. Of course, there are others, and it might be interesting to consider the question of how she should choose *between* the ways of deciding where to go to college. Could RCT be of help in deciding which method of deciding Mia should use? Can we use RCT to determine whether we *should* use RCT?

If we look at the sketch of her decision by our proposed method and compare it with our outline of how she would decide if she used RCT, some of the differences are perfectly evident. For one thing, Mia is reflective, and has enough self-knowledge to know what matters to her about college. Taking that into account contributes to putting the issue of the value she will get from one choice or the other in perspective. There is a kind of growth and wisdom that comes from struggling with and resolving a problem that is not gained when the problem is simply avoided.

The issues raised in this example are complicated. Two hundred years ago they might have been settled by custom and tradition — hypotheses about how to live that have proven themselves over large stretches of time. Of course, there are problems with using custom and tradition. The world has changed, and custom and tradition, though they change too, may not have changed fast enough. And they are social phenomena, not individually oriented, and though they are flexible, they may not be flexible enough to apply usefully to the particular case in question.

These serious problems with custom and tradition will make them much less appealing to a culture that has evolved to be individualistic, pragmatic, and progress and present oriented. But do we want them replaced by the custom of RCT? Do we want to codify the absence of reflectiveness, self-knowledge, and responsibility? Do we want to normalize the emphasis on pleasure over meaning? Do we want to encourage the living of lives that are simply sums of moments and have no purpose, no direction, no connection (unless it brings pleasure) with others? When we make the big (and little) decisions in our lives on the basis of RCT, by ignoring these things, we facilitate, normalize, and perhaps prescribe a life without them. Is this a price worth paying for, at best, a small, perhaps even illusory, increase in efficiency and clarity?

We have sketched out an alternative method of decision-making, basically a neo-Aristotelian method largely derived from Alasdair MacIntyre's *After Virtue*. Our previous discussion and MacIntyre's book address the problem of *prescriptive* psychology, but what about *descriptive* psychology; how are we to understand how people *do* think and act, as opposed to prescribing how they *should* think and act? Part of the answer is implicit in our alternative prescriptive suggestion. We believe that people should be understood as rational in a much richer sense than the rationality proposed by RCT. We believe that people can and do rationally organize their experience into coherent understanding of the world, including its causal mechanisms. We believe that they can construct and understand themselves in terms of narratives set in a social context. We believe that they can understand themselves and others in relation to purposes and goals. We believe that conceiving of and pursuing a meaningful life by defining goals and the ways of achieving them is the core of human life, and that it should be understood in that way. And we believe that our alternative account of rationality points in this direction.

To adopt our views and the practices they imply for understanding human thought and behavior entails a loss of one of contemporary Western culture's most important aspirations — that of a mathematically based scientific understanding of human nature modeled on natural science. The West has been pursuing that goal perhaps since at least the seventeenth century (Galileo, Descartes), and we do not see that the results have been anywhere near compensation for the effort. In fact, we think that one very important result has been a degraded conception of human beings together with the prospect of a further degradation that will obscure most of the subtleties of human life. We propose that we abandon the dream of a mathematically based scientific understanding of humans, the emulation of the natural sciences in regard to specifically human affairs, and return to understanding humans in human terms. The natural sciences made earth-shaking progress when they stopped anthropomorphizing nature, no longer viewing it in terms of purposes, but we think it is a monumental mistake to expect similar success if we stop anthropomorphizing humans.

We should note with some irony, however, that in making our argument we have relied in part on the very methods of science (empirical psychology) whose limitations we have been exploring. What this suggests is that science does have — and indeed should have — a prominent role in an inquiry into human nature. It is just not quite the role that most scientists expect or assume it to have. What science in general, and experimentation in particular, does is provide vivid examples or demonstrations. What the scientist must then do is embed these examples in a narrative, or an argument, that attempts to identify their particular historical or cultural significance. Narratives are not natural laws, and a science that took the development of historical narratives seriously would look quite different from most of the sciences we see before us today. Indeed, we might have to give such sciences a different name: perhaps "experimental philosophy." Of course, psychology was spawned by philosophy more than a century ago. Perhaps now is a good time to go back home.

Geologist and evolutionary theorist Stephen J. Gould wrote about the difference between the universal and the historical in the study of geology. Gould referred to the universal as "time's cycle" to highlight its repetition or recurrence. He called the historical "time's arrow" to highlight its uniqueness and directionality. He said of the distinction:

> Time's arrow and time's cycle is, if you will, a "great dichotomy" because each of its poles captures, by its essence, a theme so central to intellectual (and practical) life that Western people who hope to understand history must wrestle

intimately with both — for time's arrow is the intelligibility of distinct and irreversible events, while time's cycle is the intelligibility of timeless order and lawlike structure. We must have both.[1]

We must have both. But what we have tried to suggest and to illustrate is that in the domains of human nature, human behavior, and human rationality, it is time's arrow that should properly do most of the explanatory work.

---

1. Gould, *Time's Arrow, Time's Cycle*, 15–16.

CONCLUSION

In the first part of this book, we criticized Daniel Kahneman's specific version of RCT (in which he corrected its *descriptive* errors by elucidating a host of heuristics and biases), RCT in general (both descriptively and normatively), and, implicitly, all formal decision theory. Western culture has been trying to understand human life in mathematical terms since at least the seventeenth century, and RCT and its variants are the culmination of that attempt so far. We see the value of these theories as greatly exaggerated and the disadvantages as largely ignored.

It is true that these theories can be useful in certain very restricted kinds of cases. We have called these "closed" cases. Closed cases are those that can be framed in a way that approximates the formal requirements of RCT. Decisions like monetary bets on throws of the dice are the paradigm of such cases. The parameters for the probability of the outcomes are clearly defined (there are six equally probable sides to each die), and the outcomes are also clearly and formally defined (these numbers come up, you win X dollars). All contextual problems (how people feel about this wager, how the dice

CONCLUSION

are thrown, whether the well-dressed man next to the thrower blew on the dice) are irrelevant. We have tried to show how atypical such cases are.

Our concern is that RCT won't stay in its proper place. The temptation to treat decisions in the formal way that RCT does often leads to the attempt to reframe decisions that are not naturally amenable to such treatment. "Should we go to the beach or the art museum?" Stanovich asks, as though it is a decision like "Should we bet on a 7 or 11 at such and such odds?" But even this simple decision is not like a dice gamble. We don't know the odds that either the beach or the museum will be so crowded that they will be closed to new patrons. We don't know whether our young child will be so disappointed at the choice of the museum that he will behave in a way that makes the trip totally unpleasant for the rest of us. We can force the choice into a framing that will make it suitable for the application of RCT, but we will pay the price of losing all nuance, which cannot be quantified without significant distortion. It might seem like RCT has solved our problem, but it hasn't. First, it has not really solved *our* problem; it has solved a different one. It is truer to say that it has provided *an* answer, but so would a Ouija board. Second, quantitative calculation has not provided an answer at all. The process of framing has done the bulk of the work.

The choice between the beach and the museum is trivial. A "wrong" decision probably has little long-range significance. But the choice of whether to have a child and a family is another story, and when it is forced into a framing that facilitates the use of RCT, it contorts the issue in a truly grotesque way. It turns having children into an issue like "should I order the filet mignon?" or "should I take a vacation?" We have discussed our concern that the treatment of humans as commodities is reaching a tipping point — a point where

CONCLUSION

interactions between human beings will not only be "measured" as though they are transactions, but will become, for lack of any other way of understanding them, like transactions. Degraded understanding will lead to degraded reality. We are concerned that marriage, or having a child, will come to be understood as an attempt to acquire or preserve pleasure, rather than an attempt to establish and experience something peculiarly human that cannot be experienced in any other way.

We are further concerned that the emphasis on utility maximization will make chaotic and ineffective any attempt to control our desires for excess. We will have ever more commercial outlets offering us "everything and more." Our capacity for judgment will atrophy from both a lack of use and a lack of social legitimacy. Our capacity for thinking will atrophy as a result of being replaced by a preoccupation with counting (quantitative analysis). With that, we will lose our capacity for bold, imaginative conceptions of what to do, how to live, and who to be.

In the second part of this book we suggested an alternative: to confront the question of the purpose of what we do, and the purpose of our lives, and make our important decisions on the basis of our judgment of how the different choices accord with those purposes and the narrative coherence of our lives. We have proposed that we invert the relationship between framing/thinking and counting implied by RCT, recognizing and encouraging thinking instead of counting. We propose that we see our family, friends, and community not as sources of quantitatively measurable value, but as aspects of a dynamic human world of which we too are an aspect — the most important aspect perhaps to us, but certainly not the most important aspect per se. We believe that RCT dehumanizes the world in theory and in practice, that by atomizing in order to measure it exacerbates

CONCLUSION

our environmental and political problems, and that a return to an older way of looking at the world can help us understand ourselves better.

Life need not be like a colonoscopy (as Kahneman conceives it) — a series of moments during which we experience pain, pleasure, or something in between. Life can be the meaningful story of a character — us — trying to accomplish something worthwhile, like establishing a family, contributing to the life of the community, expanding our conception of what humans can do or our understanding of ourselves, or any number of things. Even a colonoscopy is not as Kahneman conceives it. It is an attempt to protect or improve our health by discovering whether we have colon cancer, in the best cases so that we can make more of our lives. And like other human endeavors it requires discomfort — even pain. It is not simply a series of painful moments we endure in the hope of increasing future pleasure. But we can make our lives into something resembling a colonoscopy. If we think of our lives in those terms so that we can quantify it, we are in danger of contributing to the already powerful tendency to turn our lives into exactly that. Such a change would be a tragic loss of what is best and most human about us.

CODA

Barry has a good friend who checks in periodically to find out if she's doing a good job of managing her life, since Barry is supposedly an expert on decision-making. She's a successful lawyer with a job she (mostly) likes, a good marriage, and a couple of fine children. She is close to her aging parents, devoted to helping them cope with their growing infirmities. She has a small but tight network of friends, some going back many years. Of course, her life has its share of problems. She doesn't always find the work that she does fulfilling; she spends too much time helping people who already have more money than they need find ways to accumulate even more of it. She is struggling to maintain open communication with her kids as they go through the black hole of adolescence. And she finds, as many of us do, that there are just not enough hours in the day. So her life isn't perfect (whose life is?), but she is more than pleased, overall, with the path she is on.

That said, she has a few quirks, which mostly explain her regular check-ins with Barry. She routinely buys service contracts on cars and appliances. She knows that the value of these contracts is almost certainly negative (the company selling them wants to make a profit, after all), but she regards them as insurance policies against big expenditures. She could afford to "self-insure," but the prospect of a big, unexpected expense unsettles her. She buys things she doesn't need because they are on sale. The deals are too good to pass up. She carries a credit-card balance while doggedly putting money into a savings account that earns a tenth of the interest she is paying on her debt. She does this to discipline herself into saving for retirement. She indulges her extravagant tastes in fashion accessories only when she gets an unexpected financial windfall. She does this because she knows that her tastes exceed her bank account. She watches movies until the end, no matter how distasteful she finds them, because she hates the thought of wasting money. She tends to review how past decisions have worked out and to regret the ones that have disappointed her. She is perhaps more frugal than her financial circumstances require, but she doesn't feel that she is depriving herself of anything that matters, and she wants to set an example for her kids of how to stay focused on what is really important. She regards many of her habits as unwise, but has little interest in breaking them.

This thumbnail description includes many of the biases that have occupied research in decision-making for more than half a century. So what should Barry tell his friend? She seems to be typical of most of us. Her decisions are considered, not impulsive. That is, she has reasons for behaving the way she does, even if she suspects that she could be doing better. It is easy to see how, in the case of each of the characteristics just described, Barry could give her a little mini-lecture — about framing, mental accounts, sunk costs, or whatever is appropriate — that would indicate to her why she ought to modify her behavior. But is she being irrational?

In this book, we have tried to suggest, in effect, that Barry's friend is not being irrational, and that the perspective on what it means to be rational provided by rational choice theory is too narrow and formalistic to capture what "rational" should mean. This friend has some long-term objectives—professional and social—that she is trying to reach. Her various strategies for meeting those objectives are surely imperfect, but given who she is, and what she cares about, she is perhaps doing the best she can. Sure, Barry could tell her that it doesn't make much sense to pay 20% interest on a debt while earning 2% interest on savings. But then she might tell him that because she has a lot of trouble disciplining herself about money, she has found that treating personal rules about savings as iron-clad has provided the needed discipline, and she doesn't want to spend the time and mental effort it would take to make resource allocation decisions on a case-by-case basis to maximize her use of those resources. And while she knows that "there's no use crying over spilled milk," she has also learned enough about herself to know that without the sting of regret to motivate her to make different decisions in the future, she might fall into habits that lead her to repeatedly make the same mistakes. Barry's friend knows that she could negotiate life more efficiently and effectively if she were a different person, but she doesn't want to be a different person. She rather values and likes the person she is. As Keith Stanovich might put it, this friend is alienated from some of her decisions. Either she doesn't have access to all of the processes that lead to them, or she can't control those processes. So she finds workaround strategies that keep these alien processes from having too big an impact on her life. She has organized her life to keep her eyes and efforts focused on what is most important.

In our everyday discourse, we apply the word *rational* not only to decisions but also to persons, and it is perfectly possible for rational persons to make "irrational" decisions. The reason is that "rational," as derived from RCT, is not all that we mean by rational. Rational choice theory provides us with some norms for assessing individual decisions. It does not provide us with a complete set of norms, nor does it provide us with norms for evaluating lives taken as a whole. The problem is that we use a single word – *rational* – to describe both persons and decisions. In this book, we have tried to enrich the notion of "rational" without defining it precisely. The word has profound normative implications. No one wants to be known as an irrational person. Our quarrel with the research tradition that has evolved out of the seminal work of Kahneman and Tversky is not that it has led us astray as a set of lenses through which to see and understand *some* individual decisions. Quite the contrary. It has done that job well. Our quarrel is that it has been too limited in its aspirations. It tells us a lot about the rationality and irrationality of certain kinds of decisions. But it does not tell us enough about the rationality and irrationality of all types of decisions, or of persons. What this friend really wants to know is whether she is a rational person. All that a decision scientist's "expertise" can tell her is whether she is making narrowly rational individual decisions.

Criticizing the standards of rational choice theory as too limited does not mean that there are no standards by which to criticize people's decisions. Our claim that the context of a decision affects one's experience of the decision does not mean that there are therefore no bad decisions. That approach leads to the rather fatuous tautology of the theory of revealed preference, where rationality is assumed and one uses choices to infer underlying preference structure.

Justifying sitting through a bad movie by saying, "I want to get my money's worth" is rather different from saying, "I have a tendency to be wasteful and I have found that a commitment to seeing things through to the bitter end makes me more thoughtful about undertaking a course of action in the first place." We take our criticisms of RCT to be not that any reason for a decision is as good as any other, and maximizing utility is just one reason among many, but rather that there are many good (and bad) reasons for decisions, and rational choice theory is inadequate for most of them. It is easy to defend rational choice theory against absurd alternatives. It is not quite so easy to defend it against reasonable alternatives. Sometimes the justification for a decision can be more embarrassing than the decision itself. But sometimes it is thoughtful, sensitive, and illuminating. We need a theory that distinguishes the embarrassing from the thoughtful. The study of decision-making has not done much to help us develop such a theory.

There are certainly things we can learn from research on judgment and decision-making. RCT is a useful tool, a key part of the Swiss Army knife that is rationality in full. And knowing the pitfalls to which we are susceptible is a good way to keep that tool sharp. But it is not the only tool. And it also seriously misleads us in our efforts to live purposeful, meaningful lives. It discourages us from thinking about our lives as a whole and about the impact of our decisions on other people. And it mistakenly treats framing, a necessity for rational decisions (even for RCT-driven decisions), as a source of bias. Rationality should enable people to establish and pursue worthwhile, welfare-enhancing goals and to live good lives. By itself, RCT will not produce that result. As our only tool, it may make us just the sort of "rational fools" that Sen wrote about.

And this is what Barry ought to be telling his friend. She is negotiating her way through life mindful of the temptations to which she is drawn, aware that time is scarce and that not every decision is worth her full attention and effort. She seems to have adopted strategies that work, even if they are not the strategies we might design if we were building an organism from scratch. She seems to be negotiating her life with wisdom and perspective, using all the tools in her knife. "Well done," we should say. The implicit suggestion from RCT that people who violate the norms of RCT are not living good, meaningful, and rational lives is harmfully, tragically wrong.

BIBLIOGRAPHY

Please note that we have chosen not to include citations in the body of the text itself, in the service of making the text more readable. Direct quotes are footnoted in the text, and those notes refer to listings in this bibliography. Most of the works cited below are referenced explicitly by author, title, or both in the text itself. A small set are not. Those works are in this list because they support the same points as the works that are explicitly referenced in the text.

Aristotle. 1999. *Nicomachean Ethics*. Translated by W. D. Ross. Kitchener, Ontario: Batoche Books.

Baron, J. 2024. *Thinking and Deciding*. 5th ed. New York: Cambridge University Press.

Bennis, W. M., D. L. Medin, and D. M. Bartels. 2009. "The Costs and Benefits of Calculation and Moral Rules." *Perspectives on Psychological Science* 5:187–202.

Cardenas, S. 2024. "*U.S. News and World Report*'s College Rankings Should Do Away with Peer Assessment." Higher Ed Dive, October 14, https://www.highereddive.com/news/us-news-ranking-should-get-rid-peer-assessment/729559/.

Deci, E. 1975. *Intrinsic Motivation*. New York: Plenum.

Dennett, D. C. 1987. *The Intentional Stance*. Cambridge, MA: MIT Press.

DeVoe, S. E., and J. Pfeffer. 2007. "When Time Is Money: The Effect of Hourly Payment on the Evaluation of Time." *Organizational Behavior and Human Decision Processes* 104:1–13.

BIBLIOGRAPHY

Dubner, S. 2007. "How to Cheat the Mumbai Train System." *Freakonomics*, https://freakonomics.com/2007/03/how-to-cheat-the-mumbai-train-system/.

Duckworth, A. 2016. *Grit*. New York: Scribner.

Duke, A. 2018. *Thinking in Bets*. New York: Random House.

Ellsberg, D. 1961. "Risk, Ambiguity and the Savage Axioms." *Quarterly Journal of Economics* 75:643–69.

Evans, J. St. B. T., D. E. Over, and K. I. Manktelow. 1993. "Reasoning, Decision Making and Rationality." *Cognition* 49:165–87.

Fiske, A. P. 1991. *Structures of Social Life: The Four Elementary Forms of Human Relations*. New York: Free Press.

Fiske, A. P., and P. E. Tetlock. 1997. "Taboo Trade-Offs: Reactions to Transactions That Transgress the Spheres of Justice." *Political Psychology* 18:255–97.

Fowers, B. J. 2005. *Virtue in Psychology*. Washington, DC: American Psychological Association.

Frankfurt, H. G. 1998. "Freedom of the Will and the Concept of a Person." In *The Importance of What We Care About: Philosophical Essays*, 11–25. Cambridge: Cambridge University Press.

Frederick, S. 2015. "In Defense of (Traditional) Normative Standards." *Journal of Marketing Behavior* 1:167–74.

Frisch, D. 1993. "Reasons for Framing Effects." *Organizational Behavior and Human Decision Processes* 54:399–429.

Frisch, D., and R. T. Clemen. 1994. "Beyond Expected Utility: Rethinking Behavioral Decision Research." *Psychological Bulletin* 116:46–54.

Frisch, D., and S. K. Jones. 1993. "Assessing the Accuracy of Decisions." *Theory and Psychology* 3:115–35.

Geertz, C. 1973. *The Interpretation of Cultures*. New York: Basic Books.

Gigerenzer, G. 2004. "Fast and Frugal Heuristics: The Tools of Bounded Rationality." In *Blackwell Handbook of Judgment and Decision Making*, edited by D. J. Koehler and N. Harvey, 62–89. New York: Blackwell.

———. 2007. *Gut Feelings: The Intelligence of the Unconscious*. New York: Viking.

Gilbert, D. T. 2006. *Stumbling on Happiness*. New York: Knopf.

Gilbert, D. T., and J. E. Ebert. 2002. "Decisions and Revisions: The Affective Forecasting of Changeable Outcomes." *Journal of Personality and Social Psychology* 82:503–14.

Gilligan, C. 1982. *In a Different Voice*. Cambridge, MA: Harvard University Press.

Gould, S. J. 1987. *Time's Arrow, Time's Cycle*. Cambridge, MA: Harvard University Press.

BIBLIOGRAPHY

Grant, A. M., and B. Schwartz. 2011. "Too Much of a Good Thing: The Challenge and Opportunity of the Inverted-U." *Perspectives on Psychological Science* 6:61–76.

Haidt, J. 2012. *The Righteous Mind: Why Good People Are Divided by Politics and Religion.* New York: Random House.

Hirsch, F. 1976. *Social Limits to Growth.* Cambridge, MA: Harvard University Press.

Humphrey, N. 1976. "The Social Function of Intellect." In *Growing Points in Ethology,* edited by P. P. G. Bateson and R. A. Hinde, 303–17. Cambridge: Cambridge University Press.

Jussim, L. 1986. "Self-Fulfilling Prophecies: A Theoretical and Integrative Review." *Psychological Review* 93:429–45.

———. 1989. "Teacher Expectations: Self-Fulfilling Prophecies, Perceptual Biases, and Accuracy." *Journal of Personality and Social Psychology* 57:469–80.

Jussim, L., J. Eccles, and S. Madon. 1996. "Social Perception, Social Stereotypes, and Teacher Expectations: Accuracy and the Quest for the Powerful Self-Fulfilling Prophecy." *Advances in Experimental Social Psychology* 28:281–388.

Kahneman, D. 1999. "Objective Happiness." In *Well-Being: The Foundations of Hedonic Psychology,* edited by D. Kahneman, E. Diener, and N. Schwarz, 3–25. New York: Russell Sage Foundation.

———. 2003. "A Perspective on Judgment and Choice." *American Psychologist* 58:697–720.

———. 2011. *Thinking, Fast and Slow.* New York: Farrar, Straus and Giroux.

Kahneman, D., A. B. Krueger, D. A. Schkade, N. Schwarz, and A. A. Stone. 2004. "A Survey Method for Characterizing Daily Life Experience: The Day Reconstruction Method." *Science* 306:1776–80.

Kahneman, D., and A. Tversky. 1979. "Prospect Theory: An Analysis of Decision under Risk." *Econometrica* 47:263–91.

———. 1984. "Choices, Values, and Frames." *American Psychologist* 39:341–50.

Kay, J., and M. King. 2020. *Radical Uncertainty.* New York: Norton.

Keynes, J. M. 1965. *The General Theory of Employment, Interest, and Money.* New York: Harcourt. Originally published in 1936.

Keys, D. J., and B. Schwartz. 2007. "'Leaky' Rationality: How Research on Behavioral Decision Making Challenges Normative Standards of Rationality." *Perspectives on Psychological Science* 2:162–80.

Klein, G. 1998. *Sources of Power.* Cambridge, MA: MIT Press.

Knight, F. H. 1965. *Risk, Uncertainty and Profit.* New York: Harper Torchbooks. Originally published in 1921.

BIBLIOGRAPHY

Kohlberg, L. 1969. "Stage and Sequence: The Cognitive Developmental Approach to Socialization." In *Handbook of Socialization Theory*, edited by D. A. Goslin, 347–480. Chicago: Rand McNally.

Krishnamurthy, P., and P. Kumar. 2002. "Self-Other Discrepancies in Waiting Time Decisions." *Organizational Behavior and Human Decision Processes* 87:207–26.

Kuhn, T. S. 1962. *The Structure of Scientific Revolutions*. Chicago: University of Chicago Press.

———. 1977. "Objectivity, Value Judgment, and Theory Choice." In *The Essential Tension*, 320–39. Chicago: University of Chicago Press.

Lepper, M. R., and D. Greene, eds. 1978. *The Hidden Costs of Reward*. Hillsdale, NJ: Erlbaum.

Lepper, M. R., D. Greene, D., and R. E. Nisbett. 1973. "Undermining Children's Intrinsic Interest with Extrinsic Rewards: A Test of the 'Overjustification' Hypothesis." *Journal of Personality and Social Psychology* 28:129–37.

Levin, I. P., and G. J. Gaeth. 1988. "How Consumers Are Affected by the Framing of Attribute Information Before and After Consuming the Product." *Journal of Consumer Research* 15:374–78.

Levitt, S. D., and S. J. Dubner. 2005. *Freakonomics*. New York: HarperCollins.

———. 2015. *When to Rob a Bank*. New York: William Morrow.

MacIntyre, A. 1981. *After Virtue*. Notre Dame, IN: University of Notre Dame Press.

Madon, S., L. Jussim, and J. Eccles. 1997. "In Search of the Powerful Self-Fulfilling Prophecy." *Journal of Personality and Social Psychology* 72:791–809.

Marglin, S. 1976. "What Do Bosses Do?" In *Division of Labour*, edited by A. Gorz, 13–54. London: Harvester.

Merton, R. K. 1948. "The Self-Fulfilling Prophesy." *Antioch Review* 8:193–210.

———. 1960. *Social Theory and Social Structure*. Glencoe, IL: Free Press.

Nisbett, R. E. 2009. *Intelligence and How to Get It*. New York: Norton.

Pfeffer, J. 1998. *The Human Equation*. Cambridge, MA: Harvard Business School Press.

Polanyi, K. 1944. *The Great Transformation*. New York: Farrar and Rinehart.

Pollan, M. 2002. "Power Steer." *New York Times Magazine,* March 31, 44–51, 68, 71–72, 76–77.

Posner, R. A., and E. M. Landes. 1978. "The Economics of the Baby Shortage." *Journal of Legal Studies* 7:323–41.

Redelmeier, D. A., J. Katz, and D. Kahneman. 2003. "Memories of Colonoscopy: A Randomized Trial." *Pain* 104:187–94.

Rorty, A. E. 1991. *Mind in Action: Essays in the Philosophy of Mind*. Boston: Beacon.

BIBLIOGRAPHY

Rosch, E. H. 1973. "Natural Categories." *Cognitive Psychology* 4:328–50.

Rosenthal, R., and L. Jacobson. 1968. *Pygmalion in the Classroom: Teacher Expectation and Pupils' Intellectual Development.* New York: Holt, Rinehart and Winston.

Roth, A. 2007. "Repugnance as a Constraint on Markets." *Journal of Economic Perspectives* 21:37–58.

Rozenblit, L., and F. Keil. 2002. "The Misunderstood Limits of Folk Science: An Illusion of Explanatory Depth." *Cognitive Science* 26:521–62.

Ruark, R. 1955. *Something of Value.* New York: Doubleday.

Savage, L. J. 1954. *The Foundations of Statistics.* New York: Wiley.

Schwartz, B. 1982. "Reinforcement-Induced Behavioral Stereotypy: How Not to Teach People to Discover Rules." *Journal of Experimental Psychology: General* 111:23–59.

———. 1986. *The Battle for Human Nature: Science, Morality and Modern Life.* New York: Norton.

———. 1994. *The Costs of Living: How Market Freedom Erodes the Best Things in Life.* New York: Norton.

———. 1997. "Psychology, 'Idea Technology,' and Ideology." *Psychological Science* 8:21–27.

———. 2004. *The Paradox of Choice: Why More Is Less.* New York: Ecco.

———. 2015. "What Does It Mean to Be a Rational Decision Maker?" *Journal of Marketing Behavior* 1:113–46.

———. 2015. *Why We Work.* New York: Simon and Schuster.

Schwartz, B., R. Schuldenfrei, and H. Lacey. 1978. "Operant Psychology as Factory Psychology." *Behaviorism* 6:229–54.

Schwartz, B., and K. Sharpe. 2006. "Practical Wisdom: Aristotle Meets Positive Psychology." *Journal of Happiness Studies* 7:377–95.

———. 2011. *Practical Wisdom: The Right Way to Do the Right Thing.* New York: Riverhead.

Seligman, M. E. P. 2002. *Authentic Happiness.* New York: Free Press.

———. 2011. *Flourish.* New York: Free Press.

Sen, A. 1976. "Rational Fools." *Philosophy and Public Affairs* 6:317–44.

Shiller, R. J. 2019. *Narrative Economics.* Princeton, NJ: Princeton University Press.

Simon, H. A. 1955. "A Behavioral Model of Rational Choice." *Quarterly Journal of Economics* 59:99–118.

———. 1956. "Rational Choice and the Structure of the Environment." *Psychological Review* 63:129–38.

BIBLIOGRAPHY

———. 1957. *Models of Man, Social and Rational*. New York: Wiley.

Skinner, B. F. 1948. *Walden Two*. New York: Macmillan.

———. 1953. *Science and Human Behavior*. New York: Macmillan.

———. 1971. *Beyond Freedom and Dignity*. New York: Knopf.

Skyrms, B. 1966. *Choice and Chance*. Belmont, CA: Dickenson.

Sloman, S., and P. Fernbach. 2017. *The Knowledge Illusion*. New York: Riverhead.

Slovic, P., and A. Tversky. 1974. "Who Accepts Savage's Axiom?" *Behavioral Science* 19:368–73.

Smith, A. 1937. *The Wealth of Nations*. New York: Modern Library. Originally published in 1776.

Snyder, M., and E. D. Tanke. 1977. "Social Perception and Interpersonal Behavior: On the Self-Fulfilling Nature of Social Stereotypes." *Journal of Personality and Social Psychology* 35:655–66.

Stanovich, K. E. 2010. *Decision Making and Rationality in the Modern World*. New York: Oxford University Press.

Summers, L. H. 1991. World Bank Memo, December 12. https://eml.berkeley.edu/~webfac/harrison/e181_s04/181s04summers.pdf.

Taylor, F. W. 1911. *Principles of Scientific Management*. New York: Norton.

Thaler, R. H. 1980. "Toward a Positive Theory of Consumer Choice." *Journal of Economic Behavior and Organization* 1:39–60.

———. 1985. "Mental Accounting and Consumer Choice." *Marketing Science* 4:199–214.

Tversky, A., and D. Kahneman. 1981. "The Framing of Decisions and the Psychology of Choice." *Science* 211:453–58.

Walzer, M. 1983. *Spheres of Justice*. New York: Basic Books.

Wittgenstein, L. 2009. *Philosophical Investigations*. 4th ed. Edited and translated by P. M. S. Hacker and J. Schulte. Oxford: Wiley-Blackwell. Originally published in 1953.

Wrzesniewski, A., C. R. McCauley, P. Rozin, and B. Schwartz. 1997. "Jobs, Careers, and Callings: People's Relations to Their Work." *Journal of Research in Personality* 31:21–33.

INDEX

aesthetic value, 87–88
Aristotle, 102–103, 190, 193, 199–203, 217, 248
artificial intelligence, 214
attunement, 150–151
authority ranking, 92–93

Baron, Jonathan, *Thinking and Deciding*, 71–72
Bartels, Daniel M., 77, 96–98
beach/museum example, 20–27, 40, 47, 64–65, 177, 255; value of going to beach, 11–12
beef, 129–131
behavioral decision-making. *See* judgment, and decision-making (JDM)
Bennis, Will M., 77, 96–98
body counts, 160
bounded rationality, 35
box office example, 105–111, 125–127, 176
buying a car, 11, 135–137, 205

Cardenas, Sonia, 153–154
categories, 53–54; geometrical shapes, 37–38, 51, 195; natural categories, 53; truth and lie, 51–52, 54–56
Cesarini Banhos, Deborah, 131
clarification, 17, 47–50, 56, 137–138, 140
classification, 175
closure, 33, 75; closed-world assumptions, 97, 111; closing an open system, 76–78, 97–99, 140, 142–143; process of, 17–18, 22, 196, 254
college application example, 40–46, 61–62, 180, 207–208, 249; best colleges, 41, 65, 136–137, 156; and clarification, 48–50; college rankings, 151–160; cost of college, 154–155, 230; earning potential/job offers, 155, 190–191, 229–230; good colleges, 65–67, 152, 157; law school, 68–69; liberal arts, 42, 48–49, 57, 65,

INDEX

college application example (*continued*) 80, 100, 102; quantification of value, 80–82; SAT scores, 158–159; and specification, 40–41, 44
colonoscopy, 161–163, 188, 257
communal sharing, 92, 95
comparison, 93–95
concert ticket example, 105–111, 125–127, 176
context, 75–76, 111
Copernicus, Nicolaus, 173
cost-benefit analysis, 12, 77, 96–100, 103; McNamara's metrics, 134–135
courage, 102, 197
COVID pandemic, 132–134

decisions: complexity of everyday decisions, 4–6, 70, 192; every decision is a prediction, 191–192; framing essential for, 113, 119; gambling paradigm vs everyday decisions, 21–28, 36, 61–62, 76, 140; impoverishment of, 8, 38, 196; and judgment, 193–94; and mathematics, 17; normative vs prescriptive standards for, 98–99; rational decision makers, 15, 17, 119; RCT as normative tool for, 10, 12; two essential components of, 16. *See also* judgment, and decision-making (JDM)
deliberation, 43–44, 46–47, 50, 143
Dennett, Daniel, 176
Descartes, René, 203
DeVoe, Sanford, 236
disagreement, 26–27
discovery, 213–214
disease outbreak example, 104–106, 113–114, 123

disentanglement, 18, 57, 74, 140
Dubner, Stephen, *Freakonomics*, 146–147
Duckworth, Angela, *Grit*, 198
Duke, Annie, *Thinking in Bets*, 36

Ebert, Jane, 127
economics: economic imperialism, 228–233; RCT at heart of, 30, 35; and social relations, 230–232. *See also* money; work
education, 229–230, 232; effects of teacher expectations on, 239–240. *See also* college application example
Ellsberg, Daniel, 70, 73
equality matching, 92, 198
Evans, J., 128
externalities, 130–131

factory work, 210, 218–220, 223–224, 236–237
fairness, 198
feelings, 30, 45, 122, 149–151, 163, 166–167, 205
Feinberg, Kenneth, 86–87, 97, 189
Fernbach, Philip, *The Knowledge Illusion*, 173
feudalism, 217–218
Field of Dreams (movie), 212
Fiske, Alan, 198, 232; *Structures of Social Life*, 92–97
Fowers, Blaine, *Virtue in Psychology*, 201
framing, 4, 19, 32–34, 104, 113–119; decisions require, 113, 119; effects, 122–124; and judgment, 129; and leakage, 121; mental accounting, 107–109, 149; and probability, 63–64; and rationality, 33, 141; and RCT, 34, 140–142; reframing, 96, 106; and subjectivity, 121–126, 129, 131; true cost

INDEX

of beef, 129–131; and understanding, 174–175; and value, 94–95
Frankfurt, Harry, 89–90
Frederick, Shane, 243
Frisch, Deborah, 122–125
fruit, 52–53

Gaeth, Gary J., 123–124
gambling paradigm, 13–17; essential for RCT, 36–38, 142; vs everyday decisions, 21–28, 36, 61–62, 76, 140; other gambling example, 114–115
game, 53; rewards game, 221–223, 226
Geertz, Clifford, 242
geometrical shapes, 37–38, 51, 195
Gigerenzer, Gerd, 31
Gilbert, Daniel, 127; *Stumbling on Happiness*, 82
Gilligan, Carol, 98
Gould, Stephen J., 252–253
Grant, Adam, 102, 202–203

Hirsch, Fred, 231; *Social Limits to Growth*, 160
Hitler, Adolf, 128
human beings. *See* people
Humphrey, Nicholas, 177–178

idea technology, 234–235
ideology, 235–242, 244; mechanisms by which it becomes true, 237–238
incommensurability, 90–96, 99, 102–103
industrialization, 219
intelligence, 45
intelligent reflection, 6–8
interpretation, 21
invariance, 13, 106, 123
invention, 213–214, 220

Jacobson, Lenore, 239
judgment, 51, 59, 76, 78; and decision-making (JDM), 28–29, 31–33, 36, 112, 119, 121, 173, 262; and decisions, 193–194; and framing, 129; good judgment, 194, 199; as replacement for RCT, 190–192, 196; retrospective judgment, 162, 164
Jussim, Lee, 240

Kahneman, Daniel, 29–35, 139, 261; critique of RCT, 31–32, 254; "Day Reconstruction Method" (DRM), 163, 165–166, 168, 257; on framing, 121–122; "The Framing of Decisions and the Psychology of Choice," 32–33; on meaningful life, 186; on prospect theory, 106, 113–114; on subjective experience, 125; on substitution, 60–61, 181–182; System 1 (S1) processes, 29–33, 151, 179–180, 182, 204; System 2 (S2) processes, 29–32, 179–180, 182, 204; *Thinking, Fast and Slow*, 29, 31–32, 96, 162–164, 181–182; on well-being, 161–168, 188
Kay, John, *Radical Uncertainty*, 73–74, 220
Keil, Frank, 173
Keynes, John Maynard, 58–59
Keys, Daniel, 34, 120–121
King, Mervyn, *Radical Uncertainty*, 73–74, 220
Klein, Gary, 180
Knight, Frank, 70
Kohlberg, Lawrence, 97–98
Kuhn, Thomas, 213; *The Structure of Scientific Revolutions*, 142, 204
Kulkarni, Ganesh, 146–147

INDEX

Lacey, Hugh, 209
Landes, Elizabeth, 146
language, 8, 113–114, 119; narratives, 187
law school application example, 68–69
leakage, 34, 120–121, 124–129, 150
Leonardo, da Vinci, 91; *Mona Lisa* (painting), 83–84, 87
Levin, Irwin P., 123–24
Levitt, Steven, *Freakonomics*, 146–147
liberal arts, 42, 48–49, 57, 65, 80, 100, 102, 153–154
life: good life, 183, 186, 197, 201; how to spend it, 3–4, 8–9; meaningful life, 184–190, 257; story of, 186; value of, 189
light switch example, 141–143
lost ticket example, 105–111, 125–127, 176

MacIntyre, Alasdair, 224, 228; *After Virtue*, 250
Manktelow, K., 128
Marglin, Stephen, 220
market pricing, 92–94
Marx, Karl, 235
mathematics, 13–17; and human nature, 251; mental accounting, 107–109, 149; and rationality, 203–204. *See also* quantification; statistics
maximizing, 100–101, 171–172, 229, 247, 256
McCauley, Clark, 184
McNamara, Robert, 134–135, 145
mean, 102, 200
meaning, 67, 111; meaningful life, 184–190, 195, 257
means-ends relations, 215–224; and work, 244. *See also* people, instrumentalization of

Medin, Douglas L., 77, 96–98
mental accounting, 107–109, 149
Merton, Robert K., 220, 239
money: box office example, 105–111, 125–127, 176; cost of college, 154–155, 230; diminishing marginal utility of, 14–15, 124; externalities, 130–131; monetary value, 82–87; and social relations, 230–232; stock, 111–113; and value, 100, 189. *See also* economics; work
moral development, 97–98
moral dimensions, 131–132, 192, 214

naive realism, 127
natural categories, 53
Newton, Isaac, 174

objectivity, 94, 169; objective happiness, 186; objective quantification, 88; and subjectivity, 58
Over, D., 128

people: feelings, 30, 45, 122, 149–151, 163, 166–167, 205; good person, 228–229; human engineering, 219; human nature, 209, 211, 214, 220, 236–237, 251–253; and ideology, 241–242; instrumentalization of, 146, 189, 255–256; moral development, 97–98; narratives, 187; other people, 148–151; and rationality, 32, 260–261; self-control, 198; self-knowledge, 46, 182; self-respect, 197; social relations, 230–232; understanding other people, 176–178, 198; value of a life, 189; well-being, 161–169. *See also* life; means-ends relations; subjectivity; work

INDEX

perseverance, 198
Pfeffer, Jeffrey, 236; *The Human Equation*, 228
Plato, 248
Polanyi, Karl, 210, 218
Pollan, Michael, 129–132
pollution, 145–146
Popper, Karl, 221
positive psychology, 201
Posner, Richard, 146
practical wisdom, 193, 199, 202, 206
practices, 224–225; and economic imperialism, 228–229, 233
preference, 11, 43; and quantification, 82–83; second-order preferences, 89–90
probability, 12–13; assignment of, 63–65, 69–70, 73, 79; as essential component of decisions, 16, 70, 73, 171–172; quantification of, 59, 171; radical uncertainty, 70–73

quantification, 17–18, 140; body counts, 160; college rankings, 151–160; comparative value, 87; comparison, 93–95; and disentanglement, 74; fragmentation essential to, 188; framing necessary for, 113; of happiness, 186; incommensurability, 90–96, 99, 102–103; industrial accident example, 84–86; and monetary value, 82–87; objective quantification, 88; and preference, 82–83; of probability, 59; and RCT, 160; repugnance, 95–96; right amount, 102; risk-aversion, 113–114, 182; September 11 (9/11), terrorist attack example, 87, 97, 189; of utility, 22; of value, 57–59, 80–82, 94; and Vietnam War, 134–135;

of well-being, 166–169. *See also* mathematics; statistics

radical uncertainty, 70–73, 99
Raphael, 91; *The School of Athens* (painting), 87
rational choice theory (RCT), 9–10; aim of, 18; alternative to, 171–172, 174, 183, 194, 249–251, 256; dangers of, 144–145, 169–170, 192, 244, 249, 263; defenses of, 35–38; as descriptive theory, 28, 31–32, 35, 139; and economics, 30, 35; and framing, 34, 140–142; gambling paradigm essential for, 36–38; Kahneman's critique of, 31–32, 254; as normative model, 10, 12–13, 35, 139; preferences already well-articulated for, 11, 43; process of closure, 17–18, 22, 196, 254; and quantification, 160, 171; and rationality, 32, 111, 135–137, 242–245, 247–248, 261–262; and reinforcement theory (RT), 244–245, 249; rigor of, 61–62; utility as goal of, 10–11, 188–189, 192–193, 247
rationality, 13; alternative understanding of, 171–172, 183, 204, 251; bounded rationality, 35; descriptive, 248; and framing, 33, 141; and mathematics, 203–204; and meaningful life, 186; and people, 32, 260–261; prescriptive, 249–250; rational decision makers, 15, 17, 119; and RCT, 32, 111, 135–137, 242–245, 247–248, 261–262; and subjectivity, 128; and thinking, 119, 172; and voting, 147–148
rectangle, 51–53
reflectiveness, 45, 178–181

INDEX

reflexivity, 220–221
reframing, 96, 106
reification, 211
reinforcement theory (RT), 210–211; and RCT, 244–245, 249
repugnance, 95–96
rewards game, 221–223, 226
right amount, 102
risk-aversion, 113–114, 182
Rorty, Amelie, 202
Rosch, Eleanor, 53
Rosenthal, Robert, 239
Roth, Alvin, 95
Rozenblit, Leonid, 173
Rozin, Paul, 184
rules, 97–99

satisficing, 101–102
SAT scores, 158–159
Saturday, how to spend a free one, 1–7
Savage, L. J., 19, 73, 75
Schwartz, Barry, 34, 82, 102, 120–121, 179, 184, 202-3, 221; advice for a friend, 258–263; *The Paradox of Choice*, 2, 101; *Practical Wisdom*, 51, 193; *Why We Work*, 211, 234
science, 203–204, 225–228, 252
scientific management, 210, 219
self-control, 198
self-fulfilling prophecy, 238–241
self-knowledge, 46, 182
self-respect, 197
Seligman, Martin, 201
Sen, Amartya, 243, 262
September 11 (9/11), terrorist attack victims, 87, 97, 189
Sharpe, Kenneth, *Practical Wisdom*, 51, 193
Shiller, Robert, *Narrative Economics*, 187
Simon, Herbert, 35, 101
Simon, the Magus, 95

simony, 95
Sinnott-Armstrong, Walter, 131
Skinner, B. F., 209–210, 214, 221; *Beyond Freedom and Dignity*, 215; *Science and Human Behavior*, 215; *Walden Two*, 215
Skyrms, Brian, 116
Sloman, Steven, *The Knowledge Illusion*, 173
Slovic, Paul, 173
small worlds, 73, 75
Smith, Adam, 224, 236
Snyder, Mark, 238
social relations, 230–232
Soros, George, 221
specification, 11, 17, 22, 39–41, 44, 137–138, 140
spheres, 37–38, 51
Stanovich, Keith, 255, 260; beach/museum example, 20–27, 40; *Decision Making and Rationality in the Modern World*, 16
statistics, 54–55, 73, 112, 117–118, 134, 174–175. *See also* mathematics; quantification
stock, 111–113
subjectivity: feelings, 30, 45, 122, 149–151, 163, 166–167, 205; and framing, 121–126, 129, 131; and leakage, 34, 124; and objectivity, 58; of preference, 11, 24; and rationality, 128; of utility, 10, 107
substitution, 60–61, 181
Summers, Lawrence, 145–146, 189

Tanke, Elizabeth, 238
Taylor, Frederick Winslow, 219
technology, idea technology, 234–235
Tetlock, Philip, 93
Thaler, Richard, 31, 36, 107-8

INDEX

thinking, 32–33, 119, 172, 195–196
thoughtfulness, 45
ticket-less travel example, 146–147
truth and lie, 51–52, 54–56
Tversky, Amos, 30–32, 34–35, 125, 139, 261; on framing effects, 121–122; "The Framing of Decisions and the Psychology of Choice," 32–33; on prospect theory, 106, 113–114; on understanding, 173

uncertainty, radical, 70–73
understanding, 172–175; other people, 176–178
U.S. News, 48, 50, 136–137, 151–159
utility: diminishing marginal utility of money, 14–15, 124; expected utility, 14, 107; maximization of, 100–101, 171–172, 229, 247, 256; quantification of, 22; RCT focused on, 10–11, 107, 188–189, 192–193, 247; and value, 188–190, 192

vagueness, 18, 21–22, 47–48, 50–51; fuzziness, 52–53; ineliminability of, 56, 77; need to eliminate, 64, 67; two kinds of, 48
value, 11–12; aesthetic value, 87–88; comparative value, 87; contingent valuation, 83; as essential component of decisions, 16, 76; expected value, 14; good life, 183, 186, 197, 201; incommensurability of values, 90–96, 99, 102–103; industrial accident example, 84–86; meaningful life, 184–190; monetary value, 82–87; and money, 100, 189; quantification of, 57–59, 80–82, 94; second-order preferences, 89–90; and utility, 188–190, 192; valuation, 137–138
Vietnam War, 134–135, 145, 159
virtue, 190, 197, 199–203
voting, 147–148

walkways, placement of, 211–213
Wall Street Journal, 41, 48
Walzer, Michael, *Spheres of Justice*, 92–94, 96
well-being, 161–169
Wilson, Timothy, 82
Wittgenstein, Ludwig, 8, 52–53
work: factory work, 210, 218–220, 223–224, 236–237; historical transformation of, 217–224; and means-ends relations, 244
Worth (movie), 87
Wrzesniewski, Amy, 184